W9-BQS-516

56a.29092
70

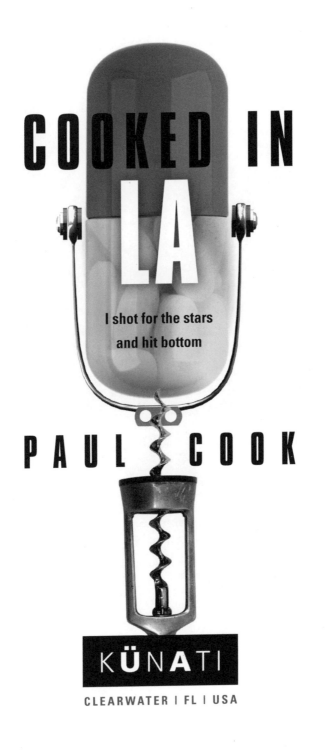

COOKED IN

LA

I shot for the stars and hit bottom

PAUL COOK

KÜNATI

CLEARWATER | FL | USA

COOKED IN LA
Copyright © 2009 by Paul Cook.

For information, contact Kunati Inc., Book Publishers in Canada.
USA: 13575 58th Street North, Suite 200, Clearwater, FL 33760-3721 USA
Canada: 75 First Street, Suite 128, Orangeville, ON L9W 5B6 CANADA.
E-mail: info@kunati.com.

FIRST EDITION

Designed by Kam Wai Yu
Persona Corp. | www.personaco.com

ISBN 978-1-60164-193-9   EAN 9781601641939
Non-Fiction/Body/Mind/Spirit/Substance Abuse/Self Help/Recovery

Published by Kunati Inc. (USA) and Kunati Inc. (Canada).
Provocative. Bold. Controversial.™

http://www.kunati.com

TM—Kunati and Kunati Trailer are trademarks owned by Kunati Inc.
Persona is a trademark owned by Persona Corp.
All other trademarks are the property of their respective owners.

Library of Congress Cataloging-in-Publication Data

Cook, Paul.
 Cooked in LA : I shot for the stars and hit bottom / Paul Cook. -- 1st ed.
   p. cm.
 Summary: "An inspiring and funny account of a young man's steady descent
into drug and alcohol abuse and his fight to regain his life and his
family"--Provided by publisher.
 ISBN 978-1-60164-193-9
 1. Drug addicts--California--Los Angeles--Biography. 2.
Alcoholics--California--Los Angeles--Biography. I. Title.
 HV5805.C66A3 2009
 362.29092--dc22
 [B]

                         2009009506

DEDICATION

For the person who needs a drink,

but knows he can't.

ACKNOWLEDGEMENTS

Neither the book nor I would be here without my beloved Jennifer.
The same gratitude goes to my parents Mary and Terry Cook.
Thank you for your love and acceptance Jacki and Rob. Quinn and Ryan I love you.
I hope you don't have to explore the dark places your father found.
Thank you for your time and prayers Mike Redmond.
Huge thanks to Jim Schoemehl for showing me the miracle.
Additional thanks to Angela Perelli Ebbott and Jamie Wagner for advice
on the manuscript and to James McKinnon for discovering it.

And thank you to GOD for fueling this talking, typing, twisting child.

Me happy at age six wearing a six-inch collar. I never would have guessed that happiness would be replaced with emptiness when I hit my adult years.

CHAPTER 1
Freakin' Frozen

Obviously I will be dead in a few minutes. My mind scrambles for answers as to how I got here. Hello? And where the hell is this terrifying place? A sweat-drenched recliner props my body up, but my chin stays plastered to my chest. I see a hallucination of images of my life, pasted together like a fifth-grade collage project, resting on my lap. The center picture shows me smiling and posing with my beautiful, short-haired blond wife. Another mental snapshot reveals me wearing headphones and laughing in front of a microphone. Those pictures depict my physical reality, and they should put me somewhere close to happy. Instead I find myself literally as stiff as a statue. My body has completely locked up. Earlier tonight we visited a rowdy twenty-something birthday party and it appears I have once again taken it too far.

The standard April showers pound this late St. Louis night. It's 1999 and I've been partying this year just like the Prince song instructs. I'm panicked, nauseated and embarrassed. This state is called the K-hole, an undesirable, drug-induced world of catatonia. I never thought I'd ever be here. My eyes will move, but that's it. Because of the ketamine, a designer drug that is used legally as a cat or horse tranquilizer, my body has been restricted to a complete stillness. I am frozen. The club music and laughter I hear create a contrast to the severity of this moment. My wife Jen keeps coming up close to my face and asking if I'm okay. I cannot answer. I cannot move. I am resigned to the fact that I'm going to fade out and die.

How did I become a statue? My recall is patchy and fragmented. Ten minutes ago a slick-haired dude put a small vial of liquid ketamine on a plate in the microwave at this after-hours party. After cooking for sixty seconds, the liquid turns to white powder. I remember drinking and talking loudly and then inhaling two long lines of that warm powder. That's how you do Special K—but not too much or you go into the K-hole. I guess I was on autopilot. Much less ketamine should be ingested than what I've consumed.

"Hello!" I think I shout. "Can you hear me?"

My lips are not moving. I might die from the fright alone. Adding to the K-hole's oddity is that it usually happens at a party if at all. This is not how it is supposed to be. Most users of Special K have never seen the K-hole, but rare stories like mine have traveled and warned partiers to cautiously avoid this mental prison.

"Just a little bit, not too much or you go in the hole," they claim, half-kidding.

I'm giving them a sobering show tonight. K-hole jail. Why am I not yelling for my wife? Jen! Suddenly, the happy collage disappears and my mind begins playing quick splashes of bizarre and appalling scenes instead. I see a red Fiero turning in front of a loaded school bus. The school kids' screams cause my head to ache heavily. Now I'm in the cab of a bulldozer and it's filling up with water from the top down. I grab the door handle to let the water out. The razor-edged lever slices through my hand. I yell for help after feeling the sharp pain. Loud crying from an infant sounds even sharper in my ears. Mixed in, I hear the sound of the water finally escaping the bulldozer cab. My eyes look down towards the splashing. This is real. I have just vomited on myself. After I hear a scramble, the lights go out and they lay me on the floor, still catatonic. I hear them console Jen, telling her she doesn't need to call an ambulance.

"He will be all right in an hour."

Jen probably thinks I've gotten too drunk. She was downstairs when I invited this ketamine torture onto myself. I slip into sleep.

Two hours later I wake up sweaty, cold and more alone than I've ever felt. I have snapped out of the K-hole. I walk around the house looking for people. It's the middle of the night and all the lights are on in the house, but I can't find anyone. Finally I find some partiers sitting out on the damp deck. I wrap a blanket off a huge queen bed around my shoulders and sit down saying nothing. My hair is matted and wet.

"Wanna beer, man?" a stranger asks.

I nod. Still telling his story, he hands me a cold beer out of the tub of ice. It sends a shiver up my arm that buries in my chest. After three minutes of struggling, I manage to crack it open. Then I sit and listen, completely shocked at what I've done tonight. Two days of throwing up follow.

These near-death experiences are enough to make a guy quit taking drugs. But I don't. Why would a nice guy like me ever risk going near the K-hole? That question is where we start. I have racked my brain, and the best answer I can come up with is the *Quest*: the search for feeling and meaning. The meaning I had once garnered from doing the right thing and encouraging people has given way to darkness, and all I can do is fill the hole inside me. It's a hole I never thought I would create by taking a couple of painkillers every once in a while to calm my constantly racing thoughts a few years ago. They have given me relief I never felt from drinking. And now this emptiness grows inside me, and I usually lose when I try to deny its ever-increasing hunger. Sometimes I overshoot the drugs or the dosage. The ketamine story of drug excess would be unique if it wasn't close to my reality every weekend in St. Louis, Missouri, from 1997 to now. For me an extremely scary hangover kills Sunday and Monday at least once every month. Many nights I find myself doubled over in pain after taking a drug that is not what it was billed as in this risky party underworld. Unfortunately, the only drug dealer screening process available is past drug-taking experience. "Weird drugs. Don't use that dude again!" But I can't blame all the trippy bad experiences on misrepresentation and greed. Sadly, on any given night, my use and thirst for drugs can scare the most toxic veteran drug users in the city. That causes sickness on its own. My new talent is for acquiring ecstasy for the entire group I am with. I am always successful even if the dealer I usually use isn't in the club, because even though the dealer isn't there, the drugs always are. This new exciting life has permanently swallowed me.

Jen and I have been married for two years. We met in college. The first time I saw her, I could not stop thinking about her. I knew she was mine, even though it would be six months before I even spoke to her. I cannot describe why, but I knew deep inside that I needed her. I felt connected to her sweet, tanned, blonde frame. I could tell that we were similar late-blooming kids. We've always been a bit smaller than most. Even though Jen hadn't yet hit her stride in college, she was gorgeous, and she has gotten better each year.

We are five years removed from college graduation now, and taking late blooming to a new level, we have become partiers later than most would have. Most twenty-eight-year-olds think about kids and houses; we only think about being rave kids and playing house music. We go out every weekend, which is probably not unlike most non-parent couples our age who drink at ballgames and local pubs on the weekends. The difference is that we go to clubs with a close group of drug-using friends. We do a lot of drinking along with cocaine and ecstasy.

However, after a year of this glee and exhilaration, remorse has begun to follow many of our partying nights. In the regretful questioning times, we hold it together by making each other laugh. Many of our best days are on the couch alone, talking, improvising skits, watching TV, and making fun of Ted, our cat. But for some reason, those positive moments don't keep us out of the clubs. My periods of guilt, insecurity and remorse rub heavily on a sweet person like Jen. Many times she doesn't know if I'm coming or going, and neither do I. However, she continues to believe in me. Her faith will soon be put to the ultimate test. Nothing could possibly challenge a young marriage quite like a move to Hollywood.

CHAPTER 2
Blue Man Recovery

Moving this freak show to the west coast is the only solution I can muster. Correct or not, I truly believe that my current melancholy reality will be improved by a move to the land of breast augmentation and reality programming. Right now I spend my nights on the radio and my days writing, both while hung over. I need to always look ahead, never at the present. When the TV show *South Park* blew up, I became convinced that creating a show like that was something I could do. Its juvenile vulgarity brilliantly parodied old stereotypes. The angle is that it's told from the perspective of four foul-mouthed kids. I have altered the winning formula a bit. *Future Dwellings* is an animated cartoon about a nursing home. It revolves around all-night nursing home raves, patients feeding each other meds erotically, and real-life aging celebrity guest stars like Regis Philbin. How couldn't this be a winner? My best friend Tom is a talented writer, and he comes on board as well. Together we develop the first script and pin our hopes on making a splash in Hollywood.

While I wait for *Future Dwellings* to pop, I start a new project, a screenplay about a cult. Our heroes are two "over-TVed" dreamers, one of whom is dying. I am also over-TVed; this is my kind of story. In fact, I have learned far too many things from television, most of them erroneous. Relying solely on television for factual information has put me in some embarrassing situations. Thanks to commercials, until I was twenty I actually thought the liquid produced during a woman's menstrual cycle was light blue.

I was off on that one.

My screenplay is developed around another philosophy I love. The dying man is a martyr; he saves the world and, most importantly, people talk highly of him after he's gone.

I'm building an arsenal of creative material to take with me to Los Angeles; now I just have to get approval from my sweet wife for us to actually make the trip. I'm not taking swings at this life alone anymore. I have to consider Jen. She has achieved a successful sales career and that must be respected. But I do believe her career could thrive even more in a bigger city. Jen is about 75 percent on board with making this frightening move. However, she will certainly insist that we begin living a better life before any move can be fully considered. That doesn't sound too lofty to me.

Most people who use a lot of recreational drugs will tell you that overshooting on dosages is just part of the life. And they are right. Going too far in my partying is a major issue, but it's just an appetizer on the problem menu of my life. The issue entrée is that I spend most of my waking moments attempting to carry around a two-ton cinder block called "perfect human approval." The need to be liked has caused many restless nights and head-heavy days. I have worked hard to alleviate this pressure, but every attempt has been fruitless. For me, trying not to care about approval is the equivalent of trying not to breathe.

Early on I learned that the best way to earn approval was through laughter. My older sister was an incredibly focused and talented tennis player when I was growing up. My mom, dad and I spent an enormous amount of time at tennis tournaments and practice. It was truly beautiful to watch her play. But in the short breaks between her long matches, I learned that I had a talent for clever goofiness. That was my time to make Mom and Dad laugh with the latest *Saturday Night Live* skit or by busting out an awkwardly funny break dance move. Being specially entertaining made me feel normal. I think I became addicted to it. What a feeling!

Over and over again throughout my life, people have tried to convince me of this common truth:

"Not everyone is going to like you, Paul."

Verbally and logically I always agree, but something deeper in me always boasts, "Yeah, right. You don't know me. I can make it happen."

And there are some positive results to back up that inner claim, but my mind and nerves are eroding because of it. And now I am seeing the effects of this flawed thinking. It manifests itself in overwhelming fatigue and sometimes furious anger. I continually coach myself to stop trying to make every situation perfect.

Jen and me in our first year of dating in 1992. Neither of us would have guessed what lay before us.

Massaging my life and the people in it is killing me. Sometimes my inner caution against seeking perfection holds its worthy ground, but when the approval heat gets turned up, I always go back to what seems comfortable. The easy way out is "likeability." There is comfort in being agreed with. But there's a big wrinkle. What about the inevitable times when my mouth or ego put people off? Usually this plunges my spirit into extreme unease. In that case, which has now become all cases, I make the life force–draining effort for approval livable by numbing myself. The only way to give this open-all-night thinking mart some relief is to consume substances. My various chemicals of choice help reality meet a hope-filled future, while altering the path taken to get here.

This roller coaster of illegal drug use is maddening. It starts with confidence and the need to blow off steam. You tell yourself you just want to be with your friends, but they aren't friends—they are the people you do drugs with. When doing the coke and ecstasy, things are exhilarating. Life is good, the impossible is possible, and laughter and approval are in the air. But eventually the eternal night ends, which for some is when the sun comes up, and for others it's when Monday arrives. That's when the outlook changes dramatically. It's a lower-than-low reality.

Jen and I wake up in disbelief at the five to six hundred dollars spent last night and the fact that we spent the middle of the night in a bathroom stall at a gay bar doing blow with three gay acquaintances. What sounds completely insane the next morning, however, sounds like a great idea the night before once you knock back that first couple of drinks. We have worked our way through most of our "nevers" in the past few years. "I'll *never* actually buy drugs. I'll *never* try cocaine. What is there for two hetero's to do in a gay bar? I'll *never* go there." At least we have a few "nevers" left.

Like, I know I'll *never* try heroine.

Many times we go to lunch and don't say a word, each knowing what the other is thinking. Why did we do that again? How will we get out of this? Maybe time will help. But in reality time does just the opposite. Give druggies time and they have just the right ammo to build up that dangerous confidence. Gaining arrogance causes us to make new plans with those same old people, always promising ourselves "it won't happen like that again." But it always does.

One thing is for sure: our weekend drug use is not going away on its own. We need help, before one of us buys the farm or worse, cheats on the other. As close as we've come to both of those scenarios, they haven't happened yet.

"We need to talk to someone," we agree.

We have admitted that this behavior is frightening, but we both agree that we are not at the point of needing a recovery center. That plunge would mean we are really far gone. So instead, we visit a psychologist.

Charesse is the most loving psychologist I have ever met. Jen and I squirm on her brown couch, which matches my khakis. If I had just worn my khaki jumpsuit, invisibility would be an option. Charesse clearly identifies that we are in a vortex of drug repetition that will not end well. Immediately she has figured out that while Jen likes to party, Jen mostly ties the drug use to the female friends that she has bonded with. Charesse decides that I'm in a different place. She comes to this conclusion mostly because, when asked, I can't remember the names of most of my coveted partying friends. I'm the problem; my anxiety is driving this fatal ship, she tells us.

"Paul, I do believe prescription anxiety medicine may help you," Charesse suggests.

"I don't know. That road brings so many side effects."

Mom, me and my sister Shannon. The worst sunburn in history waited for me on the other side of this flight. I became convinced it was because of me making those lame peace signs.

"Well, the things you describe to me tell me that you could have a condition we call bipolar type two," Charesse cautions.

"Bipolar! I'm not crazy, am I?"

"No, Honey. But just keep an open mind about bipolar medicine, okay?"

After our second session, Charesse politely shares that her son has just become the latest member of The Blue Man Group.

"Really?" I jump.

Electricity shoots up my spine. Blue Man Group is the big time. Everybody wants to get in to see their shows. Charesse's son has reached the top in the entertainment world. That's something I've always dreamed of doing. I wonder how he did it.

For the rest of our remaining treatments, when she talks all I hear is the Blue Man Group playing bizarre music on their PVC piping. "Honk, beat, beat, honk."

Charesse holds my hand.

"I want to help you put down this heavy bag of bricks, Paul."

"Me too. You know, I get the blue part, but how do they keep their faces so shiny for that whole two hour performance?"

A familiar "Paul!" blows out of Jen's mouth, scolding me to sta focused.

❧

After every Charesse appointment, Jen and I go enjoy di with a couple of bottles of wine and discuss why we simply get off the drugs. We don't arrive at a solution with Charesse I constantly hammer pretty hard that we need a geographic The genius screenplay (that I won't let even my wife read) w much faster if I'm in LA. We're ripe for success. I also ju the award for best music radio personality in St. Louis. We could make it in LA. I promise we will make new relationships out there, non-drug relationships in Hollywood. It will be different. No more defeated mornings and wasted days. It will be beaches, celebrities and stardom. Let's do it while we're young.

This cover-all move to the left coast will fix many things. Hopefully it will cause me to drop my endless, disgusting quest for painkillers. Nothing provides freedom from heavy-headed obsession like good old-fashioned pain medication. I had my first painkiller at age twenty-three after my wisdom teeth were removed. My life changed that day. It was the first time the ideas flowed without plans and pressure attached to them. Life was lighter and more beautiful. And I've had many more warm narcotic moments since then. How could feeling this way be wrong? Getting this prescribed feeling has been somewhat easy since developing multiple bouts of kidney stones since 1996. Just say those two words "kidney" and "stone" and faces wince. It's true that extreme pain swallows you whole during the time the stone is passing to the bladder, but not from the bladder to the toilet as everyone thinks. Pills have been prescribed somewhat freely since that first stone, and I've lied to doctors about them during the stoneless periods. But after a while, doctors don't just take your word for it.

"Well, if there is blood in your urine, you've got kidney stones. If not, you don't. Please fill this cup."

I'm not proud to reveal that scratching my gums with my fingernail and spitting blood in the cup then peeing on it always did the trick: thirty more Percodan earned.

"Thanks, now I'll finally be able to sleep and relax and be on the radio … and dream about where I should be."

Thoughts of ending up like Chris Farley occasionally dance in my mind.

Every time I saw the comedian on *Saturday Night Live*, I felt that I knew him. After seeing his movies, America fell in love with Chris Farley too. He seemed so jolly and funny. I was shocked to hear that personal demons caused his premature death in 1997. It also surprised me that seeing the picture of Chris Farley dead on the floor after five days of binge drinking and drugging didn't trigger repulsion in me. The three-times-too-big tongue hanging out of his mouth was oddly fascinating. I tried not to, but I couldn't help going back and viewing it over and over again that morning. I looked at it so many times, I should have made it my screensaver.

That very afternoon, I went to a doctor and lied to get painkillers. I can't explain it, but that was the reaction. You would think that Farley's ungraceful demise would have sobered me and helped keep me away from the possibility of ending up the same way. Instead, I went in the opposite direction. Deep down somewhere, I must have twisted it into a connection with Farley.

In the more lonely moments, I wonder how the type of guy who always kept a close eye on university hazing and unapproved bonfires as the president of my college fraternity got to this level of deception. I have no answer.

Actually, I've been trying to get right for a while now. Charesse suggested bipolar medicine, but my reality is already a new antidepressant every month. I'm on my fifth different feel-good right now. Other than pain medicine, I'm skeptical of any prescription relief because they create fatigue, anxiety, the shakes, gruesome nightmares that prevent sleep, hunger pangs, lack of appetite, sexual dysfunction and a really unstable, dangerous buzz when taken with alcohol or other designer drugs. I constantly wonder why I don't feel right.

CHAPTER 3
Smash Mouth, Smash Everything

It's three weeks after the K-hole and my confidence has grown enough for me to hold my head up. Tonight the radio station is having a remote broadcast at a bar downtown to encourage listeners to pre-party before they go to the Cardinals game. My Jack and Cokes are free. Three are already down the hatch, but I don't drink alone on the air tonight. Salespeople and the promotions crew all see this as the time to cut loose. We have done it this way the five previous weeks. Even though two Cardinals pre-parties remain, tonight will be the final time anyone is allowed to drink at events like this. There are many low moments in the drinking career of a guy like me. This one would definitely be voted in to my hall of fame.

The number one song on my radio station right now is "All Star" by a band called Smash Mouth. They are a fun, skaterish-type group with a rotund, jolly-looking lead singer. It must be an incredible sensation to have the number one song in the country. They can probably have whatever they want. So why is Smash Mouth's lead singer, Steve, sitting at the end of this tiny bar in St. Louis right now? It is very strange because they are not scheduled to perform any concerts in the area in the near future. My fascination with stardom and celebrity carries me down the bar to say hello.

"Hi Steve. I do nights at the radio station. We sure love 'All Star.'"

"Thanks," he says without looking up from his drink.

"I mean, really, what a great message it is about doing your best," I offer.

"Cool."

The St. Louis record rep with Steve tells me that they are in to promote the new CD and do a small show for our competition. That explains it. Steve is not at all what he seems in the Smash Mouth videos. Other than Zig Ziglar, this is one of my first celebrity meetings outside of the studio. I decide to pull back and give Steve some room and continue with my remote. A few more Jack and Cokes cause me to ponder why Steve didn't seem to like me. Maybe I didn't give him enough. I should have been better. Then I tell myself the most destructive thing I can say at that moment. "Maybe I can make him like me. Possibly we can hook up when I'm out in LA."

Another drive-by goes even worse, as I bring a pretty temptress of a co-worker with me. He doesn't seem interested in talking to the hot girl, and the mere sight of me seems to be making him sick. I step back. While also getting the brush-off, the girl decides to grab one of Steve's fries off his plate. Bad move.

"Get away from me, bitch!" he shouts.

Ouch. Awkward. I slither away, back to my broadcast station as she yells, "Screw you, dickhead!"

I look down and pretend not to hear it. Oh, crap, she is coming toward me. Now she points and yells, "Make sure that bastard's music never plays on our station again!" she orders me.

After a while, the intensity settles and the bar fills up. Mr. Social Smash Mouth is choosing to stay in the bar. He must be getting a charge out of telling people to leave him alone. He does it to a few other groups as well.

Our radio station promotions assistant grabs me from my remote table.

"Hey, the rest of Smash Mouth is at the other end of the bar and it sounds like they want to go on the air with you."

Eager to prove I'm not a total loser, I go and talk to them. We completely hit it off. After hanging out with them a bit, I learn that the rest of the band has a hit a weird patch with their big-boned lead singer too. That is why they aren't drinking together. I tell them I can see why. They even go on the radio with me. These guys are very cool.

My shift is over now. All of the radio station people are still partying with the rest of Smash Mouth, and now Jen has arrived. We are having a great time.

The guitar player, Greg, brings me another drink, the ninth or tenth of the night.

"Dude, let me introduce you to Steve myself. He's just weird, but he'll love you."

"Uh, I don't think so. You sure?"

"It will be all good."

I relent. We approach.

"Steve, you gotta meet Paul from the radio station. He's coming out with us."

"Get that fuckin' guy away from me!" Steve shouts. "You totally didn't have my back with that crazy bitch you brought over here to eat my food!"

Okay, now I'm feeling more pissed than rejected. I immediately turn and walk away. It appears that Steve just wanted me to sit there and take his abuse. Now he feels bad.

"Oh, dude, sorry, come on," Steve says

I keep walking. Greg stays with him.

When I get back to Jen, the record rep runs up to me.

"Your station was very inappropriate tonight with that girl yelling at the band and everyone is drunk. I'm calling your boss tomorrow."

"That guy is crazy," I say, motioning to the lead singer.

The record rep leaves me standing alone. I look at my drink and realize that my sometimes-coveted approval has been compromised. I feel myself losing control. It's hard to say why, but suddenly I overhand-throw my Jack and Coke glass as hard as I can at the huge brass elevator door. It shatters into a million little pieces. The sharp blades fill the crowded area. One woman loudly screams and all chatter stops. Security jumps out of nowhere. Everyone looks at me. I slither into the crowd and hear, "He did it. The radio guy did it."

Exiting the bar I think, what have I done? Drunken rage? I'll probably be fired. If pissing off the lead singer of one of the station's biggest bands doesn't do it, endangering partygoers at our event with a shattered glass certainly will.

Driving home, a hundred emotions attack me. Why did I desperately need that band to like me so much? Why couldn't I leave it alone and have a good time? It was completely wrong to freak out like that when representing the station in front of an advertiser. Mostly, my act of rage has caused me to look very bad. I can't take that. People will talk about this tomorrow. I feel like an attention-seeking loser. How weak. I start punching the ceiling of my Honda Accord. My thoughts pile on top of one another. This job was so hard earned; it will surely be gone. I scream and bash the ceiling with my right hand. With my other hand, I purposely steer the car into large orange construction drums on the side of the highway at sixty miles an hour. The construction drums fly in the air behind me. I see motorists cautiously stopping. I continue to punch the ceiling until it starts to dent. I cannot arrest my emotions as they intensify. I have lost all control.

Somehow I make it back to our apartment alive. Jen has beat me home. My right fist is bleeding. I'm still in disbelief about what I've done on the road. That "mania" the psychiatrists have described is happening right now. It just keeps getting worse: breaking my hand, appearing pushy to a celebrity, throwing a glass at a station event, endangering motorists on a highway. This rage doesn't cease at home. I can't stop, I need to get out. I run out of the back of the apartment straight through the screen door. The door sails on to the patio. Jen is scared to death because she can't understand what has tripped this episode, and truthfully, neither can I. The anger is its own entity.

Finally my blood cools and I return inside and try to convince Jennifer I am not going to kill myself. I see her to bed. She is not good with me for many days because of this frightening episode. I have a hard time living with it too.

The next morning, my knuckles are swollen and sore. I inspect my car and find the strangest evidence of last night on the front left quarter panel. A long strip of orange plastic has melted onto the black paint of the car. I hit so many construction drums at such high speed that the friction melted the plastic onto my car. Inside the car, the tan lining on the ceiling is tattered and the ceiling has knuckle imprints in it. The fury with which I hit the ceiling was powerful and dangerous. The night flashes across my memory as I sit in the parked car. My hangover saps me.

I check the newspaper to see if there were any accidents on Highway 40 last night. I breathe a bit easier after I find out there were not.

People begin to ask questions that day at work after both the nightclub/hotel and the record rep call the station. I explain it away by saying I simply dropped the glass. The pretty girl who swiped Smash Mouth Steve's fries gets most of the trouble because she appeared drunker than I at an event where drinking is not allowed. Somehow I avoid too many work consequences. It saddened me to learn that Steve Harwell would lose his six-month-old son to leukemia two years later. He certainly deserved better treatment than we showed him.

My breakdown frightens both Jen and me. We talk that night.

"You can never do that again. It was insane."

"I know. *That* was not me."

"I thought you were going to kill yourself. And for what?"

"I don't know. It was crazy. I think that whatever we were given this weekend messed me up pretty bad."

Four days before this episode, Jen and I had been given the date rape drug roofies in a club. We thought they were ecstasy. We lost twelve hours of our lives. I try to blame last night's actions on this.

"I hope that was it."

I promise to be Mr. Laidback from here on out although I know something unfamiliar is going on within me.

What is it? Am I turning into my late cousin Ren? Ren was a good dude. He looked like a young Jack Nicholson. Ren's loud, sinister laugh and jack-o-lantern smile illuminated every family gathering, even if he was hung over for most of them. After his marriage broke up, he moved into an apartment above a bar. They found him dead in that apartment last year with liquor and small cocaine residue everywhere. Ren had fired a gunshot into the TV and then into his head. By the time the police arrived, my cousin's "friends" had pretty much taken anything of value. His death hit me powerfully when I walked into the funeral and saw his two young daughters. What anger and mania makes a man take his life when he has so much to live for? I think I felt that anger last night and it scares me to the core.

Chapter 4
Geographical Cure

This town makes me sick. Everywhere I go, I see another reminder of drug and alcohol embarrassment. Has it ever worked, a geographical fix? I don't care. I just need one. St. Louis has got to be done with me, and I'm sure done with it. I've heard it before: "Moving away from your problems never makes them better." But just as I did with that advice from way back—"You can't make everyone like you"—I reject it. I believe I am different.

We need to observe the LA terrain and opportunities to see if this is actually feasible. Jen has chosen to live a dangerous social life just like me, but although she is having fun, she nonetheless hopes we will grow out of it soon. She jumped into the ecstasy boat with me a year and a half ago, probably because the stress of living with me was getting to her. My sense is that there is much more to Los Angeles than that, so to prove it, we fly out for a couple of days with my best friend Tom and his girlfriend Megan. Tom is also my writing partner on the animated cartoon about a nursing home. My six foot four best man lives in Seattle now and comes purely for enjoyment.

Driving around in this rented cherry-red Durango, we stick out more than if we wore Bermuda shorts and fanny packs. In fact, Durango is actually a city in central Mexico founded by lame, wide-eyed tourists. That fact is a very appropriate theme for us now. LA is everything we expected—gorgeous people, high fashion, hot climate, hot celebrities, and the sense of my big break is frothing over in the air, at least to me. Two long-time friends live in LA now. One is Seth, the stand-up comedian; the other is Nick Zyles, a production director for commercials and music videos. These guys are making it happen for themselves early in their entertainment careers. Zyles is a close friend from high school. He was a year behind me, and we played on the tennis team together. I like to think I discovered him like Quincy Jones discovered Herbie Hancock. I arrogantly believe people wouldn't have known Zyles was cool until I brought him out. This complex relationship caused me to be very abusive to him, the way an older brother might be. In fact we are sometimes asked if we are brothers. Zyles's absence of lips causes him to resemble Sean Penn, only he is freckle covered with light brown hair.

In our latest phone conversations, Zyles has assured me that if I move to LA, he will get me work as a production assistant on his shoots. Sounds somewhat promising. For now, I am grateful for his efforts. And to make sure they are genuine, I want to see him while I'm here to ask his advice on moving the show to Hollywood. Obviously I need more concrete affirmation on possible employment.

"P.A.ing is a $40,000-a-year job," he says. "A hundred and fifty bucks a day!"

He repeats this like a drone so much that I think he may be Rainman's twin: "We're counting cards!"

Production assistants earn $40,000 a year—if they work every day, which they don't. However, $40,000 a year would still be more than I've ever made in a year. Zyles seems extremely excited about the idea of our moving to LA. We can finally write together and make a name for ourselves. His conviction is inspiring. Back home in early high school, we were the weird kids trying to come up with some new dance to erupt into at the local teen dance club to the latest Milli Vanilli hit. I vividly recall one little number that involved our facing each other and hopping in a circle. Later that week, I almost crippled some young girl on the dance floor at Club 747 as I stumbled during the spinning portion of our jig. "Blame it on the Rain" must make her shin tingle to this day. After the incident, I crept off and bought a quick Sprite on the rocks acting like I was never even on the dance floor. That nicely epitomizes my hit-and-run style.

Right away, Jen and I notice that the hotels are different in Los Angeles. They are places to hang out, even if you're not staying in a room. After walking past a bar with a mechanical bull in it, we duck into The Standard Hotel on Sunset. The furniture and walls are all white and a girl is actually modeling in a plastic box behind the reception counter. Loud apathetic club music fills the seating area. The music comes from a modern bar area to the left of the reception counter. Jen and I grab a drink and a seat in the bar. Our friends rest in their room. I have another childhood friend from St. Louis who travels for his business. He is also in LA this week. Jack greets us with his usual sunburned face and tongues of airborne red hair. Immediately we recognize various *MTV Road Rules* and *Real World* cast members walking around.

Jack whispers, "There's a dude from *Saturday Night Live*."

"Yeah, it's Rob Schneider," I whisper back.

"Where? Oh I see," says Jen.

Rob Schneider and a friend have entered the bar about fifteen feet away. A tinge of weirdness hits my stomach. Almost immediately, I am on guard not to let another Smash Mouth episode happen. Remorse over that night is still available any time I think about music or celebrities.

"Let's say hey," Jack casually says.

"Not me, bro. I'll say 'hey' to my drink here."

"Oh, I love him," Jen says. "He's the 'You can put your weed in it' guy. I'll do it."

The Rob-inator happens to be working his way in our direction.

"But beware, honey. You never know how these guys are gonna react," I caution.

Jen gives me a dismissive look then goes for it, taking a step closer to him.

"Hi, Rob."

"Hi there, how are you guys?" Rob Schneider says like he's known us for years.

"We're great." Jen has become our spokesperson.

"What are you drinking? We're gonna grab one," says Rob Schneider.

"Jack and Diet Coke," Jen replies.

"Cool."

Schneider leaves for the bar. We giggle.

"Pretty cool guy," I said.

"Dude, think about it. He's buying your wife a drink," Jack says.

"Ah, he's harmless."

Rob trots back up to us with Jen's cocktail and he has a request.

"We're sitting right here, will you grab a seat with us?"

Just one seat is open at the table he refers to. It's right behind where we are sitting.

Jen looks at me and says, "Sure."

"Go ahead, you're good," I say.

As my wife sits down, I realize she's having a drink with *Deuce Bigalow: Male Gigolo.*

"Yeah, Jen is Deuce's next trick," says Jack.

Our backs are to them.

"Wait till he finds out she's married."

"You think he cares?"

"No, he seems like a good dude. He will care," I say.

Sitting there, my crazy mind starts to fly. Could it be that I am in the strangest of all real-life scenes from the movie *Indecent Proposal?* Instead of Robert Redford, little Rob Schneider is going to make us an offer of infidelity. I've only been in LA a few hours. This is crazy. I'm actually living an SNL skit. After Jen finishes her drink, she comes back to sit at our table.

"That was very cool. He's a nice guy."

"No flirting or hitting on you?"

"I didn't say that. But he's harmless."

ॐ

Our unbelievable recognizance mission to Los Angeles continues the next day when our Seattle friends, Jen and I sit down for lunch at an Italian cafe on Rodeo Drive. Dining on this famed street provides a good jolt of excitement. And soon Tom and I begin rapid foot tapping under the table when we overhear the twosome at the table to our left talking about the movie one of them has just finished. A younger, dark, redheaded man boasts to an older, heavier, Jewish-appearing man.

"Kevin will be recognized for his performance. It is such an awakening from living death to alive in this picture."

"I think all of them will be recognized," the older man adds.

"Deuce Bigalow" Rob Schneider and I in 2006. He had no memories of hitting on my wife seven years earlier.

Weird Al was cool and friendly, but not weird. Next to him is Greg Hewitt former mid-day talent in Y98.

Tom and I trade looks of haughtiness as we take in more of their conversation about The Director. Our girls know something is up with us, but being included in a conversation like this means nothing to them. We fill them in as we exit the little restaurant.

A year and a half later I see that dark red-haired guy on TV standing in a group accepting the Academy Award for Best Picture for the movie *American Beauty.* Kevin Spacey was recognized for his performance with the Best Actor Oscar.

Now we walk on Rodeo marveling at the huge prices in the antiseptic looking stores. Our obvious tourist vibe causes us to be approached by a dude on a skateboard carrying flyers offering us "to sit in the audience for a live late night show that is being nationally broadcast on a major network." Being curious, we relent.

Leno must be a real stickler. We find ourselves going through extremely rigorous audience evaluation. They also separate us from Tom and Megan, which makes this start to feel more like work than fun. After being security-wanded and scolded about the necessity for "appropriate clapping" I realize we are at the CBS Studios in Studio City. The four of us are deflated to realize we have run this gauntlet for *The Late Late Show with Craig Kilborn.* They seat Jen and me in the front row ten feet from Kilborn. I am so stressed about clapping at the wrong time that a nervous wheezing laugh has come to the surface. During the first commercial break, Kilborn looks down at his desk.

"Derek! I need more from these people."

Stiffly I lean into my wife.

"Hee hee hee. What a jerk. Hee hee."

The crowd is about a tenth of the size you see at Leno. It's hard to believe how distant and unfunny Kilborn is. Suddenly his coldness trips a feeling of being disapproved of. Screw this. Now

I'm refusing to applaud and I've taken to showing a forced serious face in this sea of canned laughter and glee. Kilborn is trying to deliver some lame bit where he claims he can define any word in the dictionary. He tells the crowd that we should just yell out a word and he'll give the Webster's definition. Two hours earlier in our cavity-searching audience briefing, the self-important crowd manager alerted us to this unfunny bit. He said that we should NOT yell anything out, but that "assistant producers" are in the crowd to yell out the words.

"Mollify!" A tired-looking twentyish blonde girl yells.

Kilborn gives the memorized answer.

I guess this is supposed to be unique and funny. Without waiting for him to finish his next definition I yell out the only thing I can think of that doesn't really have a definition.

"MOCK! MOCK!"

Kilborn swallows a bit, wondering what the hell I'm yelling. The crowd manager gives the throat-slashing motion to me. And after plenty of beautiful awkwardness, the six foot six TV host opens his mouth.

"Uh, did he say Marky Mark? What?"

They cut to break. Mission accomplished. I hope you feel you got "more from these people" now, Kilburrrn.

✍

Back at Zyles's apartment he begins to give me advice on moving out to LA. "You will not want to have regrets, man. When you get here, you gotta hustle."

Hustle? Obviously. In fact, I have a card with that written on it from my old tennis days.

Backstage at the VH-1 Awards in 2005 with actor Peter Gallagher. He was "The King" in American Beauty. It was the Oscar winning movie that Tom and I overheard a discussion about on our trip to Beverly Hills.

"I can assure you, Zyles, dust won't gather on these feet."

But Zyles is not talking about laziness. He says I need to inflate my experience to earn auditions and jobs and to worry about getting the right experience only after I actually get the job I'm supposed to have experience for in the first place.

I'm on board, baby.

"I'll do what it takes."

The freakiest night ever of hallucinogenic drugs ensues. It has come to be known as "The Funhouse Mushroom" night. Zyles presents us with two plates.

"Now the 'shrooms on the left are pretty good, but these over here are crazy."

We take the crazy fungus first then sit around waiting for them to take effect. The downtime is always awkward. I had taken mushrooms a few times in college. Other than pot, it was my first drug. Mushrooms were hot property in college, and up until now, the drug only created a sensation of heavy uncontrollable laughter, nothing more. So I know what to expect. A few genuine laughs might actually hit the spot now after that Kilborn turd.

As I lie on the bed waiting, a potted plant in the corner begins to bark and take the shape of a Chia pet. This only happens out of my peripheral vision; when I turn and look directly at it, the dog goes back to plant shape with no noises. The barking tree is seriously freaking me out. The funhouse is on. All we hear out of the next room is our girls giggling rapidly. Soon I find myself digging through Zyles's dirty laundry like a rat. We yell and try to hide in it. After the buzz smoothes out a bit, I become convinced that JFK Junior–looking Tom would be an Oscar-winning actor if only he'd "go for it." This strikes me after Tom starts rapping about getting shot. I turn into Stella Adler coaching Marlin Brando. Mushrooms make you leave yourself, taking everything in so intensely yet pleasurably.

"You have it, son. Your commitment is believable. Yes, I am sympathetic to your street plight. Yo," I promise.

I'm overlooking that he has absolutely no desire to do this. He's not a starving actor, Tom's a software salesman.

Finally at daylight we walk to our hotel. Unfortunately, we giggle till checkout time, getting no sleep. The harder the four of us try to sleep, the more snickering we do. When will this wear off? We are totally wiped out. Sandman cometh! A giggling mouth with worried eyes creates the weirdest of disturbing images.

⁓⁓

Back home in St. Louis, I still feel a bit crooked from all the hallucinogenic mushrooms. I've come to like this feeling, although it's a state that, earlier in my life, would have angered me. The Motor City Madman, Ted Nugent, has never drunk or done drugs. I heard him say he hated being with his fellow rockers backstage because it was like "trying to talk to a bunch of numb zombies." I previously felt the same way. In fact, Jen and I had many fights about her drinking in college. I hated any symptom that showed a lack of clarity and control. I wonder how I got on the other side of this?

I need to get advice on the LA idea from more than just the 'shroom king. Todd Newton from E! Entertainment was a local DJ here in St. Louis for years before making the move to Hollywood. He has become the hosting prototype all across the country. When a casting director is looking for a fun young host for a TV show, usually a "Todd Newton type" is also written in the breakdown. His name has now been replaced with "Ryan Seacrest type." So I track down Todd's e-mail and pop him an inquiry, expecting nothing. Boom, in forty-five minutes the guy sends me an e-mail, equipped with advice and pleasantries. Todd says that I should work on getting more camera time before coming out. He makes no mention of my script and TV show concept. Obviously the possession of either of these scripts makes no difference in being discovered because no one ever responds to my boasting about them.

Write This Down: quit waiting for an awestruck response when I mention the scripts.

Todd says it sounds like I have real potential but, "LA will always be there. Get better and get more stuff before coming out."

What a good guy—a good guy who obviously has it wrong about me and LA.

Nothing has ever been hammered out better than at Sunday lunches at my parents' house. Debates can erupt over the slightest bit of national news or political folly. And many times the chips and onion dip we munch together are the only common ground. My brother-in-law can stir it up as well as anyone, and Mom is not bashful about taking a counterposition either. It can go on for hours and from one meal to the next. This kind of fun probably happens with most families. There's something oddly fulfilling about these days. The only problem is that my participation of late has been muted by an allegiance to the all-nighter that has usually just ended a few hours earlier. In past years this aggressive and loving group of six has hammered out a solution to partisan politics as well as developing a rather kickass approach to scoring goals on the Blues power play. So, offering up a little thing like my desire for Hollywood at one of our confabs should be nothing for this think-tank to feast on. I want thoughts and opinions, baby! I'll wait for the right time when the conversation might make an easy transition to my desired topic. But for some odd reason today my bride's favorite subject has hit the round table, *Little House on the Prairie*. Have we gone soft? Please, what happened to NAFTA or the first amendment's legality of 2 Live Crew lyrics?

"Great show, tough to beat *Little House*," my sister says not looking up from the eighth-grade papers she grades.

"Oh my favorite was that Christmas episode when it snowed, and Mr. Edwards had to bring the gifts to the girls through the top window because it snowed up to the second level," Jen says with her thoughts residing somewhere in the innocence of those dusty streets of Mankato.

"Such a good family show," Mom offers.

"But poor little Carrie must have rolled down that wheat field too many times. She sounded kind of slow," I offer.

"That happened just once, Paul. They just played over and over again in the opening credits," my sister says with a smile.

"It's amazing how quick that pancreatic cancer took Michael Landon." Dad shoots some sunshine into the warm fuzzy convo.

"Yeah it was like one day he announced it and the next week Little Joe from Bonanza was gone," my brother-in-law says.

Perfect. The conversation is playing right into my hand. I see my opening.

"I can't imagine living with cancer. One of the characters in my screenplay is living with cancer," I say quickly.

No response. Jen gives me an "aw damn he went for it" look.

"A-and he's just too young to have it," I jump in again.

"To have what?" my brother-in-law asks.

"Cancer, he's too young to have it," I correct.

"He sure was and now he's walking that *Highway to Heaven*."

Mom drops in over the sink to rousing laughter.

"No, not Michael Landon. A guy in the movie I'm writing. He's twenty-two and has leukemia," I announce through the laughter.

Pause.

"Oh, that's interesting," Mom says.

"Actually I hope to move to LA soon to sell it and do other industry things too."

The silence doesn't tell me they disapprove; more it says they don't believe a guy in St. Louis with no writing experience could actually sell a script and make it in Hollywood. And I'm not totally sure I disagree. But I certainly disagree with the tension I now feel in the room.

After a few moments the silence gives way to distraction from our meal, grading papers, dishes and TV.

"Hey Ter, looks like the Billikens are gonna make the NCAA tournament this year," claims my brother-in-law.

"Eh, ya think? They have some work to do first," Dad replies.

Normal conversation commences, but I just sit and stare.

I feel like the kid in the back of the station wagon again, using a splattered bug mark on the window as the focal point for a laser, shooting street signs. "Oh, that Paul."

I've made a few passes at this topic and been given similar reactions and it's really starting to piss me off. Of course, my showing up late, forgetting birthdays and being hung over all the time is probably pissing them off.

The search for meaning and affirmation is so strong these days that any perceived criticism can set me off with no loyalties for family, friends or that blasted Todd Newton.

On the way home I ask Jen if she noticed the bizarre reaction to my screenwriting/LA offering?

"I know, that is so weird. I guess they just don't want you to leave," she says.

"Do they think I'm crazy or something? It makes me want to prove everyone wrong by actually making a success of myself out there. It's fueling me. When it happens I will shun them all!" I say, half-kidding.

༄

Although the talk of LA appears to me to have fallen on deaf ears with my parents, evidently it hasn't. After a while my dad calls and asks me to lunch. He uses that super calm business-owner-wanting-to-do-an-inventory voice. I know he means business. My dad is the most humble man I've ever known. He is good to the core and sensible even deeper than that.

As I lay out my ill-conceived plan to move this young marriage to the west, he listens. Then he stares. I talk more, knowing he thinks it's silly. Finally after getting our food he asks, "What about your preparation? You have to prepare for something like this."

Even that realistic question angers me. Calling me out on my behavior usually does. Grappling, I assure him I have a winning script here. Something he couldn't possibly understand as a State Farm Insurance agent. I calculate that he wouldn't dare go there.

"Dad, this thing is finished and it's ready to be bought (one-half finished)."

Why does a twenty-eight-year-old need this kind of affirmation and even permission to leave town for an exciting, if imaginary, opportunity? I'm not completely sure, but I know it is all about love and respect. This concern and care for my wellbeing is what positioned me for good things before the drugs and alcohol. His guidance is sound. If he were on board right now, it would fill me up. And eventually he will be.

My dad loves me, and most importantly he loves spending time with his crazy son in the same town. Also, to my great regret, my recent choices must remind him of his own alcoholic broadcaster father. When my father was young, his dad quit his radio news job without much thought and moved the family to Texas to become an orange farmer. He had no training, and they lost everything.

The similarities between my grandpa and me are not evident to me at this lunch appointment. I wish they had been.

He never actually says it, but I take my dad's vote as a "no."

Todd Newton, "no."

Zyles, "yes."

That'll do it. Let's do LA.

Both my wife and I quit our jobs before securing any confirmation of future employment. It's liberating. We feel nervous and proud. We are "Team Cook." Now all that's left is to get some travelers' checks and pack up the U-Haul.

CHAPTER 5
The Edge Of Adventure

The one-way drive to Los Angeles is 1,875 miles. We'll load up everything we own in the U-Haul and make the trip with Ted, our autistic cat. Ted doesn't handle people very well and is very skittish. If Ted is on your lap when the phone rings, you could be scratched to the point of a ruptured spleen. Usually I see him just lying on the floor staring at the wall. As I sit on the couch thinking and over-thinking, I envision Ted counting, endlessly counting. His personality is more suited to numbers than emotions. He probably thinks I am counting too. We are perfect for each other. One time I went down to our wet, dirty, unfinished basement and saw Ted standing in the back dungeon hole near the furnace just staring face first into the corner, much like the victims in *The Blair Witch Project*. I was sure the witch had gotten him.

For our road trip, we need to heavily drug Teddy. It is Jen's job to talk to the vet and get the cat tranquilizers. It is my duty to daydream about the cool buzz they might create if I take them myself.

The day before we leave, there is time for reflection and to offer our families heartfelt assurances that nothing is permanent. I also get in one last wrestling session with my brilliant five-year-old nephew, Jessie. Right there in the grass in front of the loaded-up U-Haul on this beautiful sunny July morning, I let him pin me. We all wear heavy hearts, but to Jen and me, the hard part is over and we need to see it through.

During my shower the next morning before we leave, I detect a bit of strangeness down below. Close investigation reveals that a giant tick has attached itself to my scrotum. This is as disturbing a thing as a suburban young man can ever discover. The wrestling match with my nephew must have been two against one, tick and nephew against uncle. This big black bastard seriously has a white skull with horns tattooed on his back and he has been working all night. Moses gave Pharaoh many signs that he was making the wrong choice: plagues, hail, frogs, locusts. My first sign will come to be known as "Tick on Balls." But it won't be the last. Plague-causing divinity will be with us the whole time. After using a hot match to try and burn the devil bug off my masculinity, I ascertain it looks infected. I invite my weepy father to have a look at my war wound. What a wonderful goodbye image I am offering this poor man.

After more than the necessary Bactine cotton swabbings and a tearful goodbye to both sets of our supportive parents, we hit the road.

The unknown excites Jen and comforts me. These days for me comfort comes from anything that breaks up the norm. At the telemarketing job I took right after college, life was so depressing and boring that I would cause distractions to break up the day. Burning popcorn in the microwave can create quite a stir with the office folk. I'm talking about burned to the core. When an overpowering carcinogenic odor runs through the halls, you've accomplished laudable distraction. This type of fun can kill a good two hours of a workday. It's a three-parter: the set-up, the frenzy created then the gossiping about it.

"What dumb-ass keeps misjudging the microwave cooking times?" I'd say. "I mean, there's a button for popcorn right *there*."

Moving to LA is the mother of all breaks from the norm. Maybe that's why I didn't heed the "Don't Go" advice. Additional comfort and glee run high because I truly believe in my heart that this change of locale will relieve my almost constant search for drugs. I've also sold everyone, including myself, on the "this is my destiny" concept.

Before we even get out of our neighborhood subdivision, Ted the cat is cutting loose primal screams like a lustful raptor. We grab him out of his cage, break one of the tranquilizers in half, and try to feed it to him. Immediately the medicinal taste repulses him, and we lose the element of surprise. It would take a living mouse to get him to open his mouth now. From here on out, good ol'-fashioned force will be my only alternative to get Ted his meds.

Finally we get it in the animal's beak and Jen says, "You gotta massage his throat to get it to go down." Yeah, massage the sharp object in his tender little neck; I'm sure that's not excruciating. After a while, Ted's cursing gives way to a small growl and his pupils increase to a totally frightening size. This cannot be our cat. Freakish and spooky. This is exactly how our clubbing party group looks to each other at four AM in a club's well-lit bathroom. Ted is silent.

Driving a U-Haul carting a car behind it is interesting sport. I mostly stay in the right lane out of necessity because this thing only goes about forty-five miles per hour downhill. But an interesting phenomenon of physics happens every time a semi flies by us on the left. When the truck gets even with our front bumper, some sort of wind lock builds up between the two vehicles and we feel a huge push out to the shoulder. It's like putting two positive magnets together; they force each other apart. So to counteract this mechanism, every time a semi passes us, I find myself doing the unthinkable: I direct the massive U-Haul steering wheel toward the giant vehicle flying by us, just to keep us on the road. This is totally counter-intuitive. The necessity to jerk the wheel toward a collision to avoid actually leaving the road thousands of times on this trip causes a strange, fearless mental twist. Abandonment of these driving laws has dusted my already out-of-whack ego with a few more grains of self-importance.

About one hundred miles into our journey, the same vehicle passes us twice. It's a small, haggard white pickup carrying assorted furniture and mattresses, and beneath that junk, on the lower left, is a small wooden cage with a cramped dog inside. The rear bumper and bed of the truck almost touch the ground. Knowing nothing about cars I say, "His shocks must be blown."

I wonder did this guy in the white pickup make the same decision to pursue stardom as we did, because for most of our 1,875-mile trip, we will be tandemed with him. It is like a bizarre dream because he always appears to pass us two times for each time we pass him. Maybe he's got a tiny bladder and every time he passes us he pulls off at an exit to relieve it then, speeding up when he resumes, he catches back up to us. And now that the highway hypnosis is running high, I consider that maybe there are two beat-up white trucks with dog cages tag-teaming down Route 66. Who is this guy? Is he bringing a screenplay to Hollywood too? What about that poor dog? Maybe we aren't as unique as we think. Is this the gold rush?

Jen says, "I feel bad for that little dog. He looks miserable."

"Yeah, that's a horrible thing to do to an animal," I reply.

"Screw you both," growls Ted.

The long day of driving ends in Oklahoma City. The next day as we're making our way out of Oklahoma, a storm that feels like the rapture hits. Suddenly the sun just goes away; winds swirl. Jen grabs my attention from the road.

"What the hell is that?"

It looks like twenty mini-tornados spinning on each side of the road, and suddenly, like a shotgun blast, hard rain pounds the windshield. Visibility is zero. I am literally driving and seeing nothing. I tell myself cars are at least moving on the highway and I should not pull over because I would probably rear end one of the other cars seeking relief on the shoulder. Our hearts pound. The thought of imminent calamity is on our faces.

"Pull over!" urges Jen.

"I can't. I can't see at all! I'll hit a parked car."

I am locked in. Rain pounds like gravel on the windshield. My senses feel cat-like, minus the tranquilizers. The next five minutes seem to take a week. Gradually a patch of light blue becomes visible through the windshield.

"It's breaking up."

The first vehicle I see is the beat-up white truck with the dog in the cage. I can't believe it.

"Why did he just flip us off?" Jen asks.

"We must have been going slower than the jerk-off liked during the Armageddon." What a nightmare.

"Is our car still back there?"

I am positive our load is a little lighter now. We will have to check on the cargo. Thankfully, Ted is still out cold in la-la land. The swirling storm nightmare is over.

A successful campaign of survival has worked up some rumblings of hunger. We notice huge signs advertising The Big Texan restaurant. This place promotes a free seventy-two-ounce steak. Who could possibly want to eat that much red meat? Maybe that blinding downpour painfully transitioned us to a bizarre world between heaven and hell, where beasts devour half their body weight in beef every day. Nope. A quick drive by the restaurant reveals that we are indeed still on "over promise, under deliver" earth. The Big Texan is a big anti-climax.

To this point, we have quit our jobs and made the emotional break from our hometown. We have avoided certain death from a sideways monsoon, and we've managed to drug the cat twice. A feeling of victory fills the U-Haul cab. What can't we do? Over my life, I've learned that a question like this is a red flag. A red flag not heeded. "What can't I do?" almost always seems to usher in some form of overstep followed by pain.

One of my buddies in college had a friend who won the Iowa State Lottery: $2.3 million. This guy bought a Winnebago. For spring break in my junior year, we decided to drive that motor home to Arizona State University to take in the parties and beautiful girls. En route to ASU, I convinced the other four guys that a detour to Vegas would be fun. The convincing took the simple purchasing of an Elvis "Viva Las Vegas" cass-single at a truck stop. The next 300 miles were my leg to drive, so Elvis was great background to support my persuasion. Easy prey. I'm sure they gave in just to shut me up.

We pulled into Vegas with high hopes, created by me. But in the end, every guy lost most of his money. On top of losing a ton of cash, my added punishment was developing pink eye in each eye.

"What a great idea, Cook, douche! Now we're off course 350 miles and we're broke."

The Viva Las Vegas cass-single raps me in the head while I put in some truck stop Visine in the back seat.

My wife, Ted and I are now on that exact same stretch of road where I began my Las Vegas sell job seven years ago in college. That proved to be such a fruitful trip that I decide to start working it again. Capitalizing on the air of victory that surrounds me, I break down the detour and its advantages.

"But where would we park this thing," asks Jen,

"On the strip, baby. Come on, I need the juice!"

"Paul, we have our whole life in this U-Haul. What if someone steals it?"

She's right, I'm looking to fill the hole. Why would I risk it all for one or two exciting nights? We bag the Vegas idea, and I make her pay for being an adult by giving her the silent treatment for an hour. At the end of my light pouting, remorse follows. This is a woman who has already been through hell for me, seen me almost die, watched me out-selfish the selfish, and quit her job to jump on my so-called star. Her reality checks like this one have probably kept me alive, but that doesn't stop me from sucking the joy right out of the U-Haul like an Oreck vac. I do not deserve her.

Now the U-Haul goes thirty-five miles per hour at top speed. There has got to be something wrong with this vehicle.

"Maybe if we turn off the AC," Jen suggests.

That suggestion gives us a mere extra five miles per hour, but that's progress.

"Good call."

Silence.

"Sorry about the Vegas idea. You were right."

"I just don't want to always be the drag."

"No, you aren't. I need you to reality-check me sometimes. I need that."

"I'm not saying it wouldn't have been fun. We'll be close enough to check it out once we get settled in LA. There are so many places

I want to see."

I grab her hand.

"This is gonna be great."

For at least one thousand miles of our trip, we sit holding hands. She obviously doesn't know I need her more than she needs me.

With no AC, the cabin heat must have awakened Ted. We are now nearing the Mojave Desert and doing it without any cool air. Suddenly Ted begins to let up guttural cat screams of a new tone.

"I'm gonna get him out of his carrier and let him get some air," says Jen.

Ted's matted hair and dry nose alert us to his diminished health. This counting kitty has been part of no less than five moves in the last five years with us. The mind of Ted is complex. When he was a kitten, we tried to potty-train him. We kept finding a wet stinky corner in our crappy apartment, so we knew he had not been using the cat box. Jen would give Ted small spanks and say "No!" every time the corner was wet. It was strange to us when we realized Ted only used his pee corner when it rained. You never know what's going on with animals. We were disgusted when it occurred to us that the corner of the apartment leaked when it rained; it wasn't Ted at all. Maybe that's why he is so skittish. He's been proving the self-fulfilling prophecy by urinating on the couch every once in a while since then.

Right now, he's in a heated drug-withdrawal misery. Very strange. Ted just keeps opening his mouth like he wants more air. Open, shut, silently and slowly, open, shut.

"What the hell is he doing?"

Fresh air and angry kitty must not mix. After a couple more breaths he makes a run for the brakes and gas pedal area of the U-Haul. I manage to pin him with my right wrist while still hanging

I regret that I drank too much at my own wedding reception. Every time I hear about a young dude getting married I grab him and caution him not to drink too much because you'll remember that for the rest of your life.

on to a Dorito. I hold the enormous steering wheel with my left hand. He's slipping from my wrist lock, and I'm still refusing to drop the chip. I mostly have his tail now. If he gets loose down there, surely his frenzied head will get jammed under the brake and we will end up in the strangest car fatality ever. Is this how we're gonna go out? Jen tries to grab Ted around the midsection.

"PHITFFRAAAR!!!!"

Like a reflex, Ted flips around and bites her hand. This cat has entered the third dimension of crazy, totally out of character. Maps, drinks and cat hair are flying. We have an insane cat screaming in the cab of our U-Haul and we are screaming too. His hissing promises he will bite any and all comers.

Bring it, bitches!

The trip is taking a toll. We finally manage to bat our lovely house pet into his cage and throw him behind the seat. Crazy situations happen to most people in the singular; they seem to happen to me on top of one another and all at once. This is one of those times.

We have to get some air in this joint. Our U-Haul has a very rudimentary, circa 1980s-type sunroof. A gunk-covered twisty dial on the ceiling of the cab is the only tool. You spin it and basically the big hatch lifts up allowing fresh air to get into the cab. Twist it the other way and it closes. Calling this a sunroof is too generous. I crank it up. Yes, fresh air. Noisy, fresh, hot air. Like Hannibal Lecter, Ted jerks his caged head towards the rush of air like he just heard an enormous tasty moth flutter its wings. All the benefit the fresh air brings us is erased by the annoyingly loud whistling steel noise. But we continue to creep along Route 66 at about forty-five miles per hour in a growling capsule of heat and hope.

"Please put down that crappy sunroof." Jen can take it no more.

"Can you do it? I gotta keep us on the road."

Twist, twist, twist. Slowly that bad boy must be going down. Nope.

"Maybe you need to go the other way," I offer.

That doesn't work either. There is no way that thing is broken in the open position as we are heading into the Mojave desert with no AC and a crazy cat on board. The thermometer tops 104. This is unbelievable. We pull over to get a closer, sweaty look at the problem. I decide I am going to "man" it closed by forcing it. Now I'm on top of the cab at a gas station, trying to pound the little roof door down. It won't budge. The arm holding it up is locked like a Jim Brown stiff arm.

"Jen, hand me that two-by-four we're supposed to put behind the tire when we park on a hill."

Now I'm losing my temper trying to leverage it down with this long piece of wood. The wood snaps.

I yell to the heavens, "You have got to be kidding me! No way!"

I am at my wits' end. We slither back on to the highway.

After a couple hundred more miles, we can take the heat no longer so we stop to find a motel. I call home to my parents to give them the status on our trip so far. They give us some great news. The program director at KBIG Radio in LA called after hearing the demo I sent him. This nationally known program director wants to have a meeting when I get to LA. What a jolt of hope. Maybe I actually could be on the air in the second biggest market in the country. Coming from market twenty, you always have your doubts. And this program director is big. As I doze off that night, I think maybe this decision was not crazy to the core.

In the middle of the night my hopeful slumber gets startled. "Good Christ, what is that crazy noise?" I say to Jen. Out of a dead

Ted The Cat and the couch he urinated on in 1998. At this moment Ted is joyfully pondering another road trip.

sleep, I realize I'm in a hotel room. The noise sounds like what happens when Tickle Me Elmo's batteries are running low and Elmo enters a falsetto demon state by himself in the middle of the night.

Elmo's high voice "ECK!" deepens to super low "HeeeeEEEE."

"Sweet Jesus, we have a poltergeist!"

That exact type of noise comes from under the bed right now and only a strand of kitty sound is mixed in. Ted is already crazy, but now he also has a drug-soaked brain. And he obviously does not approve of La Quinta Inns. We hear banging on the walls from next door.

"Shut up!"

There's really nothing like tackling the cat in the middle of the night to force meds down his throat. It's beast control. A switch has flipped in my brain, and somehow it feels right. "GET OVER HERE MUTHER!"

I pry his ungrateful mouth open and deliver the goods. I then free him from my death grip and he continues yelling, but after a minute or two he's back to crackhead.

As we whistle along down the road the next day, I hang on to the thought of that radio op at KBIG. When thoughts drift to worry, remorse or fear, which often percolate in me, I bring my mind back to KBIG as a reservoir of positivity.

CHAPTER 6
Try To Fit In

Traffic and heat greet us as we drive into Southern California. We sit in a jam that starts in Ontario, Ca. This is obviously just an aberration. But at least it gives me an opportunity to hear "my new" radio station, KBIG 104. The blonde lady who played the singer on Ally McBeal is the first artist we hear. What? She's not a real artist. And why was she always singing someone else's hit on that show anyway? Listening more. Ew, this is a tad lame. Maybe it's just one song. We keep listening. More Celine Dion, Selena, and Madonna. What? This is a station for gay people! And in a world where sounding real on the radio is the goal, these DJs are puking their voices all over the place like Casey Kasem. I feel like I'm back in the '80s. Before long, it gets a bit more hip, but not much. Well it's not like the station I came from, but it is market number two, and I'm in if they'll have me.

Unlike most men, I will pull over for directions, but then I'll get distracted in the convenience mart and totally forget those directions. Upon realizing this, I'll refuse to go back in. Jen was giving me directions around my hometown within the first year of her being there. And now Jen points the U-Haul in the direction of Culver City. We have a two-week reservation at the Extended Stay hotel there. And when we find an apartment, we'll just move in.

Culver City is home to many major production studios, and we recognize it right away. Excitement is building. This is a special place to me. I have dreamed about making this move my whole life.

We pull off the Howard Hughes Expressway and our temporary home is right there next to Dinah's Chicken. We unhitch the car and back the U-Haul up against a wall, so no one will break into it. We are anxious to get out and tour around our new sun-soaked home.

Driving around on Sunset feels great. The attractiveness and activity really jump out at us. Strangely, everyone seems to be completely aware of each other, always making eye contact. We have lunch on the deck of a bar called Red Rock. I see the bass player from the Goo Goo Dolls drive by in a new Volkswagen Beetle.

"This is gonna be cool."

Jen spots Nathalie from *The Facts of Life* later, and I totally miss her.

"You didn't miss much; she looked angry."

After getting back to our room, I make the call to KBIG. Ronnie Kann wants to see me later that afternoon. Scramble time. Jen and I cruise to Glendale together.

"I like you. You sound like Seacrest," Ronnie says.

"He sounds like me."

"We were this close to hiring him last year for mornings (wistfully looking off). Okay, we do have one opening for you doing weekends. I want you to come in and tryout live on the air tonight."

"Tonight? You got it."

"Yeah, do two to five AM. We are union so you get paid for this. Fill out your paperwork with Andy and leave the tape of your show under my door, and I'll call you to let you know if you fit in."

"Any pointers?" I ask.

Long pause.

"You see out that window? They took that shot in the beginning of *Erin Brockovich*. Gorgeous. Remember it?"

"Oh, wow. Yeah." I have no clue.

"Air Advice: lots of energy. The positioner is K-Big 104 LA, and Orange County's Upbeat Mix of 80s, 90s and today!"

I repeat it.

"No, no, no!"

And just like in Howard Stern's movie *Private Parts*, this guy starts coaching me on inflection perfection.

"You have GOT to go up on the upbeat!"

So we go back and forth with me yelling "UPBEAT mix of the—" and him correcting, "NO, NO!, up*beat* mix!"

Finally he gets tired of correcting me and says, "You got it. Good luck. Bye!"

I'm in Hollywood for three hours and I already have a paying job, sort of. Pride is running high, but I'm incredibly tired and I have to stay up and try out for this station all night. Staying awake won't be the problem, but sharp creativity and good radio formatics could be. Then gradually, my fatigue gives way to that familiar fear. The second guessing begins to riddle. I've become the kind of guy who always loves to know he has a job but never really wants to work. But now it's action time.

As Jen and I look at apartments in Brentwood (where the O.J. murders took place), I practice my "up*beat* Mix!" These Los Angeles neighborhoods are amazing. Splashing pools and manicured lawns are the decor. Beautiful people walk around everywhere, holding either Coffee Bean cups or Jamba Juice Smoothies.

As I drive to KBIG that night, I hear the regular evening guy talking so loud and pukey that it sounds like someone has his balls wrapped in a rubber band. Where am I? This can't be real. I've been feverishly working for the last five years to sound natural on the air. This departure is going to be a tall order. After further reflection, I surmise that even if I get the job, I think I'll be so miserable I'll want to off myself. So I decide to go over the top with my voice like Wolfman Jack would do.

"KBIG 104! LA AND ORANGE COUNTIES' UPBEEEEAT MIX OF THE 80'S, 90'S AND TODAY! I'M PAUL COOK, HA! STEVE WINWOOD NOW!"

Yuck.

After three hours of that, I shove the cassette under Ronnie Kaye's door while snickering, and I leave.

The next day, I call Ronnie and he says, "You nailed it! I was worried you would try to be all alternative and totally kill the energy. But you did really well. KBIG is yours if you want it."

"Oh thank you so much. That means a ton coming from you. But I'm not sure KBIG is the best fit for me. I just don't want to seem ungrateful."

Ronnie jumps in, "I understand. I don't know if they have any openings but would you like me to call STAR for you? We are the same company."

STAR would be a much better fit. Danny Bonaduce is the morning host and Ryan Seacrest is on in the afternoon. I thank Ronnie again and tell him I'd be grateful for his help.

～♂～

After sleeping during the day on Friday, we decide to hit Hollywood that night. And we will do it with a fellow confirmand. Seth has lived out here for three years. We have gone to church and school together from the beginning. We were confirmed in

Danny Bonaduce and Gretchen Bonaduce in 2005. They got married after their first date and divorced a year after this picture was taken. We are Backstage at the Vh-1 awards, four years after I left LA. Danny had a hit show in 2005 on Vh-1 called Breaking Bonaduce. It probably caused that divorce.

the United Church of Christ back in St. Louis in 1985 and have since abandoned many of those Christian principles. He is doing his work for award shows on the red carpet these days and also performing stand-up comedy. Everyone back home is rooting for our lighthearted, lanky friend to make it big. After meeting up with other St. Louis transplants at a bar on the Sunset Strip called Dublan's, we decide to hit a bar on Hollywood Boulevard where Jeff Goldblum is rumored to be playing in a band.

I loved Goldblum in *The Fly*. His appearances in the *Jurassic Park* movies have made him a wealthy man. Actors can be found playing music almost every night of the week in LA. For many of them it seems that music is their true love. I find myself wondering, why do they forsake what is attained with such difficulty for amateur guitar riffs? Or in Goldblum's case, the keyboard.

As we enter we notice that the walls of this bar are made of liquid. The water runs straight across the wall and from the ceiling to the floor with glass between you and the water. The rushing water sound appears to be calming for most, but it makes me think I have to pee. Jen and I have never seen anything as modern as this. A Red Bull and vodka cost twelve bucks. Evidently water walls don't grow on trees. When you order that drink you should just say "Gimme a System Jerker." The alcohol and taurine (super caffeine) mix feels bizarre. I like to feel different. We spot Goldblum right on entry. This is exciting; for my money, he is the coolest guy in show business. He introduces his band.

"Hi everyone. We are the Swinging Chads!"

He's a pretty good musician too. I stand to his right, about ten feet off the stage. When the first song ends, he looks directly at me and says, "Do you play?"

"Yes I do." In reality, I took seven keyboard lessons in the eighth grade. I can only play the beginning of seven Van Halen songs and "On The Dark Side" by John Cafferty.

"It's great, isn't it? Where are you from?" Goldblum looks out.

"My wife and I just moved here from St. Louis."

"Good luck."

Not wanting to overstep, I walk away. When I tell my buzzed wife that I just had a conversation with Jeff Fricken Goldblum, she says, "No way! Oh, I always wanted to tell him something."

"Well, maybe we'll see him again when the band takes a break."

Sure enough, twenty minutes later he long strides right by us.

"Jeff! This is my wife, Jen."

"It's my pleasure to meet you. How long have you two been married?"

"Four years."

"Nice, that's wonderful! You guys look good together."

"Jeff, I have always wanted to tell you that you have the best walk in show business," Jen offers.

"Well, thank you." says an embarrassed Goldblum with a pause, "Nice meeting you guys."

He walks away attempting to hang on to his famous saunter, only the compliment appears to have tightened his Achilles tendon. You know the feeling when someone draws attention to a physical attribute you possess? You try not to do anything different, but it is impossible. My wife has made Jeff Goldblum lose himself in a way. What a great start.

"Best walk? You had to go there? What the hell was that?"

"It's true," argues Jen.

Seth sneaks up.

"Your obsession with Jeff Goldblum is freaking me out. I thought you were gonna tell him you wanted to skin him and wear his flesh as your own. Next time slow down."

The next day, we travel up the Pacific Coast Highway to Malibu to have Greyhounds at an outdoor restaurant-bar. We suck them down like water. The walls of the bar feature old pictures of famous surfers. We throw the drinks and mahi-mahi meals on the Visa and life is all good. As we drive back down the PCH, we listen to STAR, the other station Ronnie was talking about. It's like night and day. An old school Kasey Kasem sound is replaced with a cool spunky girl. Lara lures you in by chatting with callers about life and pop culture. Jen and I look at each other because we have never heard a girl on the radio sound this good. But that is bad. Suddenly I start to feel like I might not be good enough to work on this station. Forcing optimism, I check the messages on the spiffy complimentary voice mail at our tidy Extended Stay in Culver City. A message from the program director at STAR 98.7FM causes a near drive off into an embankment. After a spirited conversation sponsored by Grey Goose, they invite me in to offer me a job on STAR Radio. April, the STAR program director, lets their Saturday night guy go to give me Saturday and Sunday nights. Since writing scripts and doing on-camera work are my goals, just weekends at STAR will be perfect. My emotions have roller coasted from dirt low to king high.

I meet Ryan Seacrest at my first interview.

"Wow, you are loud, Paul," is the first thing he says to me.

"Sorry, it's just good to meet you. I'm a big fan." Not really, but I keep hearing that I'm like him, so why not be a fan of myself.

"Well, thanks. Welcome to STAR."

I learn quickly that this guy is a star. Even though he is not yet nationally known, you get the feeling that it's in Ryan Seacrest's future. People talk about him everywhere in the city, and soon I actually do become a fan. At this time I begin to feel a little-fish-in-a-big-pond sensation shrinking my confidence to minnow size. The fact that I was offered two radio jobs in the first twenty-four hours doesn't seem to inflate me like I thought it would. However, plenty of cheap pinot grigio from Whole Foods does just the trick to fight the anxiety. Maybe that's why I talk so loud; I'm generally semi-buzzed. But then again, people are always telling me I'm loud, whether I'm drinking or not. Could I be the real-life Jacob Silge? He was the volume-challenged character Will Farrell played on *Saturday Night Live*. Everything he said, he shouted.

I have been put in a position to win. Things are looking up, but pangs of fear begin to creep in on me like never before.

In the weeks that followed, I did my shifts on STAR, and April seemed to like them. But radio is not why I'm in Hollywood. I'm here to sell these scripts, do some auditioning and get an agent. I have always envisioned that this will all be possible by showing everyone my unbridled, contagious charisma. Only problem is, I'm finding that I'm unable to muster that magic I was born with. It is being blanketed for some reason. Maybe I have lost it for good. In my mind, only liquor can bring out my personality. Obviously this is not a new concept for me.

When I earned my big break doing evenings full-time in St. Louis, I was amped up and ready to go on the air that first time. But an hour before the broadcast, I escaped the building and bought a big bottle of Orange Mad Dog liquor. I downed that foul cheap elixir while sitting in my '88 Accord in a bad neighborhood. It turned out to be one of my better shows. I drank away the pressured expectations.

Shopping at the Ralph's on Wilshire in Santa Monica right now, I think about picking up a bottle of that "vitamin C" Mad Dog for old time's sake. I'm here because I've been scolded by Jen and told to get "all new supplies." We had to throw out the surplus of toiletries we brought because I discovered a legion of ants had taken over half our U-Haul at the Extended Stay. They were going after the cat food in the truck. My brilliant idea of backing her up to a foliage-covered wall for security purposes was just the opportunity the little bitches needed.

So the signs that I may be acting outside of the "plan for my life" are starting to mount. You've got TICK ON BALLS before leaving, TINY KILLER SAND TORNADOES on the road and now ANT-INFESTED U-HAUL after arriving. We go unscathed over the next few weeks, which are filled with high hopes.

Over that time we take many trips to the beach. Jen canvases the area with résumés, and I get more comfortable in my on-air position. Also we find an apartment in Brentwood, a one-bedroom for $1,250 a month, no cats allowed. I build Ted a secret compartment in the closet with a moving box. He runs for his life to get in the box if someone knocks at the door, a phone rings (real life or on the TV), the toilet flushes, or the alarm clock goes off. Where are those kitty tranquilizers?

To sell my screenplay, I first have to finish it. It was supposed to be done months ago, but I just couldn't bring myself to write during all that obsessing about Smash Mouth and the K-hole. But that is behind me now, 1,875 miles away. While Jen is off interviewing with Heinz, the LA *Times*, and Cintas Uniforms, I sit on a metal lawn chair by our Melrose Place-like apartment pool and write. I need a gruesome scene to carry me into the third and final act. How about a cult member with Down Syndrome? His lungs are larger than normal. He grabs victims and holds them at the bottom of pools to show his power. He'd have to operate near a resort where he puts pool-goers in danger, then he saves them, persuading them to join his "church." Oh, this is wicked.

During this brilliant thinking time, I first meet L'il Raj, a small twenty-three-year-old who looks about sixteen. Dark hair, tan skin, glasses and acne. He is skittish like Ted. Oddly, that both irritates me and endears him to me. I've seen him before, loitering around our new apartment. Everywhere he goes he carries a small black vinyl bag about the size of a fanny pack. Every time I see that, I say to myself, I bet he has drugs in that bag. Well, it's time to find out. He's on the approach.

"How ya doing, man?" I offer

"You guys are new, right?" L'il Raj replies.

"Yeah, we're from St. Louis. I'm Paul."

"I'm Roger. I used to party with Sandy, the girl who just moved out of your apartment."

Party? Too easy. I remind myself I am not going to pursue drug relationships here in LA. This is just fact-finding. I'm doing nothing. Lying to yourself is quite easy if you want to. You just need to activate that dangerous power of rationalization.

"Sandy, yeah, we met her." Pause. "Ya know, I thought you partied."

I get a big smile from L'il Raj. "I think you'll have fun here."

If I had known the places I would go with L'il Raj and that he had every drug ever invented in his apartment at that time, I would have tied myself to that metal lawn chair and plunged into the pool like a resort-dwelling Down Syndrome cult member. But it appears I had to experience each of those empty moments on my own.

CHAPTER 7
Welcome To The Cube Farm

Back in St. Louis, I had started corresponding with an entertainment temp agency. The Comar Agency places personal assistants with celebrities and they put office employees in production companies and with networks. Evidently, people in Los Angeles call in sick a lot, because these businesses always need temp help. Getting the call from them to go do some temp work tomorrow makes my wife happy. The thought of my working nine to five warms the cockles of her work-ethic pumping heart.

The FX cable channel needs a data entry person for the next couple of days. I should do this for Comar, because it will help them know I'm a good guy to call for the bigger things. FX is on Santa Monica Boulevard in the same building as Fox Sports and right near the Fox News Channel.

They set me up in a cubicle cataloging beta tapes of commercials. I even have a computer with an Internet connection, but they frown on personal Internet use. Having worked only in radio since the Internet became prominent, I don't understand these restrictions on surfing. It's required in radio. At the end of my first day they tell me this temp job is open ended, and I should plan on returning every day until further notice.

The best I can tell, the commercial traffic department I'm working in is mostly full of number-crunching type-B personalities, except for the dude in the cube to my right, talking on the phone all day about the independent film he has maxed out his credit cards trying to make. His name is Carlos. The only other creative is a hostile Prince wannabe who runs the beta-tape storage room. I am shunned by him about four times a day when dropping off my tapes after cataloging.

Hmmm, structure. This gig might be okay. I get a lunch. I stay out of trouble. And I can read every screenplay ever written while I'm supposed to be working. I find it curious that these office folk try to throw at least one party a week at lunch: birthdays, Halloween, going away, newcomer celebration, best decorated cube, best lunch, best idea for a lunch party.

This is weird to me because they appear to be the most miserable gaggle of folks ever to walk the earth. Disgust oozes. I am unable to attend most of these awkward lunch gatherings. The food repulses me and the conversation reminds me of the first time you meet your girlfriend's parents. Besides, lunch is my free time to check out the city and possibly grab a nap and some TV. I get an hour, but if you keep a good lookout as to when your supervisor leaves to eat, you can stretch it into an hour and forty-five minutes. Just make sure she sees you working right before she leaves. Get her with a nonchalant hallway pass.

"Barbara, I think I'm getting this thing down!"

"Great, any questions you have just let me know after I come back from lunch."

"You got it, I'll be right here plugging away."

Then bail quickly. When you come back from the slumber, make it known that you worked through most of her lunchtime and that you must have left for yours right when she got back. There are a variety of ways to do this, most of them involve making sure she hears it in a loud hallway conversation.

Logging tapes is easy, and I'm not sure it really serves a purpose.

I average reading about a screenplay a day. M. Knight Shyamalan wrote the best one I've read when he penned "The Sixth Sense." I spend my remaining six hours touring the building, analyzing the vending machine goodies and worrying about making it in this city.

On recent nights, I've been getting assaulted by my mind while I'm sitting on the couch. For some reason, I can't seem to let go of things I said and did during my drugging St. Louis days. Alcohol is in the picture in LA, but no drugs. I believe these overpowering thoughts are happening because the fog is lifting. Or the damage done by the psychotic drugs—ecstasy, antidepressants, cocaine, and ketamine—is starting to manifest itself in paranoia, worry and remorse. In those days we didn't really mortally hurt anyone except ourselves, and we kept our fidelity. But these small regrets and embarrassments can't be put away no matter how hard I try. This is when I really start to rely on Jen for support. Far more often than ever before, I check with her to see if things I did were "okay" or not that "big of a deal."

At first she constantly says, "That is so not a big deal."

But then my out-of-the-norm frequency and need to ask wears on her. "Why are you worrying about this stuff in the past?"

"I'm not sure. But was that okay?"

"Yes! Quit it."

Generally the nightly wine or daily Bud Light and Jack Daniel's tend to settle these thoughts down. But after the liquor runs out, mind mugging commences.

My discovery of paddle tennis has helped. Exercise has always served my mind more than my body. Zyles and I play on the walk in Venice Beach right by Muscle Beach. This activity serves my ego well. Tourists walk by looking at all the shops and vendors on the boardwalk, and many stop to watch this interesting game of mini-tennis. Being seen as local is what I've always wanted.

I remember walking around Williamsburg, Virginia on a family trip, with a plastic sword and three-corner hat from the gift shop. Looking like a soldier, I dreamed that everyone thought I worked as a professional war re-enactor.

Zyles and I pick up paddle tennis pretty quickly since we have a background in actual tennis. Our knock-down, drag-out yelling matches over line calls also divert attention our way.

"Out? You gotta be kidding me! Zyles, you know the lines are in bounds, right?"

"Shut up! I make five hundred bucks a day!" Zyles brags for no reason.

"What?"

Cheap shot.

⤴⤵

Life at FX is starting to feel pretty satisfactory. I've been here a couple weeks and now everyone knows I'm on the air at Star 98.7 on the weekends. I always see them mentally trying to figure out why a guy on the air at that great station is a temp in a cube for seven dollars an hour during the week. Radio doesn't bring in the money most people think.

I've fallen in love with a certain potato potpie out of the vending machine in our Fox break room. Everyday this warm creamy treat makes a euphoric appointment with me. My increasingly puffy face is evidence of a love connection. Today I am surprised to see Bill O'Reilly eating in our tiny lunchroom with his very old parents. He is extremely polite and quiet with them. They all talk with their inside voices. O'Reilly's dad looks like a shorter, eighty-year-old version of his son. Mom and dad are a one-piece unit, sitting closely, not wanting to be fussed over. I think, should I leave them alone?

"Ding!"

My Tater Pot Pie is ready in the microwave. Nah, I think I'll sit and eavesdrop a bit. Bill Fricken O'Reilly—one of the most hated men in this city—is sitting right here! Prince wannabe doesn't even notice him when he grabs a grape drink out of the machine. I try to let the purple one know by moving my eyes so that he notices Bill Fricken O'Reilly. Prince wannabe looks at me like I'm retarded. Walking out, he says nothing.

O'Reilly carefully unwraps a frozen chocolate éclair ice-cream bar from the vending machine. His father uses a fork and knife to eat the ice cream like prime rib. The popsicle stick shoots out the side. O'Reilly whispers quietly to them and they share a few reserved chuckles. It's just me and them in the snack room and now it feels like I'm intruding. After a few short moments, I leave. It was interesting how sweetly he handled his parents. You would expect something more brash and aggressive.

"Dad here's your chocolate éclair. Go! Mom, looking good. What say you!?"

"Well, Bill this—"

"Nah, Nah, Nah. You're wrong! And I'm outta time. And you're being unreasonable, but you get the last word."

Dad offers, "Ya know tourists in this t-t-town—"

"GOTTA GO! GOTTA GO!"

⁂

Zyles's girlfriend Kerri is also from St. Louis. He met her at

Missouri State. She is a beautiful, younger version of Shania Twain. For her birthday, Zyles takes us to The Sunset Room for dinner. This is a very trendy place for celebrities to eat and party. After dinner, we go to the dance area. Jen has been hitting the Red Bulls and vodka pretty hard. Her drunk eyes and fidgety body display a familiar contrast. I have been matching her drink for drink with Jack and Coke.

Earlier that week, during my FX lunch, I had an interview at William Morris to talk about my latest short-term whim of becoming a trainee agent. I met a very nice, slick agent during the interview. To show my thanks for his kindness, I use the business card he gave me at that interview as my own at the Sunset Room.

"You're an agent at William Morris?" some dude asks.

Everyone in LA constantly asks what you do.

"Yeah, it's not that cool," I reply. "People always want something from me."

"Hey, I want to introduce you to someone," Dude says.

"You got it."

He walks me back through the restaurant and introduces me as "Robert, an agent at William Morris" to the most skanked-up porn star I've ever seen. She is hammered and her lipstick is all over her teeth. Her eyes light up.

"Hi," she meekly squeals like Paris Hilton.

"Charlotte wants to start doing more mainstream acting," Dude offers.

"Well give me a call. We'll talk about it."

I hand her the business card. You might think I'd be disappointed that I wasted my one William Morris business card on a skanked-up porn star, but I have no regrets. The delight in her eyes was well worth it. I wonder how that phone conversation went on Monday when she called Robert.

On the way home, we have to pull over on the 10 so that Jen can heave. After a few more stops for my weary wife, we finally arrive at the apartment. As she plunges onto our bed, she weakly says into the other room, "Happy Berfday, Kerri!"

The rest of us are heavily buzzed and not ready for the night to end. What a great opportunity to introduce Zyles to L'il Raj, who's been lingering outside our door anyway. L'il Raj invites us into his cruddy little apartment for a smoke. Cigarette? No. Weed? Nah.

"How about a smoke of opium?"

We're up for it, but in our current diminished state, it's hard to figure out all the moving parts to smoking opium. The little black gummy drug is on a long stiff wire. You need to heat up a metal hanger with a lighter. Then you touch the hanger to the gummy substance and inhale the smoke through another weird bong. Yes, with all of this paraphernalia involved it looks like advanced drug addiction 101 in here. We giggle through the weirdness. Soon Zyles and I are tackling this like two Iranian princes. Zyles takes on the aggression of a pro wrestler.

"HAAAA, LET'S DO MORE!" yells Iron Sheik Zyles.

As the WWF's "Mean Jean" Okerland might, I manage to negotiate a move of all the opium equipment back to my apartment minus L'il Raj. The kicker happens when I decide to heat up the hanger with the gas stove burner. My opium buzz puts a huge delay between turning on the gas and actually lighting it. Click. Click. Click. POOOF! A burst of flames two feet high fills the kitchen. Then the fire disappears quickly, taking my eyebrows with it.

CHAPTER 8
Money In Dem Hills

Jen has been offered a wonderful job at Cintas Uniforms. This opportunity will save us since she is earning more than she ever made previously. She deserves it after all that time working with the old boys as a food broker. Jen's days schlepping for some fat, lazy, arrogant man are finally over. The only obstacle standing in our way will be a drug test.

Two weeks earlier, Jen tagged along on a trip over the hills to Burbank to visit my friend Seth. On that day, fear charged through our sunburned bodies as Seth brought out a giant blue four-foot bong to blow on. Weed has never been a drug of choice for either Jen or me. It makes us weird. I don't need more strange thoughts. And she doesn't need more bladder-bursting laughter. Nonetheless, with the excited newness of LA in our present, we partake on this Wednesday dusk.

Seth dives in, "Cough, Cough! Happens everytime."

"What the hell are we doing?" I ask.

"I'm scared," says Jen.

Looking down through the long smurf-like member, I see a swirling tornado of cannabis fumes levitating towards my worried peepers. I take it in. The smoke disappears as in Ron Howard's *Backdraft* movie.

"HERE!" I say in a high Papa Smurf voice.

The old "here" hand-off is the best thing about pot. Breathe out the air in your lungs and say "Here!" and you got the sound.

"YES!" yells Seth as he grabs it.

It takes two people to operate this Death Star of drug paraphernalia, one to light, the other to partake from four feet away. Now the video camera is on. Seth and I compete in the "White Guy Dance Party." The test is who can come up with the most hideous and lame moves. I am certain that Seth has unhinged his arms from his torso during one number. That gives him the title, hands down.

"I'm hungry. You wanna grab the best ice cream on the planet?" asks Seth.

On the way, Jen breaks a time-spent-laughing record culminating in a pee incident in Seth's back seat. Jen reluctantly enjoys her mint chip and wet shorts, cracking a smile in between self-scolding head shakes. She is so embarrassed that we never tell Seth. His mom came out for a visit a month later.

"Seth, good mercy! Your car smells like cat pee."

❧

Heavy coffee intake puts me in the place I need to be for radio. Then beer and wine sustain me after coffee brings the jitters. Sometimes the process is reversed. I'm the Saturday night fun guy on STAR. Energy and fun. Coffee and liquor. Answering the radio station phones in LA is much more fruitful than in St. Louis.

"Hey, this is Star!"

"Seacrest, what are you doing there on a Saturday night?"

"Oh, this is Paul; I just kind of sound like Ryan. What are you doin' tonight?"

Click.

Everyone knows Danny Bonaduce from his Partridge Family

days, and you may have heard he was accused of beating up a tranny one time in the '80s. But since those days, he's been doing radio and doing it very well. When I lived in DeKalb, Illinois, I listened to Danny's show in Chicago and it was truly great. Radio is what he was meant to do.

I've learned that Danny's morning show at STAR does well, but Ryan Seacrest's afternoon show is even more popular. Seacrest's afternoon show sounds like a morning show. His partner Lisa Foxx operates with incredible ease on the radio and women listeners seem to really love her. As far as I can tell, that's the big difference between St. Louis radio and LA radio: the women are much better here. Since people have been telling me I sound like Seacrest, it's super weird to now be working at his station. As I mentioned, he is absolutely poised to blow up huge. In fact, both of these men are volcanoes waiting to erupt—Ryan's career and Danny's emotions and addictions. I see myself as more of a Ryan, but possibly I am closer to Danny.

Existing at air staff meetings with these talented people is quite a challenge. I am basically reduced to a piece of furniture in the corner. At my old radio station, I was fun, motivated and full of ideas. But now, no matter how hard I try, the "Ol' Paulie Power Play" is not charged. People close to me know the "power play" as a moment where we choose for my personality to dominate a situation. Sometimes this would be necessary when two groups of strangers were getting together for an event. Possibly the other group was being unkind or stuffy. The Paulie Power Play puts them on their heels a bit. It could even send other aggressive personalities into an introverted state. I wouldn't describe it as being mean, just big, wild and affable. Sometimes that's all it takes.

But this is LA, home of the big boys. Now I've become the

introvert. Fear grips me, and strangely I have developed a very weird physical habit that I cannot stop with all of my will. I find myself putting my two thumbnails together, matching them up. For some reason they need to match perfectly; if they don't, I scrape one down a bit. I look down and focus on this all the time, especially when I am quietly thinking, which happens a lot in these meetings. This neurosis is new and while it is comforting to me, it has to be off-putting to others. I don't know where it came from and I have never seen anyone do it before. Am I losing it?

This fear needs to be overcome. That small fact I know. Los Angeles is not the place to turtle up and lose your courage. So in a move to draw out the real Paul, I take an acting class. It is my first since a three-month workshop I took in my seventh-grade summer. Back then, our workshop ended with a big performance in which I was the lead. I felt great about my performance, but there was silence from my parents on the ride home. When I asked what they thought of my acting, my mom simply said, "You seemed very self-conscious."

This was really a very harmless comment from my mother. She probably meant that I could have practiced more, creating more comfort with the material on stage. But harmless leveled at a painfully sensitive person can leave its marks. It has been my goal to never "seem self-conscious" again. But awareness of this goal would not help. In fact, maybe it hindered. For me, it is either self-conscious or over-confident, never the desired middle ground.

I'm taking Terry Berland's Commercial Acting Workshop. I have heard that many celebs get their big break pimping some product with extreme frequency before a television audience. To me, this seems like a back door to getting noticed and I'm all for a shortcut. The class is made up of seasoned actors, and then there's this disc jockey who sometimes smells of wine and liquor. So far, the most notable thing about this class is that we sit on Dudley Moore's old shedding white burlap couch. And it also sits on us. He donated it to the acting school. When I eat my imaginary chocolate brownie in front of the class and camera, long white bits of fabric from Dudley's couch sit on my shoulder, cheering me on.

"Use the space!" says the burlap couch. "Make bold choices with the copy!"

But rehearsing my commercials at home with Jen nearly always leads to hostile thoughts. It seems to be an opportunity for Jen to take the stress of the workday out on me and my performances. Eventually the class will be reading a McDonald's spot before a real agent and I need practice.

"McDonald's make their burgers with less meat. Do I look twenty percent smaller to you? I di—"

"UH! I'm not feeling it," Jen interrupts. "You have dead eyes!" She laughs.

"Okay, but please say it more constructively."

"Where are you looking off to? I'm right here?"

"The camera is usually above you. Jen, you suck at this."

"I'm just trying to be like a casting director. Don't you want that?"

Later that night, a knock on the door startles us. A nice-looking thirty-year-old guy named Chris introduces himself as our neighbor. Dark hair, looks like he's from the Midwest. We hold our conversation in the apartment hallway on the second floor overlooking the pool. He is an attorney who works for the California prosecutor's office.

"Let me know if you ever need a ticket taken care of."

"If we ever get moving above the speed limit with all this

traffic!"

"HHAHAHAHALOL."

We all hold the laugh for way too long. L'il Raj comes out of his apartment. He has a knack for noticing any and all who make it out of their apartment.

"Hey guys," L'il Raj says as his voice cracks.

"Well, nice meeting you guys," says Chris. "I'll be seeing you I guess."

"That's for sure!" Jen replies. "Bye."

"What's up dude?" I ask.

"I wanted to see what you guys did with Sandy's apartment," answers L'il Raj.

After looking around, he appears to like Jen's home decor touch.

"Man, I hope we weren't too loud smoking that crazy shit the other night," I say. "Our next door neighbor works for the city."

"Chris? He's a big crack-head," replies L'il Raj.

I laugh.

"What?" asks Jen.

"Crack-head Chris." L'il Raj throws away.

"No way."

"Yeah, he and I bought a ball one time and he spent all weekend cooking it up in his microwave. It was a little too intense."

Jen looks at me, I look down. Where in the world are we?

CHAPTER 9
Bipolar Two Electric Boog-A-Loo

The moments I spend worrying are increasing by the day. Small rituals sometimes give me comfort or prevent it when they are not completed. I start to wonder if I'm becoming obsessive compulsive. I look at my thumbs a lot. The hours I spend matching the nails together are even worrying me. Being with people or being alone doesn't change this ritual. When I look down at my thumbs, people ask, "What are you looking at?" I don't have an answer. I also wash my hands more frequently than normal. I was seeing a psychiatrist back in St. Louis. His diagnosis was bipolar type two. The main symptom of type two is anxiety and a cycling of up and down moods.

The thumb matching and other new OCD rituals and symptoms, plus the worrying, obsessing and not feeling right in my gut have caused me to seek medicine from a psychiatrist here in LA. Despite the side-effect hell I endured in St. Louis, obtaining medicines is what I do best. My psychiatrist, Roger Dom, resembles Father Dowling from the *Father Dowling Mysteries*. And that is appropriate because in this city my wife is constantly mistaken for the nun played by Tracy Nelson on that show. In fact, we saw my bride's doppelganger in person one night at the Hamburger Hamlet in Brentwood. The similarities were minimized when the two appeared next to each other in the same room. Jen looked like the "before" picture shown during a "don't smoke and tan too much" seminar. Tracy Nelson has enjoyed the outdoors and a few

Luckys in her time.

With the exception of needing all payment up front with no submissions to health care providers by him, Dr. Dom appears to be a kind man sitting in his soft light wonderland office. Soft orchestral music lightly plays in the background. He makes his love of the arts well known in our small talk. The Doc was over the moon for the movie *Chocolat*, or as he would call it "Shock-oh-lot." Descriptions of what was going on in my head must have "shocked-oh-lot" too. Almost immediately he puts me on the very potent drug depakote, pronounced dep-a-coat. It's a drug used by epileptics and, in much higher doses, by bipolar patients. Because of our fascinating *Chocolat* talk, I will always call my new medication "Johnny Depakote." Using him, or it, I will experience daze, hunger and chopped up people in my nightmares. My OCD tendencies do lessen though, so I continue to take the enormous 2,500 milligrams a day as directed.

Now at the strangest times, I feel extreme hunger like never before. My stomach forces me to pull over for a meatball sub at Subway. The to-go order is gone before the car starts. Johnny Depakote fun is just beginning.

∽⚬∾

The Comar Agency does what they promised. They place me at the FX Network in the traffic department, and while it is not "entertainment," it is near entertainment. They have just called to see how I feel about being a personal assistant for a well-known producer.

"Jerry Bruckheimer needs a new personal assistant. Have you heard of him?"

"Sure, *Men in Black*, right?"

"Totally," the Comar rep says.

"Interesting, how much would something like this pay?"

"That's the good part. The job is twelve hours a day. With overtime you will make close to sixty thousand a year."

"Great. What would I be doing?"

"You will take care of his needs. He has two dogs and one has cancer. You'll be spending time with them and taking the stool samples to the doctor for the sick doggy. You will also organize his hockey team."

Damn, I hate other people's dogs. "Uh ... I'm not sure this is for me."

"And you'll be running scripts up to Nic Cage almost every day."

"What?" I can win that dude over.

"Yep. You will be doing a lot of script-running to big-time actors."

"Cool. Just tell me what to do."

"We'll set it up. Just show what a great team player you are."

Zyles calls.

"JERRY FRICKEN BRUCKHEIMER! Are you kidding me?" screams Zyles.

"Yeah, he did *Men in Black*, right?"

"No! Are you crazy? *Con Air, The Rock, Armageddon, Coyote Ugly*. Every big movie comes from him."

"Yeah, but I won't be on the professional side."

"Dude, it all runs together. I heard he has hired many of his personal assistants to be producers for his company after a while. This is huge. Look at it this way. Bruckheimer Productions is the one paying you."

After thinking about it, I realize Zyles is right. LA is more a relationship city than a talent one. Getting in with this guy will be key. I have generally enjoyed good success at winning people over. This is my big break. As long as I don't miss the interview because I am forced to pull over for a sixer of Fat Burgers to satisfy this psychotic hunger. The final interview is one on one with Jerry Bruckheimer himself, but that comes after four meetings with various other people at Jerry Bruckheimer Films over the next few months.

Big Break. I lie awake in the middle of the night watching Jen sleep so peacefully. She is silent, cozied up and beautiful. Her face puffs up just a bit when she sleeps causing her to appear even more content. Out the window the sky is light gray. The city makes no noise either. The only thing I hear is Ted grooming himself down on the floor. Many nights we are nocturnal partners like this. I ponder what is in front of me over and over again. I hope I have what it takes to deliver on "my big break."

Moving to Los Angeles helped remove some old obstacles in my life. The need for prescription pills is one of those. Many nights I would hate myself for looking in friends' and family's medicine cabinets for old painkillers that I convinced myself were no longer valuable to them. Unforgivably, I took meds from people who ended up really needing them. And embarrassingly, but deservedly so, at least five times I swiped and ingested drugs that were not pain medicines at all, causing me extreme sickness. A couple of unexplainable incidents like this can make an amateur pharmacist out of any pill popper. I had a run of this for five years. All blame goes to me, but many times I would swear someone outside my body was doing the pill snooping. My only choice was to swallow the stolen pills my alter ego had pocketed in order to forget that indiscretion. And now here in LA, as my perceived need for pain pills has decreased, my daily drinking has replaced it. There's such excitement in this city, but a huge spine of unbearable anxiety runs through it for me.

I've been in LA for four months now and tonight I am set to attend a radio station staff party intended to build closeness. Rock and roll bowling will be our vehicle to interpersonal cohesion and fun. All the big dogs will attend—Seacrest, Bonaduce, the program director April (who I can't get a read on), Lisa Foxx, Lara Scott and Jaime White, Danny's chirpy sidekick. What to wear? How to act? Certainly I have to kill a four-pack of mini-wine bottles in the Universal City parking lot before making my appearance.

"Gag! Cough! Fricken white zin!"

I walk into the all-neon bowling alley at The Universal City Walk. Someone introduces me to Bonaduce's sidekick, Jamie White.

"Hey! Nice to meet you, Jamie."

She jumps on me, legs first, as I'm tying my bowling shoes. We tumble over onto the slick floor of a bowling lane. As we sort out the tangled limbs on the hardwood, I think, "You crazy bitch!"

She gets up, saying nothing more to me. I was just a pawn in her quest to look like a fun, wild girl. I've used that *M.O.* to look like a fun, wild girl too. Uh, boy. Jamie gets canned a couple years later.

One of the most down-to-earth people at the party is Danny Bonaduce himself. He pleasantly inquires how I like LA while he pleasantly pounds many drinks. My kind of guy. Back at one of the scorers' tables a few other female rock 'n roll bowlers have spotted Seacrest. They are on him like Danny's *Partridge Family* brother David Cassidy. I hang close to sponge the zest. Seacrest uses my name every time he talks to me, a virtue I wish I possessed, but I can't seem to remember anyone's name.

The night ends with the shoe attendant having a hard time finding Bonaduce's boots in the square wooden boxes where they replace bowling shoes. Danny jumps over the counter, completely startling the tattooed dude. Danny grabs his leather cowboy boots and jumps back over the counter. Tattooed Dude says he's going to call the police. Danny leaves and gets in a scuffle in the parking lot with another man. After a certain point it appears that Danny may be a bad drunk. I like to think I'm a pleasant, story-telling, sometimes exaggerating drunk, if there is such a thing.

The hangover that morning is a toughie. I throw back seven hundred and fifty milligrams of Johnny Depakote and within minutes I feel better, but I am certainly no more productive at work. I feel like Donnie Darko in front of my computer screen. It is sucking me in. This depakote is strong stuff. I can hardly read a script now because of uncontrollable staring. That is not cool. A couple weeks ago, I found a running cartoon rabbit online. I copied that running rabbit onto the desktop of my work computer. He just runs in place all day. I log hours every day just watching this little white fella jog. It's calming in an odd way.

A voice startles me.

"Paul, could you come see me when you have a natural break in your current task?" asks Barbara.

Barbara runs the department. Busted. I wipe away the drool, straighten my sweater, and head into her office to receive my medicine.

"Paul, how are things going?"

"Pretty well. Still learning, but I really enjoy the work."

"Are you really?"

"Yes, I like numbers."

"Well, with Rosa Marie leaving us for Oxygen, we're in the lurch.

We'd like to offer you a permanent, full-time job here at FX in the traffic department."

"Wow, what a compliment."

"We can pay you $26.5K."

Twenty-six thousand dollars a year in LA? I better get free Andy Capp's Hot Fries out of the vending machines, cuz that's the only way I'll eat.

"Oh, Barbara, thank you very much."

"I don't need to know today."

"Okay, let me talk it over with my wife."

"This could be very exciting for you, Paul."

"Ya know, I can feel that. Thank you."

"Let us know."

"I'm betting I'll be jumping at it. On an unrelated note, did you get my request for a personal day on Friday?"

"Uh, yes, we'll cover for you."

My shortsightedness knows no bounds. I am offered the compliment of a full-time job to work, and I wrap it up with an inquiry about not working. Barbara should have known right there she was dealing with a distracted man.

The personal day that I inquired about so smoothly is for me to visit Jack in Phoenix. He was the friend observing Jen's speed date with Rob Schneider. Friends since age seven, we have damaged slightly fewer things in our twenty-three-year relationship than the Janjaweed have done to Sierra Leone looking for diamonds. Hilariously memorable moments also seem to follow us.

About three years ago, Jack was diagnosed with the very convenient illness of Adult Attention Deficit Disorder. A prescribed dose of a form of Ritalin has helped him avoid the need to race every single motorist at every stoplight on his way to work. This drug calms and focuses Jack. I have found that it produces a cocaine-like effect in me. Before LA, asking for a couple of these blue pills before going on the air became somewhat of a ritual for me. And very much unlike me, Jack usually gave them up. Unfortunately, my self-consciousness about these requests passed the limits of tolerable embarrassment, so I began taking tablets of his much-needed medicine when he was not looking.

I'll never forget the time he paid for me to be in a golf tournament with him and while he was out chipping on to the green, I snaked a few pills right out of the golf cart. During the awards ceremony after the scramble, they fell out onto my chair and Jack discovered them. I denied that I had taken them. Writing this now I realize what a horrible friend I have been to this man. The extent of this damaging betrayal could not be calculated at the time of the infraction, but it would have its consequences.

Jack's longtime girlfriend has just broken up with him for the final time, and to celebrate, he has gone out and earned his third DWI. I come out to console my lifelong friend. Obviously this is also a trip to get hammered in different surroundings.

Jack is a better-looking, shorter version of Mark McGwire. He sweats out his liquor with heavy workouts and his physique displays this. I barely recall him unloading both Jen and me on our bed one night a year ago after we were given roofies instead of ecstasy at a club. He probably saved our lives that night.

Zyles and I start drinking heavily at LAX before our flight. Jack is unaware that Zyles is coming on this mission of brotherly love. They are distant friends.

Delusion and arrogance mask the reality of how stupid it is to smuggle marijuana onto a plane. L'il Raj fronted me the small package that resides under mine right now. As I've mentioned, pot is not my thing, but I have no pills and the liquor is starting to be less effective. The fact that these substances are so necessary in my daily diet of life angers me. I was told that in high school and college, drugs were all around me. I truly recall never noticing them. Now that I'm a living victim, I notice every pill or narcotic within a forty-foot radius. My "drug-dar" is a gift to my addiction and probably a fast lane to my demise.

Jack picks us up and we continue drinking at one of Phoenix's off-track betting establishments. Between races, we talk about his DWI and breakup. He appears to be a sad man, a sad man willing to go along with the party for companionship.

Back at his Tempe, Arizona, condo, we drink more. Another hometown friend shows up. Rudy has taken my place as the friend who actually has the ability to care about others. Jack has flown Rudy out to be with us. I light up my Bob Marley on Jack's deck, but our host is disgusted.

"Man you brought pot on a plane? You gotta be better than that. I always thought big things were in the cards for you."

This is strange, because Jack was the first person I ever saw do drugs. One day during our sophomore year, after I picked him up for school, he unwrapped a little aluminum foil package and put a pile of dusty moldy hallucinogenic mushrooms on his McBiscuit. Maybe he envisions a better path for me than the one he will take, which must be categorized as being a good friend. But now, every time he sees me doing a drug, it angers him, probably because he has seen me steal his own medicine. He always just says, "You're better than that." Many people incorrectly think that these days.

I'm tired and dragging big time. I need a pick-me-up. I put out the joint. Rather than going back through the sliding doors to the room where everyone is drinking, I go back in the other side to

Jack's bedroom. There I start a frenzied search for his Ritalin. The rummaging is borderline vandalism. What am I doing? How can I be doing this? Knocking starts at the door.

"I'm taking a shower!" I yell.

He's now banging at the door, and I can't find those little blue pills. As I open a dresser drawer, I see Jack standing on the deck looking in at me. Discovered, I stop immediately and take my shower. Nothing is said.

Jack refuses to sit with me at the club that night. He sits at the bar with Rudy, downing Stoli like he's trying to break a record. I hang out near the dance club, and the Paul-Cook-bulldog-for-drugs mindset has been activated. X is the goal. But lethargy and slur have stolen my charm. It seems that most of the Arizona clubbers are convinced I'm a cop. I'm half-hoping a cop comes and smothers my endless search.

At three AM, the bright closing time lights go on in the club. In the parking lot I am tailing Jack. I push him like a brother and begin yelling at him.

"What the hell is wrong with you?"

With an extra forty pounds and additional four inches of height, he turns and runs at me aggressively. We begin grappling in a hugging-type position.

"Hey, you ripped my shirt!" I say.

BOOM!

I feel a punch to the side of my face. We've been through a lot since kindergarten, and we've both wronged each other over the years, but a full-on knock to the face? My ears are ringing. This isn't happening.

"Did you just punch me?" I'm still grappling.

BOOM! Again I feel his giant, gaudy silver ring break the skin on my cheek bone. I start backing up quickly while holding on to him. With all his weight coming my way, I step to the side sharply pulling him with me, and he flies to the ground. He must be too drunk and not know it's me.

"Jay, it's me, Paul! You just punched me twice. It's Paul!"

Jack says nothing as he stands up. Then he cracks me again, same spot. I feel it from my Adam's apple to the small of my back. It sobers me immediately.

"Let's go, fucker," I yell.

He swings another huge right. I duck it, and he misses. Immediately I unload on my lifelong friend with swinging rights and lefts, all straight to the face. He falls straight back to the pavement. A crowd of exiting clubbers has gathered.

"Stay down," I yell at him. "What the fuck are you doing?"

Blood drips from my eye onto my shoulder. He struggles to get up again. I jump on him, striking him more in the face. From the ground he kicks me in the ribs to get up.

Finally, our friends jump in through the big crowd. I see only blood in my left eye and flashing lights in my right. I run away before the police grab me. After regaining some sight, I duck into a restaurant and ask the shocked hostess to call me a taxi. My face must be a bludgeoned mess.

I try to sleep at the airport and clean myself up in the bathroom. I have a black eye, a large cut on my cheek bone, and it feels like I have a cracked rib. I fly back to LA early that morning, leaving my things for Zyles to bring back.

Rudy would later tell everyone back home that I beat up the bigger man. Our twisted friends laughed about this tragic event. Writing this right now, I finally see my part in what caused that fight. Early in my life I was taught the right way to act, but for some reason, I abandoned many of those lessons. It has become my *M.O.* to perceive that you have wronged me, then use that notion to excuse my inappropriate behavior. But I push on, numbing and forgetting.

Isolation takes hold of me after the Phoenix brawl. The only reaching out I do is to my best friend, Tom, and to my mother. By now, Jen is traveling back to the Midwest every week for her sales executive job with Cintas Uniforms. She feels for her wounded husband, but being the family breadwinner takes precedence right now. Tom doesn't return my calls for more than a month. Maybe he is just taking a break from the toxic pus I routinely send through the telephone receiver. So the only person left is my mom.

I have written Jack a letter describing how I see what happened. At this point, my wrongs have not yet occurred to me. I explain that I took no pills from him at his condo and that his clocking me in the face repeatedly was out of line. I also admit wrongdoing in taking pills previously from him at the golf tournament. When I tell my mother this, she becomes furious that I have extended even the most limited of olive branches to him. She promises me that Jack will use the letter to embarrass me. Sitting there, lonely, battered and abused, I become bitter for being criticized for trying to reach out. Her reaction to the letter is more than I can take right now. For the first time ever, I let my mom have it.

"I can't believe you are trying to criticize me on this!" I say that over and over again, causing her to hang up.

Self-pity and self-inflicted drama ensure that I take virtually no sober breaths in the next few weeks. The only time I am not drinking is when I'm at FX, or when I'm asleep, which is frequently. Sleep helps the isolation go better. There is no break in the constant vibration of fear.

Providing a small burst of optimism, I learn that my third entertainment industry friend from St. Louis has relocated out to LA. Steve is a Bob Costas look-alike and that's appropriate because he is a sportscaster. During Mark McGwire's steroid-evident run for Roger Maris's home run record, Steve called home runs number fifty-one and fifty-eight on the Cardinals' flagship station, KMOX. He is coming out to do some work for Fox Sports Radio. He actually wants me to be his partner on his nationally aired Sunday night radio show.

National show. Fear. Ass lock. Fear. Must deliver.

As I run through the possibilities while sitting in my cube at FX, I feel even more fear, which paralyzes me. What the hell is this? As I run through the possibilities of a great opportunity, I watch that bunny rabbit run on my desktop. He is the only thing moving. By now, FX has not only given me the task of cataloging commercials but also updating them in the system for revisions to air on the network. But my effort and interest in this has come to a screeching halt. I can't stop staring.

Many opportunities lie before me in this city of opportunity. But the Depakote prescribed for me by Doctor Dom is completely sapping me. I'm operating somewhere between sad and agitated. And what the drug doesn't steal, the alcohol sucks right up. My little desktop bunny just runs in place. Look at that little guy. He calms me. By now my cubicle phone is on its fifth ring.

"Paul, you over there?" Carlos, my next-door cubemate tries to alert me.

I wrestle with some papers.

"Paul, your phone!"

"Hey, FX this is Paul."

"Paul, this is Mary Anne at Jerry Bruckheimer Productions."

"Mary, how are you?"

"Mary Anne."

"Oh sorry, how are you doing?"

"Great, we'd like to see you again for Jerry's assistant job. How about 2:30?"

"Fabulous! I'll be there."

"Just tell the parking attendant you are here to see Mr. Bruckheimer."

"Thanks Mary Anne."

I must have earned another meeting because I did pretty well in our first low-key chat, spending a ton of time telling them that I'm an action-oriented guy and that nothing is beneath me. I learned this lesson well when I first got to town from an opportunity I screwed up big-time to be the assistant to Britney Spears's acting manager. Yes, *acting*. I got through those interviews nicely, but on the third and final interview I spotted a bunch of screenplays in his office and I began talking about my screenplay.

"Paul, I really like you," the acting manager said. "But I'm going with the other guy. And next time you try for a job like this, don't talk about your script. We manage those people, we aren't them."

So I stay on task-oriented virtues with Bruck's people. Steadily, I'm starting to feel that this wonderful opportunity could be mine. And part of the uncertainty I feel goes away. From time to time, I feel an amazing sensation of hope and light. I know I won't have enough time to drink and drug if I get it. Surely, I'll find my way out of this apathetic quicksand and get back to discovering Paul Cook, Successful Guy Who Gets Things Done. Certainly I am capable of realizing the magnitude of the job and steering myself clear of the juvenile behavior that has sapped the last four years of my life. I begin to make a small card of things to keep in mind with

Bruckheimer.

"I'm a planner!" Actually I'm a dork.

"Just wanna be part of the team. Helping others get the glory is my glory." Liar. Cubemate Carlos enters.

"You got finals coming up? What's with the flash cards? Mid terms?" he says.

"Yes, in fact I'm learning the great world of Verbal Advantage. Whether you know it or not, people judge you on the words you use, Carlos. 'Capricious' is the word of the day."

"Really?"

"Nope."

"I heard you mention Jerry Bruckheimer. Is that a joke?"

At the risk of laying out a stereotype, Carlos doesn't look like he'd be named Carlos. He's just a dark-haired dude with no Hispanic accent. He has become my work friend. Many of our days are spent talking movie aspirations and drugs. I tell him someday he needs to try ecstasy. What a great prospective friend I am.

"Yeah, I can't believe I have an opportunity to be his personal assistant."

"Wow, for a producer that is a cool thing. They can help you get work after the gig."

"I heard that. And he's pretty huge. I'll get you working with me, Carlos."

CHAPTER 10
Rollin'

Steve the Sports Guy and I have a good chemistry on the air. It comes from complete lack of respect for one another. This razzing generally makes for good sports talk. He's been given a weekly national sports talk show. We are going to create our good chemistry on his FOX radio show on Sunday evenings. I have obsessed about this show enough. We're on. It's time to jump into the studio and hope that my fog will lift.

"We continue on Fox Sports Radio. I'm Steve Schlanger. You've got the NHL playoffs in full force and the NFL draft coming this weekend. 1-866-Get-On-Fox to tell us what you think. Who do you want your team to draft? Paul Cook is here to break it down too."

I jump in, "Oh Steve, this is an awesome time of the year. Thirty professional football teams are gathering in their green rooms to decide what young prospect to take."

"What is this, Jay Leno? Green Room?" Steve corrects.

"Uh, you know what I mean, idiot. Green room, w-wu-war room, same thing." I can't breathe.

Time stops. Steve's eyes get huge as he's trying to figure out what I'm talking about. My rapid blinking appears to be signaling ships in the harbor. His on-air pause feels as deep as the Grand Canyon.

"Ya-you, you sure, Paul? We'll be right back on Fox Sports Radio."

OUT TO COMMERCIALS

"What the hell are you talking about?" yells Steve.

"I'm not sure. Shut up! Let me catch my breath."

The amount of caffeine I've ingested to get me up for this ten PM broadcast is blood-sugar dangerous, but I've been so sluggish, I needed it. The beverages I've tackled this hour include a large coffee at home, two Starbucks cold frappucinos on the way to Fox, and a Red Bull right now. My heart is a roar! My mind has literally lapped itself. Energy and ear-catching phraseology are what I need. Instead the power I'm getting is that of an out-of-control space shuttle booster. I feel only the heat. But for some reason, this extended caffeine cocktail has put Hubba Bubba between my synapses. Thoughts are racing but not registering.

"Welcome back to Fox Sports Radio. We're talking NHL playoffs right now. Paul, you're an NHL specialist, who looks good? What about those surprising Kings?"

"Yeah—"

A good broadcaster never says "yeah" when he agrees with his co-host. If he agrees, he just comments without a "yeah." Rookie mistake. Red flag to a decision maker.

"Steve, the Kings are doing much better than expected in their first round match-ups between a first and seventh seed. Who would have guessed they would be giving Detroit such a run?"

Steve looks away from me like he's disgusted. I realize it is first and eighth seed, not first and seventh. There are eight teams from each conference in the playoffs. So far Green Room/War Room. Seventh seed/eighth seed. These are big mistakes.

"Okay, lets see what's up with Chad in Buffalo. Hey, you're on Fox Sports Radio on a Sunday Night with Steve and Paul."

"Hey guys, great job. How do you think the St. Louis Blues will do in their match-up against Colorado?"

This call is coming from the next room, not Buffalo. It's a talk-show softball thrown my way to get my confidence back.

"Well, Chad, this year makes twenty-five years straight in the NHL playoffs for St. Louis. That is an achievement all by itself," I reply.

"Oh, twenty-five? Wow," says Chad.

"I never thought it would happen but Pierre Turgeon has finally learned how to score in the playoffs. He is now showing why he was a first-round pick. And with Chris Pronger and Al MacInnis on that blue line, you always have a chance."

"Great job. Thanks guys."

The show meanders on with a few more embarrassing lapses mixed in with some good comments. At the end Steve seems to think it went okay. Obviously I don't believe him, but I still hold out hope the job will be mine. I can't wait to hear.

The next day, in another session with my psychiatrist, Roger Dom, I explain the patches of zombie-like numbness I'm living. He tells me that it takes time for the body to get used to the medication. I have found that psychiatrists all say that. It's easier said than done when you're not the one dealing with the sapped energy and the horrific nightmares and sweats each evening.

"How much are you drinking?" he lays on me.

"Honestly, about a bottle of wine a day." I low-ball it.

"Hmm … Paul, I believe if you continue on that path, you will likely become an alcoholic very soon."

That word makes me shiver.

"Alcoholic!"

At this time, my vision of alcoholism always comes with

homelessness. I know I'm not alone in that assumption.

"Ya know, doc, most people refuse to look at themselves. They spend their lives evaluating what others are doing wrong, but they never turn the camera around. And when they eventually do, they are applauded. I used to think this was never my problem. I am overly self-evaluative, constantly running myself through the defect detector. How can you spend so much time looking at your own flaws and still not have any of them fixed? Am I looking at the wrong things?"

The doctor just sits. The dead air causes my heart to race. Right when I open my mouth he says, "I believe that you feel things so intensely that it causes you to over evaluate yourself. If we can attack this anxiety correctly, you will be able to look at the appropriate things and eventually trust yourself more."

༄

The waiting game is over. It appears that of all the irons I have in the fire, two have gone frigid cold. Word has come back from a faceless job title that Fox Sports Radio is going to take a pass on Paul Cook. Evidently, the industrial-sized coffee cocktail I ingested before the broadcast did not produce the desired effect. It is appalling how many situations I've gone into with the idea that consumption of a stimulant would aid me. You would think I had experienced some prolonged success to reinforce this thought. I have been perked up from time to time with a cup of joe before going on the air, but never by the extreme amounts of coffee I've been playing with lately.

Extremes: that is who I am. I guess addiction has been in the cards from the very beginning. I've always needed more and never been able to control that desire. Back in grade school, I remember never enjoying a snow day because I would spend the entire time worrying about getting another one the next day.

My second ice-cold iron in the Hollywood fire is my animated show about a nursing home. I have just discovered that another company already has an animated show of the same type in development. Every time I pitch my concept to someone, they tell me about Jerry Seinfeld's company working on a show with the same theme. From St. Louis, I sent out our first script to anyone with a 310 area code, trying to gain interest. Seinfeld's company began development shortly after that time. Coincidence? Probably. A great scriptwriter once wrote, "The chances that someone will steal your script idea are small, but the likelihood that another writer will also think of it is great. So work hard to develop your ideas quickly."

Oddly, my best friend Tom's former longtime girlfriend lives out here too. Ruthie resides in Hermosa Beach, south of where we live in Brentwood. She is not hung up on opportunity, celebrities or glitz, even though her beautiful blue angel eyes would look great on camera. Since moving to LA, Ruthie has worked to foster her spiritual side, and it really seems to suit her. I have known her for close to twenty years. She was the shy pretty girl in the class who always lent me a pencil when needed. I will always feel some guilt when I see her because of what happened on our senior cruise to Cancun.

We were in a big group hanging out at Carlos and Charlie's. She and her friends had purchased a bucket full of Dos Equis bottles. She was sitting down chugging her beer and I was standing with my back to her. I turned around and accidentally elbowed the glass bottle in her mouth. I cringed when I felt that it was a solid blow.

Sweet Ruthie spent the rest of the senior cruise looking like Ellie May on Hee Haw with a chipped-out front tooth. I pretty much apologize for that every time I see her.

Both she and her husband are heavily involved in a controversial program in LA called Landmark. This is a program enjoying great popularity on the West Coast these days. Members learn how to live happier, more efficient lives by taking classes about life. And as if Landmark's self-evaluating and betterment isn't enough, they also attend a non-denominational church called Agape. "Uh-gah-pay" is Greek for love. Ruthie and her husband frequently invite us to participate in both Landmark and Agape. We have only taken them up on church.

The godless, self-sustaining life I'm living would have you believe that thoughts of faith are impossible. And you would be right. Faith in anything is impossible. My need to control proves I'm living without faith. But that doesn't mean I don't have a small belief in God. I've always been searching for something to fulfill me. If it would happen immediately and on my schedule, maybe we could find out. And it did go down just like that for me once.

I'll never forget being struck with a massive amount of Christmas Spirit one winter. This serenity-based exhilaration hit me at a midnight service on Christmas Eve. I was a freshman in college and had never felt a lift like that before. I floated through the next two days of my life in what must have been the presence of God. And then it faded. Gone. I didn't have the maturity to realize that maybe it was a teaser, a divine preview. So the next year I chased it like a drug, trying to feel that way again. I began playing holiday music in my car on December 1 that next year. Johnnie Mathis, Burl Ives and The Chipmunks filled my red Cherokee. This was quite a contrast to the Pearl Jam and Nine Inch Nails that pounded out of my friends' autos. I put up Christmas lights in my dorm, and I made gift lists. But the feeling from the year before never came.

Attending the Agape Church in Culver City, California, with Ruthie and her husband, we see that this is a loving place. I love the pastor's message. Endorphins flow from it. He reminds me of Zig Ziglar, the motivational speaker I idolized in junior high. But many times throughout the service, the congregation is asked to hold hands in unity and pray. In my current state, this is too much for me. It cuts the good feeling right off. Our chats in the car on the way home prove that Jen and I aren't there yet.

"I don't think I'm smart enough for this church," says Jen.

"Yes, you are. You just think they're saying more than they are."

"I'm telling you, I don't really understand it," she insists.

"I'm not a fan of the hand-holding. I held hands with that creepy guy for the better part of forty-five minutes. It makes it hard to listen."

"I don't mind that so much," Jen admits.

"Yeah, you were on the end just holding my hand. According to my calculations we held hands fifteen minutes longer this time than last week."

We laugh at our callousness. But there is one small thread of doom. If the Agape Church is God and God is right, maybe we'll never be right.

To change the mood, we ponder our beach plans for the rest of that Sunday. The Sabbath in LA is generally more fun than Saturday. Back home, people spend it resting and getting ready for the work week. Here people party and hit the beach. It is truly awesome. Most traffic heads south to the Hermosa Beach area and so do we. But the trip can take a while, so we always bring huge plastic cups filled with pinot grigio and ice to sip as we travel. Delicious. That's where we gain our inner warmth.

Back at the cube, when I'm not looking at the rabbit, I plan a trip back to St. Louis for Jen and me. We will grace the city on a special weekend for the first time since moving. St. Louis holds the second largest Mardi Gras celebration in the United States, boasting up to five hundred thousand drunk freaks in the street on that day alone.

Mardi Gras is the perfect time for a visit because Jen misses her friends and I miss the ecstasy. After a no-frills flight, the cell phone buzzes like a hive with St. Louis friends eager to hook up. The next morning we scurry into Mardi Gras Central in Soulard, Missouri, with the old party bunch. It's ten AM and cocaine is already being bumped around in the bathroom at one of the many taverns. Ecstasy is on the way. I am the only person not to partake in the white stuff, but I am no saint. Cocaine before X completely ruins the effect, making them both unnoticeable.

This all sounds so seedy. But there is more to it than that. Quite unlike what you usually hear, these partying couples really care about each other. Drugs are what they do when socializing. For Jen and me, it has only been a few years, but for them, this illegal fun is what most of them have done since high school. In fact, it is so completely normal that no one really talks about the drugs. Sadly, it is a given. Two people will go off to the bathroom while conversing about the Cardinals. Those two will return, still talking about the redbirds. The only thing slightly unusual will be a hand-off of the little cocaine bottle back and forth. But that is standard for them.

Today's festivities will take place under a tent behind a bar participating in Mardi Gras festivities. Rain pours off the sides of the white tent. The Johnnie-on-the-spot is in no man's land. Party goers must step in the mud to enter the teal depository. But that's a small price to pay to make valuable room in the bladder for more Bud Light.

The X has arrived. I go into bulldog mode.

"How many you want?" says the dude with the X.

"Four. How much?"

"Twenty-five a piece."

I dig in my pocket and look at the ten or twelve people having innocent fun talking under the huge tent. Oh crap! There's a guy from my fraternity over there. Norm voted for me for president. When he graduated, I spoke to our fraternity about Norm's great work ethic and dedication. He can't know what I've become. He won't see me. I'm too good at this. I peel off five twenties and hand them to the dude with the X. He hands them to me in the plastic wrapper that a pack of cigarettes comes in. The plastic makes a crinkling noise as I shove it into my jeans pocket.

"Have fun."

"They good?"

"Ohh yeah."

They always say that. It must be like an oath or something. As I walk away I look at the wrapper: sure enough, four green pills. Giving no thought to the five hundred milligrams of Depakote I ingested just an hour earlier, I immediately pop an X tab, smashing it up with my tongue. A disgusting, bitter taste hits my buds. Yup, that's real X. It's interesting and strange that when you are living this life, things that would repulse a normal person represent victory to you. There is also a chemical-created, overwhelmed and uncomfortable feeling that precedes the high of ecstasy. For most, these twenty minutes are hell. I've come to look forward to them.

I break another in half and put it in Jen's hand because a full tablet is too potent for her. She reminisces with another friend from our college. Good God, is this a college reunion? She downs it with a gulp of Bud Light. To me this is a waste because she has already visited with Mr. White, but it was only half of my stash.

More fraternity brothers arrive. Hugs, secret handshakes and stories are shared. I introduce my new friends to the old ones. These factions know two completely different Pauls. At first glance, the whole group looks the same, but each group seeks a different "fun." The old guys are mostly in sales or mortgage brokering. Their crazy days are behind them. I'm ready to have one right now. Uneasy feelings are beginning, both chemical and social.

"Cookie, you have filled out," says one college friend.

"Ey, it looks good. We all get fat!" says another, rubbing his belly.

"I'm more of a man now," I reply. Actually, I was more of a man in college than now. The ecstasy is kicking in. Sounds are changing and it's getting hard to hear.

"We haven't won the Grand Sage's (the top fraternity honor) since you were president," says the first college friend.

"Yeah, I know," I proudly admit.

In my ears, my voice sounds like basketball personality Dick Vitale. The deep drawn out voices signal that the pill is working. I slam my beer. Now I'm getting cold chills. I peel away from the college crew to my drugging friends.

"How's it going for you?" someone says. "Good?" In drug talk that means "Has your X started to work?"

"Not really." I say.

Dealers always say the drugs are good and I always say they aren't working. I guess that is my way of trying to get a freebie.

Another beer is down and my head is expanding and shrinking like an alien pod. My jaw tightens. What little remains of my personality these days is gone for the night. Deejay Paul is taking on the role of casual listener. Casual listeners catch about every third sentence on the radio because they are busy with other things. I am busy flushing my system with a dangerous load of serotonin. The second pill goes down my trap.

"Man, you got hammered pretty quick!" says the first college friend. Pause. Zombie stare from me.

"Celebrate!" I yell. "It's Marthy Grap!"

I'm flying. My college friends take occasional breaks from proudly sharing baby pictures to notice their old leader. They can't believe what they are seeing. To most of them, I appear way drunk. But three of those guys dabbled with drugs in college. They know that the locked jaw and huge pupils mean something more than Bud Light. These men looked up to me. Through my buzz, I see their sadness. They don't have to say a word. I've seen that look many times lately. The most powerful look of disgust comes from Betty, an old fraternity brother who was gifted athletically but at times partied too dangerously with drugs. Like most, he's got his act together now. As I'm jumping around and over-explaining just where in the hell I think my career is, he shakes his head and tightens his smile while looking down. He probably didn't think he'd ever recognize the side effects of this drug on me. I observe his expression in a quick flash at the time then remember fully later. Even though I dismiss his look now, I know that it will be the main ghost haunting the lonely attic of my mind in the very near future.

What a pivotal moment. The strong man I had worked hard to be has fully collided with the oppressed man I now am. "I saw you guys at the Rams game about a year ago, but I lost you in the crowd," says Norm.

"That Super Bowl was exciti—," Jen starts.

Without waiting for her to finish I babble. "Juju, right, I know. Can I, uh, uh?" Clarity strikes. "Sorry, I know I'm making no sense."

Moments like that happen on X. That brief snap back to lucidity haunts you.

"We gotta sit you down," Jen says.

She sits me with the new crew. They also talk about what in the hell is wrong with me. I am scaring both the college crew and the drug camp. My poor wife is forced to worry about me yet again. The party continues for about another four hours in this tent, which seems like ten minutes to me, then the drugging camp heads to an all-night party. I leave behind my car keys and my dignity.

For the entire trip back to Los Angeles, I am haunted by my behavior at St. Louis's "Marthy Grap" celebration. I ponder calling one of the three college friends who witnessed how I've been living. I've done this a lot over the last couple of years. I make calls the day after to see "if I was okay" when I clearly know I am not. As I scroll through my cell I see that Jerry Bruckheimer Films has called me while I was out of town. Excitement erases the remorse. Maybe this is my way out.

At the layover in Phoenix, home of the Paul Cook Street Brawl, I call Jerry Bruckheimer Films.

"Paul, we have been very impressed with you. I like your approach and your fresh demeanor."

My stomach is doing flips. I walk around the gate as she talks. Every time there is excitement on the phone, I walk nervously.

"Well, thank you very much. I just can't wait to do all I can to help Jerry and you."

"I thought you'd say that. Jerry can meet with you on Wednesday. Is that good for you?"

"Yes, I hope he likes me."

"He will. Don't be nervous. Just treat Mr. Bruckheimer like a regular guy."

Yes! Jen is excited. Maybe the entertainment success I've promised her is within our grasp.

"I cannot believe this," says Zyles. "I have been out here for eight years and I've never even smelled an opportunity like Jerry Fricken Bruckheimer! I hear he's starting to get into TV stuff."

"Oh, well, I hope he keeps making movies," I say.

"He will. This is the highest-grossing producer in Hollywood."

"He must be with the four crazy interviews I've been through for this."

"Just one left. Later, man."

"Hey, tell him about our reality show concept!" Zyles asks.

"No way! I'm talking only about being a guy who gets stuff done."

CHAPTER 11
Made Ya Flinch

Talking to my psychiatrist generally leaves me defensive and exposed. However, I do believe this man is trying to help me.

"I feel really hungry a lot."

"Uh-huh." Doctor Dom takes notes.

"But the hand washing and OCD stuff that first brought me to you have gone away."

"Uh-huh. The nightmares?"

"Hell, yeah. And, man, they are freaky. Is that normal for Depakote?"

"Not really, but maybe for some."

"Sometimes my head is a bit foggy and I have this big interview coming up to be Jerry Bruckheimer's personal assistant."

"Still drinking?"

"A little."

"How much is a little?"

"Mostly just wine."

"How much?"

"Not sure, maybe a bottle every two days."

"Paul you have a form of a condition we call bipolar. People with this condition will sometimes self-medicate with alcohol, but you don't have to anymore. The medicine should be helping you. And using them both at the same time is not a great idea."

"Okay, I will really work to limit my consumption."

"Yes, give it a chance to work."

I go the next day and a half without drinking. At times my head feels uneasy. At other moments, I am confident I could climb Mount Everest in shorts. My Bruckheimer interview is tomorrow. Sitting at my FX workspace, I ponder the possibility of winning Jerry over and working my way up at Jerry Bruckheimer Films.

Maybe it will turn out like this:

At a major movie premiere in 2010, Jerry will say, "Paul was, at one time, my personal assistant, but I always knew he had great judgment and a talent for pictures. I have every confidence that his first film will be a production success."

The track record shows that I can do this. In radio, I worked my way up from intern to part-time on air, to full-time evenings to afternoon drive-time host. That hadn't been done before. So, while my self-esteem is in the hamper, my ego is running high. Doctor Dom tells me this can be a lethal cocktail of human emotions.

"Pssst!"

Donelle is a copy traffic manager for Fox Sports. He sort of trained me, as much as you can train a guy when the trainee constantly says "Sure, got it" after every direction. Donelle is from the Philippines. He brings the double threat of extreme gayness and enormous front teeth. He's leaning into my cube right now.

"Cook, the sheet has hit the fan."

"What, Donelle?"

"Jue messed up. There are errors."

"How?"

"Jue haven't been doing the revisions."

"Donelle, what are you saying?"

Donelle pops his head over my cubicle like a prairie dog.

"Oh sheet. Here she comes."

Barbara, my boss and the lady who just offered me a position at

FX, enters the crowded cube.

"Donelle, grab the weekly congruity reports and meet us in the conference room. Come with me, Paul."

Oh no, the sheet has, indeed, hit the fan. The walk to the conference room is comparable to ascending Everest. From another cubicle, I think I hear a muffled voice whisper "dead man walking."

Barbara and I sit at a big table. Folders and files line the walls.

"Paul, have you been updating the spots, making revisions when they come in?"

"Yes, when a new spot comes in with a new number, I log it and file in the commercial room for air."

"Revisions don't have new numbers. That's our issue. We have a great many commercials that have not been updated. These clients want refunds from us for running outdated spots."

Donelle saunters in with a big document log.

"Paul, have you been making sure your work matches the weekly congruity reports?"

"I have never heard of a congruity report."

"What?!" Barbara barks. "Donelle, did you ever show Paul how to use these reports to check his work?"

"I thought he was updating the revisions. And I thought I deed."

"I have never seen those," I promise.

"But you still should have been updating the spots. Guys, this is a $43,000-loss for FX."

Silence. Doom rings in my ears.

"Barbara, I am so sorry."

"Donelle, you need to check his work at the end of each day. Paul, *this* can never happen again."

"It won't."

Wow, I'm a real dirtbag. My hands feel shaky, I need a drink. No. No alcohol. I have Bruckheimer tomorrow. I can bail on this FX mess if I get that job. I'll be one of those creative types who hides behind the notion that "Office work just wasn't for me."

Back at the apartment, I put more pressure on myself to impress Bruckheimer, since the FX job might be crumbling. I set out to perfect my Bruckheimer Mental Reminder List.

*Nothing is beneath me

*I love lists, love getting things done

*DON'T act like a fan of his

*Team Pla—

Jen arrives home from work.

"Hey." Kiss, hug.

"Girl, I messed up at FX."

"What? What happened?"

"I wasn't trained right on something and I lost them a bunch of money."

"How much?"

"Forty-three grand."

"They aren't holding us accountable for the money, are they?"

"No."

"Well, that's good. People make mistakes." She laughs. "I guess that full-time job offer has been unextended?"

"I think that's a given, but she didn't mention it. Man! I really messed up."

"Look, FX traffic assistant is not that important to you. Don't let it destroy your head."

"I just don't know what's wrong with me."

Jen hugs me. The anxiety that was building diminishes. She

smells so pretty and good.

"This is all new. There is nothing wrong with you, Paul. I don't wanna hear you say that. We got pretty comfortable in St. Louis. You are just trying to find your way."

"I worry I never will."

"I *know* you will. Think about Bruck. You've been through all these interviews and they love you. Just one left."

"I gotta nail this."

Jen starts putting her folders and travel bag away.

"It's exciting. Making one of your reminder notes?"

"You know it."

∾

Today is the big day. I will be one on one with the highest-grossing producer in Hollywood. My appointment is at lunchtime, and I'm trying not to get my hopes too high because he has postponed twice previously. Obviously, I feel anxious walking into FX, especially since I haven't had any medicine (alcohol) in two days. My shrink also said that drinking too much can render the Depakote useless. So maybe the prescription will now work to its fullest.

The plan is to play it low-key today. Without stopping to talk to Carlos or spending the usual fifteen minutes talking to my other friend Lyle, I will go straight to my cubicle and work in a diligent, organized manner. Head down, Bruckheimer notes in hand. I can feel the whispering remnants of my mess-up still in the air. Everyone knows about the revenue loss. I just need to get to the cubicle—I'll be safe there. I tell myself I can breathe when I get to the cube. I'm close, making the turn.

"Hi, Paul."

"Oh, hi, Barbara."

She leans on my desk, looking at the white rabbit running on my desktop. Her pleated gray pants suit bulges at all the wrong places and there is barely enough fabric to cover her enormous ass.

"We have another loss. Please come to my office."

"Paul, yesterday we were made aware of losses for incorrectly run and outdated spots that equate to $43,000. The actual broadcast day was three days ago. For the actual broadcast day two days ago, we have just seen a loss of an additional seventy-seven thousand coming from your desk."

"No! Thirty-four grand more?"

"No, Paul."

"No?"

"Double the day before."

"What? That's crazy."

"Paul, today is a new $77,000 we will owe back in ad revenue. We're in big trouble here."

I can say nothing. My head finds my hands.

"You will no longer be scheduling spots. You are only to data entry the miscellaneous info. Are we clear?"

"I am so sorry."

She straightens her tiny jacket. "Okay, please excuse me."

The thought of being potentially liable to assume personal responsibility for the money is all I can think about, but I don't inquire if she is thinking this too. What a blow to the gut. I have lost FX $120,000 as a temporary employee. Being temporary might be my only saving grace.

I tell myself that the money doesn't matter because this isn't my desired field—as if the money will be counted differently because it's not my first choice for a job. I guess I'm hoping that perspective will help me sleep better at night. But no matter how I spin it, I have become a huge liability, reaching total loser status. This is unfamiliarly comical, but only for a moment; my pride won't let me stay there too long.

I decide to gather myself in the bathroom three buildings away at Fox News. I sit in the stall and struggle to get my mind over this cataclysmic event, knowing that the biggest interview of my life happens in just two hours.

Keep your eye on the prize! Bruck in two hours. Sweet Jesus, I better get this job. Staying at FX will create shame that is too much to bear.

Why in the hell haven't they fired me?

I bet Barbara had already put in the paperwork for me to become a full-time employee of FOX. She doesn't want to look bad firing a guy she backed so heavily. Maybe she's going to try to pin it on Donelle. He does deserve some blame here. I was moved from data entry to updating commercials pretty quick. Maybe in all the haste, he forgot to mention the congruity reports. Either way, he certainly must have told me about updating revisions, which I didn't do and don't remember. But Donelle is as good of a guy as any to get whacked for this. Being in damage-control mode has sapped me of what little upstanding character I have.

∽◌∾

The home base for Jerry Bruckheimer Films is an incredibly cool place. The building resembles a giant airplane hangar, only it is chicly finished with all-glass offices and spacious hallways that are suspended in air. There are no walls other than the giant hangar shell. Strangely, it's very homey. I sit on an uncomfortable blue modern couch. With resume in hand, I go over "the list" in my head:

"Nothing's beneath me."

"I just want to be part of something good."

"I need no glory."

I ponder whether I should I also include "I have recently crippled the FX television network while in a delusional daze, causing astronomical revenue losses."

No, get that out of my head. Slay the dragon. Remember confidence. I will slay the dragon today.

Two other people have joined me on the blue modern couches.

"Mr. Bruckheimer will see you in a minute," the pretty brunette receptionist promises.

In unison, a younger guy and I say, "Thanks!"

"Oh, are you here for the Jerry job, too?" he asks.

"His personal assistant?"

"Yep. They said there was one other guy."

I size him up. Good looking. Probably twenty-four. Clean cut, dark hair.

"Yeah, you from LA?" I ask.

Stupid question. Nobody is from LA. "No, I'm from St. Louis, Missouri."

What thuh! "Me too!"

"Oh," he throws away.

"What are the chances that two guys would be left to go for this job and they'd both be from St. Louis?"

He seems less surprised at this than I.

"How 'bout those Blues? President's trophy," he says.

That brings a Fox Sports flashback. More failure flashes in my mind, jangling my nerves.

"Yeah, I—"

The other guy interrupts. "'Scuse me. You guys are gonna be working directly with Jerry?"

He's in his mid-forties and looks like Jan or Dean from the Southern California singing group.

"One of us is."

"That should be a great springboard," says Jan. "Very cool for you."

"Are you here to see Mr. Bruckheimer?" I ask.

"Sort of," replies Jan. "I'm dropping off a script he requested."

"Oh you're a screenwriter. I'm Paul, I wrote a screenplay."

"I'm a script writer."

The receptionist breaks our threesome.

"Mr. Bruckheimer is ready for you now."

Ass lock.

She stands in front of the other dude from St. Louis.

"Good luck, man," I say. "Tell him you're here for the audition."

"Yeah, right."

"Just kidding. You seem like you'll be great."

"Thanks."

She walks him back to the big metal stairwell. To my eyes, he seems calm and cool as he enters a mammoth board room in the back corner upstairs.

"So this isn't a screenplay you are dropping off?"

"No, it's a script for a TV show about crime scene investigation. Jerry made notes and I was hired to do the rewrite."

"I had heard a rumor that Jerry was breaking into TV."

Jan gets jumpy.

"Actually, I'm not totally sure what this is going to be."

I've noticed that everyone in LA talks too much, but no one

wants to be caught doing it.

As I write this, it's hard to believe that I was actually talking with someone about the infancy of CSI, a genre of programming that would triple the already great empire of Jerry Bruckheimer. It was his break into TV and it would require him to gather many more producers, directors, and actors to fill out all these popular TV shows—CSI, CSI Miami, CSI New York, Cold Case, The Amazing Race, Without a Trace, and Close to Home. Before TV, Bruckheimer produced two blockbusters a year. Now he'll be producing a major chunk of primetime TV. I don't know it at the time, but I am talking to Jerry Bruckheimer at the best possible moment.

It's been just ten minutes and the other St. Louisan is already breezing by me like he's seen a ghost. This has to be good for me.

"See ya," I say.

There's no reply from him.

"Okay, Paul, it's your turn," says the receptionist.

"Let's do this!"

When I get up to the mammoth board room, I see that it holds a massively long, all brass table. It looks like the kind of table Bruce Wayne has in his dining room. The great Jerry Bruckheimer sits on the other side of the short end. Time begins jerking and swirling.

"Hi, Jerry Bruckheimer," he extends his hand.

"Hi there. I'm Paul Cook. It is so nice to meet you."

For a small guy, his voice is powerful and resonant. I feel it in my gizzard. Peripheral vision is now gone. I see only him.

"Let me have a look at your résumé."

I hand him the fourth résumé I have given them.

"Sure."

There's nothing but silence as he views it. I guess they haven't told him what a great guy I am.

"So you're on the radio?"

"Yes."

I feel a weird tightness in my neck. I try loosening it up a bit. Physically moving my head is very difficult.

"Radio is something I do part-time. It's a small job on the weekend. I actually moved out here to sort of get away from radio."

What in the hell is wrong with me? I have never been this nervous talking to someone.

"So, Paul, what do you want to be when you grow up?"

An uncontrollable twitch has now started in my left eye. It is on the side of my face closest to him. Has he noticed?

"I am a planner. And I make lists. I love to accomplish those tasks. Eventually I want to help put motion pictures together."

I carefully avoid the word "producer." There's now a heavy pulsing in the same side of the neck as the eye twitch. He pauses and just looks at me. I feel my head favoring a slight jerk towards the direction of the tight neck. This is like an 8.0 earthquake to me. Does he see it?

I remember reading a Web site where Bruckheimer was quoted about how he built his empire. He seemed to take great ownership. Protecting the integrity of Jerry Bruckheimer Films was something he said he worked tirelessly to do.

"So there's a lot of radio here. How can you help me?" Bruckheimer asks.

"Well."

Pause. Massive Twitch Left Eye. I feel it pulsating.

"Well, I worked very hard to build a successful radio career."

My eyes must be popping out. Now his eyes are popping out.

"I know that I can get things done for you. It's not easy to get on the radio in LA."

This is crazy, my head is now forcibly shaking. Think Katherine Hepburn.

"I was able to get that done in my first day here. Imagine what I can do for you with a bit ..." I pause to move my head back and forth like I'm loosening up, "with a bit more time."

For some reason with the combination of all the factors coming at me, I know I am now coming across angry and a bit unstable. Bruckheimer just stares.

"Okay, well it's nice to meet you."

"Thank you very much."

I shake his hand while I stand. He looks past me to the window.

"Who else do we have?"

His secretary says, "That's it."

He looks disappointed.

My body and twitching head float down the airy stairwell and out to my car.

"What the hell *was that*!? Twitching!" I yell. I take a deep breath. The plague ceases. I dial up Jen on the cell.

Half a ring and she picks up, "Hello? Did he cancel again?"

"No, I just got done with him. Horrible. Simply horrible."

"What? I bet you did better than you think. Remember you always think they are horrible, then you always get the job."

"Jen, I had uncontrollable twitches in my eye and neck. I actually felt my head jerking."

"No way!"

"I've never had anything like that. It must be that damn Depakote. I'm so pissed."

"Well, how was Bruck?"

"A bit taken aback by the freak he was interviewing."

"I bet he didn't even notice."

"I don't know how he couldn't have. Either way, the twitches changed how I talked and what I said. I think I even came off mad at one time."

She laughs.

"I'm so sorry I'm laughing. I can't believe this after all the times you have interviewed."

"Damn!"

"Did they tell you what the next step is?"

"No, they just showed me out. I'll call them later. It can't be good."

"I'm so sorry," she offers in a sweet voice.

"Yeah, now I've gotta get back to FX. They found that I lost them another seventy-seven grand today."

"What?"

"Jen, I don't think I can bring myself to really even talk about it."

"I understand. I love you."

Defeated. "I love you too."

Have I lost my big opportunity in one twitching moment? What the hell was that? I ponder this question over many Bud Lights, two boiled artichokes and melba crisps after FX that night. Not drinking is out! What good did it do me anyway?

For the next couple of days at FX, not a soul talks to me except Carlos.

"What can ya do?" he says in his laid-back way.

"Read screenplays, take long lunches and feel sorry for myself. I can do that. But I totally have to do a better job here."

"That shouldn't be hard. She has stripped you of most every one of your duties."

"But she's still paying me."

"Yeah. We could drink at lunch. I was wondering, you were telling me about your partying times. Have you ever tried something called glass?" asks Carlos.

"No, what is it?"

"Got tired at a party last weekend and a guy gave it to me. I guess it kept me up."

"Never heard of it. Is it legal?"

"No. It was in aluminum foil."

"Huh? If you are looking to stay up and keep drinking, the white stuff works best."

"Yes, we have to do that sometime together."

"Definitely."

Drug talk is horrible. It primes the pump.

To date, I've been in a no-holds-barred brawl with one of my best friends, found a tick on my balls, played footsies with a drug-induced death, drove a crippled U-Haul through a hell storm, set my eyebrows on fire with opium flames, and been stricken with uncontrollable palsies during my biggest career opportunity. I'm hot!

Feeling so low, in a self-imposed downer, I tell myself I have to live a little. Zyles wants me to fly to Vegas with him for a highschool friend's bachelor party. Money is tight. You may ask, how could I possibly ask my wife for this? When pleasure consumption is all you know, questions like this never enter your mind. Besides, she feels bad for me after my current failures.

Instead of flying, I'll drive by myself for a one-nighter, then I'll head back the next morning to get back for my Saturday show on Star 98.7. The ride there feels very short and I do my best thinking when driving alone. I'll convince myself to shake off these negative results and begin seizing LA like I'm supposed to.

CHAPTER 12
Highway Hypnosis

While driving, I pass the area where Sam Kinison was killed. The shouting comedian was killed while driving to Laughlin, Nevada, from LA. I recall just the spot because I saw the *E! True Hollywood Story* on Kinison. I have always thought that when you can take in a *Behind the Music* and a couple *E! True Hollywood Stories*, it's been a good night.

Maybe I like them because I am basically operating one notch above rock bottom myself. The notion of "rock bottom" is the dramatic climax to all of those stories about celebrities. This also explains why I chose to view the pictures of a dead Chris Farley. Maybe I like those stories of entertainers rising and falling because eventually most of them *do* rise again, somewhat.

The entire bachelor party stays at the Hard Rock Cafe Hotel, a wild place, perfect for a "Pauly Power Play." As I mentioned earlier, this massive cockiness can put strangers into a timid state, making the people in the party feel more comfortable. Those who are with me enjoy being in the group. It's all I know how to do in group situations. Insert your "cry for help" diagnoses here.

I arrive at ten AM and the guys are already at the outdoor pool bar. I'm not surprised that it is already on with nine of my closest high school friends from St. Louis at the Hard Rock. We all see it as our duty to outperform the rest of Vegas on the shock-o-meter. There is a blind peace in being loud and crazy, not worrying about the reactions. This is going to be just what I need.

"Let's do this!" I shout across the pool. "I'll take a White Russian!"

"Great! A nice glass of milk baking here in the sun." Boom, my stomach drops. It's Jack. My street-fighting friend from a couple months ago sits on a lawn chair by the pool.

"What's up, dude?" he offers.

Awkwardness and regret swallow my confidence. What can I possibly say? I hold my arms out.

"Get in here." I hug him.

Huge cheers come from the other side of the bar where everyone else drinks. Somebody yells, "Get between 'em!! They're gonna throw again!"

More laughs.

"They've been giving me shit, saying you kicked my ass," says Jack.

"Well that whole thing was wrong."

"Yeah."

"You still wearing that big fricken ring?"

I point to the platinum ring that tore up my cheek bone on three blows.

"Sorry about that. I don't remember any of it."

"Eh, we'll be okay. This place is awesome."

"Oh yeah, it's gonna be a good time."

We join the other guys. There are lots of drinks.

After getting some suntan lotion put on my back by a very friendly girl, who I am told was actually a prostitute, I go up to a room with a bunch of the guys to clean up.

"Pick-me-up?" one of them asks.

We do coke for an hour, which feels like thirty seconds, then I head back down to the casino where I lose most of my money at blackjack. Then I hit the number ten on the roulette table playing my nephew Jake's birthday, the tenth. The three hundred and fifty bucks put me ahead.

Twice that money will be gone by the next morning after the strip clubs, drugs and gambling. It is a good time like Jack promised, but now the sun is coming up. Finally, with no sleep, I decide to drive back to LA.

It's six AM and I am completely roached. The bright sun feels so strong that I have every sun visor, paper bag, and piece of clothing hanging around the windows to block out the blinding rays. It looks like I have been living in my car. I hit the highway with a headache, extreme fatigue and two grams of cocaine. I am so locked in that I never think to snort the cocaine to try and perk myself up for a fighting chance at surviving the long drive home. Crazy if I do, crazy if I don't.

Now I'm back on the same route that claimed Sam Kinison, probably in the same mental state. During the next four hours of driving, I fall asleep at least eight times on the road. Somehow I wake just before hitting the middle road divider each time. I should have died. And the cocaine would have taken my good name with me.

Somehow I make it to the outskirts of Los Angeles. It takes all of my limited brain power to make the call home to tell Jen I'm alive. I hope she doesn't hate me. She answers.

"HEY! Can you pick up some Bud Light on your way in?"

"It's ten AM. What are you doing?" I ask.

"We've been up."

"Oh, no."

I certainly can't look down on this.

Jen has also been up partying all night with Martha, another friend in from St. Louis. She is my drug bulldogging female counterpart. When we were working a club for feel goods, there was none left for even the sickest of partiers when we left. Evidently, Martha bulldogged in this city of strangers for some coke with Jen last night.

When I arrive at our apartment an hour later with a stomach ache and a twelve-pack in hand, both girls are asleep. Jen is sick the entire day.

My binge continues that night at work. I convince myself that the only way I can get through my air shift is to bring the white pony along for the ride. Falling asleep on the road is one thing, but checking out while on the air, that is just unacceptable. I vow that I will not use unless it is absolutely necessary. This is always a losing proposition. I am setting myself up for an internal argument that can be torturous.

"Am I tired? A little bit would make it better. No, then I would need more. This is wrong. You are on the air for God's sake. I need it. Screw it!"

I check the halls for employees. No one is there on a Saturday night. Now I wait for a two-song sweep where I don't have to talk. I dump out a little pile on my left side by the carts. I fold a piece of paper to sit up and block the drugs. In case someone enters I can do a quick cover-up. I cut it up, sniff it. Now I am not tired. I feel better. I talk over a song intro.

"It's another Amazing 80s Weekend on Star 98.7. This is the 80s band The Church!"

Nice. And just five more hours left on the air. Damn, I feel good. I need water. I grab a bottle out of the vending machine, passing numerous pictures of Seacrest with bands. Lucky bastard.

Feeling good back in the studio, I wonder if I could feel better?

Eight minutes have passed and I'm feeling lower than four minutes ago. I wonder if I could feel better?

The problem with a drugging lifestyle is that it causes you to repeatedly ask yourself "How am I feeling? Could I feel better?" This is a question you never think to ask yourself before drugs. Before, you never evaluated how you felt, except when you were ill. It was just you. But that all changes with drugs, inviting a new type of hourly neurosis into your life. That neurosis intensifies during actual use.

Now that the first bump of the night is in, all defenses are gone. There can be no level-headed evaluation. More down on the table, more up my nose. This sucks. I cannot find that first feeling. I get close, but side effects follow. Now I'm squinting and I can't talk right.

When my replacement arrives at 12:45, I am a jittery mess. I don't look him in the eye. My ears are ringing. My jaw is locked up, shifting from side to side. He must notice this.

Paranoia is all I am now. Does he see that I am worrying about him seeing me worry (paranoia about the paranoia)? How will I get home without getting pulled over? How do I hide the remaining cocaine? I can't throw it away. I put it in a small pocket in the golf bag in my trunk. On the entire ride home on the 405 southbound, I contagiously brake every time I see other red brake lights. Hell has been realized. I am worth nothing.

Most of my drug consumption happens when Jennifer is out of town. Those are the times I need L'il Raj. When Jen is back, I am full of remorse and I avoid him. He has come through with drugs on many occasions lately. But much of the time I spend using with L'il Raj is not enjoyable since he won't quit prattling on about how he and I need to grab a nice dinner sometime. He seems obsessed with eating together. It's the same old story. I wish he would get the point of our relationship: I talk to you for drugs. I am friendly for drugs. It's shameful, but let's be honest about it. I certainly can't be honest to my little friend; the drugs would go away. I relent to his pressure.

We choose a restaurant in Santa Monica, my treat. It's a nice place. My little drug fiend friend has decided to order everything off the menu and do it in all courses. Mineral water, apps, salad, main course, side item, and, sweet Jesus, he wants to share a dessert. I didn't know he ate at all.

"This sweet potato ravioli appetizer is delicious!" I give him.

With his elbows on the table and his hands locked by his face, looking me deeply in the eye, he lovingly grabs some lint off my shoulder, never even glancing away from my eyes. At that point I realize we are on a romantic date. Check please!

Unfortunately, this wouldn't be our last quality time together. A couple weeks later, we take a nice Sunday drive into the Hollywood Hills to see his drug dealer. I have to wait in the car so I "don't get shot" while L'il Raj creeps off into this guy's mansion to buy some vicodin.

I wish I could say I am 100 percent willing to live this lifestyle, but unlike all of my friends, I'm not. Without second thoughts, I wouldn't feel so bad all the time. All of my use comes with bitter reflection. Maybe this is my conscience. I sit in that parked car waiting and thinking about how, at one stage of my life, I was "a good kid" on student council. It felt good to do the right thing back then. And now I'm alone in the Hills, waiting to not get shot. What the hell am I doing?

It's March of 2001, and we have been living in Los Angeles for nine months.

"Jerry Bruckheimer has taken a pass," Mary Anne tells me.

"Why?" I wonder if Bruck scolded them for bringing a defensive, flinching mess into his presence.

"Jerry is just like that sometimes," she replies.

"That really sucks. Did he mention anything irregular?"

"No. We really liked you. I'm so sorry."

"I appreciate it and I understand. Thanks for all your assistance."

I feel bad for Mary Anne. She told him I was the guy. I obviously wasn't the guy. That might hurt her image in Jerry's eyes. I let them all down. A couple years later, this failure will be revisited every time I turn on CBS. At least five shows end with JERRY BRUCKHEIMER as the creator. Every time I see it, my gut churns.

What a week. Now that the job I was counting on has disappeared, I have to be on time to work. My Jetta zooms through a neighborhood shortcut to make it to work at FX quickly. What's this? I discover that my favorite shortcut has been compromised. Cars line this small neighborhood street. Where in the hell have all these people come from? Self-pity doesn't pick and choose, it blankets. I bang on the dash with total fury. Why me? Losing company money and showing up late, sounds like "employee of the month" achievement to me.

Usually I shoot through this little neighborhood connecting Brentwood to Olympic. Take the left on Olympic, go a couple miles and I'm there. It's fifteen minutes tops. Anxiety convinces me that in the no-brainer choice between causing a dangerous auto accident and being late for a dead-end job, the latter is much more important. I have favored this misappropriation of importance too many times to count in the last three years. Hell, I might just survive a direct collision with a two-ton metal bullet, but obviously no one survives being tardy.

For some reason, although my self-esteem is in the hamper, my driving confidence is through the roof. I will need to chance it! I shoot across Olympic without optimal space and make the left. As long as somebody isn't floating in the turn lane, I'm good. Not good! Here comes a red bullet. Suicide Lane Suzy is flying. My front bumper scrapes the right side of her Devil Geo. Contact! We have bumper on metal contact.

You'd think she would be a little more attentive to details, working at Microsoft (at least that's what her business card says).

"Oh gosh, you came out of nowhere there," I tell her. "I am so sorry."

"Yeah."

"Are you okay?" I ask.

"Yeah, it's just the scratch on the car. That's the only thing."

I give her my info, which is my father's State Farm Insurance Agency. At least this will be a smaller claim than they are used to receiving from me.

It's funny how barely scratching the paint off the side of someone's car with no dent can cause major chiropractic damage. Either Suicide Lane Suzy blew out a disc or she's having an affair with the chiropractor because over the next two months, she claims to see the doctor every day because of our scrape.

So I am encountering failure on all levels: career, psychosis, finances, and now I'm even a higher high-risk insurance gamble. My father must be proud. He has been victimized with a dirtbag son.

Back to now: Barbara, my boss, doesn't notice my accident-causing, late-arriving scurry. She probably doesn't want to. A day later, she discovers another small loss of $12,000 at FX. She lets me know it's no longer "good business" to keep me around.

"You can come back after lunch or just stay home," she tells me.

"Barbara, I am sorry to have put you in this position."

I've been saying that phrase so much lately that I consider creating my own clothing line called MEA CULPA! We'd kill at fashion week.

"Paul, I know we messed up training you and I, too, am sorry for this."

Getting other people to take responsibility for my mistakes was not something I was raised to do, but I'm getting pretty good at it.

I have been fired. This feels weird. I have been canned and I deserved it. Not many people can say that. I'm not sure why I linger in the halls for a longer-than-normal time. The time I refused to spend with everyone before is now freely given. It must be my way of checking with everyone to see if I am hated. They seem not to care about the damage I've done through those huge mistakes. In fact my coworkers think I got a raw deal. At least they make me think that. And that's probably what I would say to a guy if he'd just been fired too, even if he did suck.

I gather my screenplays, delete the porn from my computer and say a goodbye to the running white rabbit. Rabbit is the only thing I leave behind as a reminder of my presence. I see that he's too busy running on my desktop to return sad goodbyes. I understand.

"Give 'em hell, little fella," I whisper. "Give 'em hell."

Then I look in on my cubemate.

"Well, that's it. Later, Carlos."

"I'll call you later," he says. "I might have Kings tickets."

"Thanks, man."

Carlos is a good man. His nonchalant kindness is just what the doctor ordered. Carlos will personally experience my same fate three months later for getting to work late more times in one year than actually being on time. What a raw deal.

CHAPTER 13
P.A. Paybacks

Okay, let's look for the silver lining in my latest failure. I will now have more time to work on being an entertainer in this city. That's big. And usually I made about fifty dollars a day at FX. Now I'll be working with Zyles as a production assistant. P.A.-ing is hard work that earns you a hundred and fifty dollars a day. I'll spend my mornings unloading equipment and the midday running around for people. Afternoons are the agonizing loading up of all the crap you unloaded that morning. We move big stuff around like purposeful little beavers.

I'm out to prove I can do what I'm told. I have to show that if I'm given something to do, I can do it. I have always lacked consistency. Doing what I'm told a couple times is one thing, but what about following directions every day? And can I do what I'm told when it comes from Zyles, my old high school friend? He's the guy I used to boss around. Hopefully he has forgotten about that.

It's definitely a new wrinkle. On the radio in St. Louis, I told the interns what to do. Now I'll basically be an intern. It's amazing what you'll do when you are out of options. I would much rather cruise the Internet all day for some big entertainment opportunity, but I need to do this for Jen. We are a team. She has cancelled some of her ambition in favor of mine many times. I will shut up and do the heavy lifting for once. I only hope my over-thinking head will allow me to just do what I'm told.

My production assistant career starts with an early-morning

coffee run for the director, producer, Zyles and everybody else with a latte addiction. The director on this commercial is Jason Reitman. This twenty-four-year-old kid will make $25,000 for two weeks of work on a Heineken commercial. This is possible at such a young age because Jason has been noticed for creating a gaggle of hilarious short films with his producing partner Dan. Dan is Zyles's even-keeled boss for all of our gigs. Jason's great eye runs in the family; his dad, Ivan Reitman, directed *Ghostbusters*, *Animal House*, and a ton of other comedies. None of us know it now, but son will soon bypass Dad in critical acclaim when he writes and directs his first feature, *Thank You For Smoking*. After that, Jason Reitman will even be nominated for the Academy Award in 2008 for directing *JUNO*.

"How will I know I'm doing the right stuff? I ask Zyles. "I don't really know what to do. Will you train me on the job?"

"I know you're new. You worry too much. I'll take you through it."

Although I am basically a gopher, this side of the entertainment world immediately seems surprisingly exciting. Before production begins I'm needed to help lay down the foundation for the shoot, which is acquiring the equipment, making sure the client (advertiser) is happy, getting everyone to the right places and making sure all those people feel important. Then we take everything back to the rental places and create the reports at the end that detail everything we just did. Zyles basically oversees all of this. I am really surprised to see how efficiently and effectively he does his job. He appears to have a genuine talent for this.

Right now, I've been charged with labeling the audition tapes and making sure copies are made for the director and the client. Watching the auditions is very interesting. I want to be a commercial actor or host, so watching people do it is a great benefit. I find it helps calm my auditioning anxiety to actually see it being done. The other P.A.s hang in a sort of network. They are all friends and have worked many other jobs together. A couple of factors have caused a bit of unfamiliar shyness in me. One is that obviously I'm the rookie. The other is that I've been failing so much lately I don't have any reserve of confidence to call on. I can be seen passing the perceived awkward moments, looking down and matching my thumbnails in deep concentration. Obviously this closed-off stance is just the encouragement other P.A.s are looking for to include me.

"Did you see how well his thumbnails match up? That Paul looks like a real good-time guy."

"Neato, ask him to help us tape up this chair so the talent can stand on it!"

But I do find some comfort in the fact that I have my childhood friend running the show and showing me the ropes.

"Paul you've gotta get over to Sunset Rentals for that dolly and tables," he instructs.

"You got it. Where is that?"

"You don't know?"

"On Sunset?"

"Paul, you have to know these places. MapQuest it."

Zyles writes down the address. A bit chilly on the bedside manner, but that's cool. I can do this.

"And keep your cell on. Is it charged?"

"Oh yeah, charged and ready to ring, boss."

I wait for a goodbye. He doesn't look up. I'm too sensitive. He's got a ton to do. It's work time. But I bet I would have said goodbye and maybe thanks.

The huge white truck I'm driving maneuvers its way through LA traffic. I cruise along on the 10. The sun shines powerfully, and that's saying something with all the smog hanging around. Loud sports talk from the radio bounces around the cab. Ahhh, it's good to be out of that producer's building. Just me and a list. My phone rings.

"Yo?"

"Where are you?" Zyles asks.

"On the 10."

"You should be on La Brea by now," Zyles barks.

"I'll make it, Mom."

"Hey pick up lunch for us on the way back. Call me when you get closer. And when you get back you have to grab a check from me and get some cash for us."

"Okay, you mean after I eat lunch?"

He just laughs and hangs up.

Zyles would later send me out to Blockbuster for DVDs so he could watch them for fun that night with his girlfriend.

"Yes, I also heard Spielberg's *A.I.* was good, but does this really fall under my job requirements?"

More laughter.

"Just do it."

Beep. Click.

"Hello?"

If money weren't tight, I wouldn't put up with this power-trip crap from Zyles. I wasted the opportunity to get uppity when I almost brought the FX network to its knees. No, I will just grin and take my orders. But I'll still dream about selling my script for more than $100,000 so I can bail on this gopher gig. So many people have my script that I worry that the idea will be ripped off. Is this a normal worry, or am I living in the anxiety? Sometimes I think I see pieces of my screenplay during shows. I constantly tell myself I've been thieved. Luckily I have registered the script with the Writers Guild of America, but I find out that really protects a writer from nothing.

One day in between grunting orders at me Zyles mentions a friend who won $45,000 on *Hollywood Squares*. Pop culture quizzing and bright, hospitable contestants: I can do that. So getting myself on a collision course with Whoopi Goldberg and *Hollywood Squares* instantly becomes my new focus.

After peppering the *Hollywood Squares* Web sites with many contestant requests, they finally relent. The effeminate H.S. rep leaves a message about my tryout.

"Paul Cook, this is Kyle with *Hollywood Squares*. We would like you to participate in a show tryout next Thursday in the Valley."

Damn, if I clean up on that show, I can sit out the year and work at getting my screenplay purchased. On top of that, I'll be able to finish the script for that episode of the Geena Davis sitcom I'm writing.

The Geena Davis Show? Yup, I decided that I could break into the writing world out here by helping a struggling show get better. Nobody at *Friends* is going to give you a look; they are too successful. Only the desperate and almost cancelled will look for a shining bit of fresh hope. Academy Award-winner Geena Davis is trying her luck in a sitcom. In recent years, huge movie stars have moved to TV and done very well.

Geena plays a single mother with two young kids and a crazy best friend. Early episodes are horrible. Awkward writing can make the best actor look uneasy and off her game. And I'm betting because she's Geena Davis the network won't pull the plug too quickly in an effort to see if it will catch on. They have to be searching for better writers at this very moment. I'll gut my way in like usual. This seems totally plausible to me, but my best concocted plans are always humorous to everyone else. Maybe I am living a sitcom? Or a sit-sadgedy.

"Geena Davis? I think that show got cancelled already," says Steve, my Fox Sports friend. He calls to give me crap about anything I bring up because he's still bitter about over-extending his neck on our sports radio tryout.

"Check again, dickweed. They were saved at the eleventh hour."

Steve laughs hysterically on the other end of the phone.

"Man are you reaching! Geena Davis, that's funny."

"Wait and see. There is an Emmy coming for this script I am about to finish," I promise.

"Oh, I'll wait."

∽◌∾

For the second P.A. gig that I'm working on with Zyles, Dan and Jason, I won't be needed for the shoot, which is taking place in Vancouver. The job is a commercial for Great Stuff, which is a foam that fills cracks in your house. I've been told I would just get in the way. So my duties will be complete after one final important task. Zyles has charged me with getting two gigantic beaver suits delivered to the shoot location. He and the crew have gone ahead to Vancouver to get ready. The only thing they are waiting on is the completion of the beaver suits. I'm supposed to pick them up on Saturday in the Valley, pack them up, drive the suits down to LAX, and send them out of the country. For that I get a hundred and fifty dollars. Ho hum.

Zyles lectures me. "The entire shoot is weighing on these suits. A $500,000-job. Be very careful. If they both don't fit inside your Montero, you have to go and rent a U-haul and take it down the 405 that way."

"They'll fit," I promise.

"Do you understand? Do not put any part of those things on top of your damn car. They will fly off, ruining the whole gig."

"Don't worry, boss. You will receive two spic-and-span beaver suits from LA on Saturday. Just let me know if you need me to pick up any DVDs for you to watch on your lonely nights in Canada, maybe some Ju-jubes too."

∿∾

Jen and I have come to love Whole Foods Market. Generally every day around the time she comes home from work, I will go to Whole Foods for a couple bottles of wine and some of their fresh dinner-type foods. I can drink my dinner without food, but Jen gets hungry.

I always feel a tiny lift even just preparing for drinking. A spring in my strut carries me across the parking lot, head up; you never know who you might see out in Brentwood. We have eaten burritos next to Joey from *Friends*, watched Clint Eastwood drive by in a big car packed with kids, and eavesdropped on *JAG* at the Hamburger Hamlet eating with his family.

LA is different from St. Louis in many ways. Obviously, the weather, traffic and overall beauty of the people differ. But one thing you wouldn't guess to be strikingly different are the common rules about personal space. These people stand right on top of you in line. It happens everywhere. Even normal out-of-towners notice this. I almost gouged out a dude's larynx with the *Air Force One* DVD at Blockbuster on Christmas Eve for extreme personal space invasion.

"Hey Dude! Check my prostate while you're back there. It's a growing problem not a going problem," I say while looking straight ahead.

"What? Chill, dude," he says. "I have somebody double parked out there."

"Well, the back of my shoes ain't for parking either."

Now at Whole Foods I have my two-liter bottle of pinot, some cheddar crisps, and a smelly Latin gentleman inside my handheld grocery carrier.

"The line ain't gonna go any faster no matter how on my ass you get," I snap. No response. We scoot up another notch. El Siamese Twin moves right along with me. I can feel him breathing. I exhale loudly. This has become a normal exchange for me here.

"Damn!"

People are looking. Now I've become this week's freak having a breakdown in the store. My eyes are moving back and forth quickly. I give a "Yes, I'm crazy" look to the cashier as I pay. When I walk out, I do the demonstrative turnaround to give my linemate the stink eye. We lock eyes. Damn, this is one good-looking tailgater. Oddly, that makes his invasion of body space privacy acceptable. He's got LA validity. How dare I go toe to toe with that. I'm pissed and twisted up.

I march back through the parking lot looking like Whoopi Goldberg crossing the street in *Ghost* with those red high heels. When I get back to the apartment, I tell myself I'm losing stability. Must chill. Where is my companion and savior, the corkscrew?

CHAPTER 14
Nice Beaver!

Saturdays are Jen and Paul days. Usually we go to either Malibu or the Century City Mall in Hollywood. The mall is a very scenic outdoor shopping area with cheap, cold beer. We love to sit in the courtyard and people watch. And the place is always packed with impatient, frantic shoppers trying to gain entry. Trying to get in quickly, I attempted to jam the Montero into the low hanging sedan garage entrance last week. Our SUV was literally stuck halfway into the parking garage. Would-be shoppers verbally blasted me while I inspected the embarrassing damage. So we've decided to give the Century City Mall a break from the Cooks for a while. It's perfect timing because today we're taking our newly scratched-up Montero to the Valley to pick up two very important beaver suits.

When we arrive in this very strange looking industrial park, only one beaver suit has eyes. Zyles has contracted a shady artist character to have the suits done by now. I realize now that the hopes of Zyles's half-a-million-dollar shoot weigh on two strange freaks, if you include me. Luckily, we have grace in the flesh with us, my wife Jennifer.

Mascots are funny, especially on that rare occasion when two teams' mascots get into fisticuffs. There is something about those big fuzzy limbs flailing violently that comes off as comedic. The comedy is magnified when you think about how someone could be brought to physical rage while wearing such a fun-intentioned costume. Will it be hilarious to experience violent rage over a mascot suit while driving on the nation's busiest highway? Let's find out.

After beaver number two's eyes finally get glued on, I give the artist his eight-thousand-dollar check. These rodent-looking mammals are enormous. During pack up, I discover that only one beaver fits in the Montero. This is not good. Zyles made no bones about the fact that both costumes have to be inside a vehicle during transport. But now it's too late to get a U-Haul because the Vancouver-bound plane is leaving in an hour. So I make the call to put beaver number two on top of the Montero, undried eyes and all.

"Got any wire or string for this?" I ask.

"You sure you want to do this?" asks beaver suit creator.

I'm starting to think Zyles told this guy to keep an eye on me to make sure I don't try and tie anything to the roof. But he's got his eight grand. What does he care?

"Let's throw it up there. We'll be fine."

"You think you can cart this five-foot by five-foot box down the 405 in LA traffic on a breezy day like this?" asks beaver costume maker man.

"Well (pause) that's my job, (pause) sir," I assure him. "I've done it many times before." Lie.

I am just now realizing the irony in the fact that the exact same luggage rack that made us too big for the sedan entrance at Century City Mall last week will be the very thing we are relying on to carry us through this dangerous mission. Forsaken and left for dead a short time ago, it's now indispensable. I dub the luggage rack FIGHTING PAUL KERSEY. Kersey (Charles Bronson in those *Death Wish* movies) is tattered and torn, but now he/it has meaning. What more could a luggage rack ask for?

Unfortunately, overconfidence prevented me from bringing

rope or adequate tie downs for an audible like this, so I'm forced to search the beaver workshop for cable, cords or lassos. Good Christ! Time is ticking. Doesn't this freak have a lanyard lying around anywhere? I'm starting to lose my happy. Finally we discover some twine that is basically layered plastic. Luckily, the box fits perfectly in our partly-bent luggage rack. Things are looking up. But my wife has gone cold on the idea.

"Paul, you sure about this?" she asks.

She can lightly squeal my name like no one else.

"Hell yeah. But we're gonna have to hold the rope."

Cocksureness fills the vehicle as we negotiate our way out of the industrial park with box in tow. Sure we haven't broken the ten mile per hour milestone yet, but this beaver is locked in.

The Mitsubishi Montero is already a funny-looking vehicle. It seems too tall for its wheels. Add on a huge five-foot-square box, and it looks like the SUV has doubled in height. I see the beaver creator illustrating this to his laughing lackeys with hand motions as we enter the outer road.

"We'll go very slow," I assure Jen.

A breezy day? Holy crap, there are forty-five-mile-per-hour winds out here today. We catch a gust of it as we turn onto the 405.

"Windy, but we're good," I say, voice cracking.

Jen must not be that concerned for beaver safety because she has already checked out, reading US Weekly. That's good because I don't need her "ideas" making me more nervous. My hand is out the window pulling down on any slack from the twine, as we scoot along the right lane of the 405.

"But in a second you will need to pull on the rope outside of your window so we can keep this thing down," I tell her.

"Okay," she says without looking up from the Fashion Police

section.

More frightening gusts of wind alarm me. Slowing, I check my rearview mirror for impatient LA drivers riding my bumper. All I get is a big eye full of Brown Beaver Box number one. I begin to visualize the shoot with one fabulous looking beaver mascot. Standing next to him is a production assistant with simple brown sweats, spray-painted brown shoes, and pantyhose on his head with big happy eyes drawn on with a Sharpie. What if I only deliver on half the mission? Would Zyles pay me $75 on the $150-gig? No, I would definitely have to leave the country; I am sure of that.

Suddenly I realize I have let my side of the rope slip a bit. There is no slack. It is so tight I can barely get my fingers under the rope. My world stops when I comprehend that the beaver box is levitating above our car only connected by the twine; it no longer touches the luggage rack. Basically, we are carrying a giant 200-pound beaver kite down the highway.

"JEN! Grab your side, we're gonna lose this thing!" I startle her.

"Oh, pull over!" she yells.

"There is no shoulder to pull on to!"

Jen hits the button to bring her window down more. The open window causes the *US Weekly* to flutter back like a rabid bat smacking the beaver box in the back seat.

"Pull at the same time to bring it down," I order.

The gusts fade away, allowing us to tether the box back down to the Montero roof. Our grunting is almost orchestral.

"Damn it, Jen! Why weren't you holding your end?"

"I didn't think it needed it."

"Fuck, you're killing me!" I snap.

"You don't have to be such a jerk! I don't need this crap."

"I will be blacklisted in this city! Christ! The Reitmans. Remember *Stripes*. Damn it!"

Along with her shrieking, I now hear Zyles's voice in my head.

"If this beaver suit flies off the back of the car on the 405, it will be smashed to tiny brown bits. And you will cost the production many tens of thousands of dollars."

I can't let him down. I should have prepared better. Prepared! Now I hear my dad. My head spins with three voices swirling in it, all yelling "BEAVER! BEAVER!"

"Jen! It's happening again! Grab your damn side!"

"I'm trying."

"No, you weren't. You suck at this; stay in the game, damn it!"

"I hate you!" she says as she grabs the white twine out her passenger-side window.

"Hate? That's great. Just do what you agreed to do," I say.

"You are such a mean person! Don't talk to me."

Five minutes of rope holding pass quietly.

"All right, I think we're gonna be oka—"

"I'm serious. I don't wanna hear your mouth, ever again."

The beavers stay stationary through sixteen more miles of silence. And by some miracle we arrive at LAX unscathed. Well, the beaver suits do. Our relationship is a bit tattered.

To send boxes of this size out of the country, you have to go to a sub-terminal and get them logged as cargo. Blithely, the attendants accept our word about what the boxes contain. They ship them right on through to the airplane. Obviously, their pre-9/11 nonchalance does not strike us as strange.

A couple of Red Hook beers at Red Lobster allow us to look back at the "Furry Fury on the Four Oh Five" with a big laugh. A successful delivery helps to chase away any ill feelings. I doubt there would be any smiling if beaver bits covered the interstate. I apologize for treating her badly and throwing her into an impossible situation. This is a familiar speech. The good news is that in most every situation, we both completely lack the will to stay mad at one another. Even in my sickest moments, I don't want to hurt her, though my emotions do sometimes.

But I do live completely in the extreme. In the heat of our fights, I think the only answer can be divorce. When we get along, she is my soul mate. The middle ground eludes me. I have mentioned this to other men before and they all say "Yeah, I have felt that way too." Maybe this is the average Extreme Man condition.

While eating those delicious Red Lobster biscuits, we daydream about *Hollywood Squares.*

"Whoopi and Jm J. Bullock don't know The Paulie Power Play that's coming their way," Jen says, still trying to feel better. "I just witnessed it firsthand."

"Nice. I think Jm J has been axed. But certainly I know those quizzing fun facts."

"You totally do."

"And all they do is make a lame joke when they don't know the answer. I just hope they pick me to be on the show."

"We need it, Paulie," she takes a drink. "They'd be crazy not to pick you."

∽✺∾

Right when I arrive at the *Hollywood Squares* tryout, they give me a multiple-choice quiz. How many states? Presidents? Generic stuff. The first time I took the ACT I got a fourteen. I was a sophomore and I ended up taking it four separate times, never getting higher than an eighteen. I just couldn't sit still that whole time. All of those words and my future depending on it—that was too much pressure.

The ACT was more of a people-watching event for me, followed by depression because of how poorly I knew I performed. I pulled my hair out at the fact that I just couldn't focus. Of course, patience shouldn't get all the blame. I'm not the sharpest dude in the world. The *Hollywood Squares* test is much easier than the ACT, but it brings the same anxiety.

"If chosen for the show, you need to bring five different outfits because we will record that whole week's worth of shows in one day," says the associate producer. They begin to train us in the art of playing *Hollywood Squares*. Isn't this tic-tac-toe? I think I can manage.

"You don't want to ever leave your opponent an opportunity to win an easy game if you get the wrong answer; that's the skill of winning. So never go for a straight three-across victory if your opponent has two squares near by," the contestant producer scolds.

This puzzles me, throwing off all the schemes and rules I've always applied to tic-tac-toe. I feel my confidence waning. What's this? When do I get to be witty?

We then break into a mock game, complete with fake celebrities. My counterparts repeatedly guess wrong on the most basic of pop culture questions. Thankfully, it is not yet my turn, because I'm still trying to wrap my head around this newfangled way to play tic-tac-toe. It just doesn't make sense to me.

"The celebrities will notice if you are playing without using the *Hollywood Squares* blueprint we have shown you today. Everyone will know you are a rookie."

Celebrities laughing at me to themselves? I don't need that. Anxiety builds. Thanks a ton for that little bit of encouragement.

"And make sure you don't forget to smile a lot. Paul Cook from St. Louis, you are next going against Tabitha from New Jersey."

We have been told not to say we're living in LA or that we're an actor. They frown heavily on those two things. A married disc jockey from St. Louis is my identity. This is go time. Breathe. I tell myself to feel good. Slay the dragon. Bring it, bitch. I am the X. My turn.

"I'll take Craig T. Nelson, please."

First question: "Okay. Craig T. Nelson, Russell Crowe was a little-known actor when he starred in this western with Sharon Stone."

The stagehand playing Craig T. Nelson says, "That's easy, *Tombstone!*"

I jump in, "Sorry, Coach, I do not agree. Obviously, that was *The Quick and The Dead.*"

"Paul, you have to wait for our host, Tom, to ask you what you think, and you don't need to give the correct answer if you disagree."

"Oh, sorry 'bout that. I got excited."

Laughs from the other contestant wannabes.

"But you are right, Paul. You get an X."

"Watch out for this guy," another wannabe contestant in the front row says.

My blood is pumping. I have an X. Now I have to consider this weird strategy while Tabitha takes her turn. She picks a stand-in Joy Behar from *The View.*

"In a recent survey, 87 percent of women say they would go crazy without this mechanical device."

Fake Joy says, "Tell me about it! I need two, one for the bedroom and the other for the family room. It's a television remote control."

"I agree with Joyce."

Contestant producer butts in, "Okay, guys. It's very important that we get the stars' names right. It's Joy. Joy Behar."

Wow, these people are sticklers.

"I agree with Joy," Tabitha says.

"Nope, it is the dishwasher," says fake Tom Bergeron. "Joy's square gets an X. Paul, your square."

Since Tabitha correctly used the *Hollywood Squares* formula, my new X is not near the other one. This makes it impossible to get three in a row on my next play.

"I'll take the Smothers Brothers."

"Commander in Chief William Jefferson Clinton became the second president ever to do this?" fake Tom Bergeron quizzes.

"Balance the budget!" says the fake Dick Smothers.

"Paul, what do you think?" asks the fake Tom Bergeron.

"I disagree."

"Another X for Paul. The answer is, he was the second to ever be impeached. Tabitha?"

Piece of cake. I look around. I will be on *Hollywood Squares*. Is confidence the reason I gradually begin to notice that my breathing pattern has changed? Suddenly I'm feeling tightness in my cheek. NO!

"Wolfgang Puck for the block," Tabitha chirps.

Tragically, the twitching has started again in my eye. The outside part of my left eye is pulsating. My required *Hollywood Squares* smile is gone. The lack of smile is the first thing the producers notice. This red flag has directed all attention to my fluttering face.

I put a finger to my eye subtly massaging it, trying to bring more blood flow to the tic. Damn! I am doing so well. The game is now secondary. Fake Tom Bergeron hasn't noticed.

"Mr. Puck, much European cooking uses this ingredient to add an aphrodisiac to the recipe."

"Eh, booday othor," says fake Wolfgang.

I hear a smattering of laughs. I swing my head quickly in the direction of the other contestants. The giggles echo. Surely everyone is amused by my alien-like face.

"What?" asks fake Tom Bergeron. "Booty? What?"

"European body odor," the fake Puck replies.

Big laughs from everyone but me. I force a big toothy Tom Cruise smile, but I'm cooked. And now my neck tendons look like cello strings, my head favoring the left side. Do I run out sobbing?

The crowd producer addresses the other contestant wannabes sitting in the crowd. He faces them but keeps his gaze on the world war happening on my face out of the corner of his eye.

"Now, guys, when something like this is said, as contestants you need to laugh."

"I kid," says fake Wolfgang. "It's sweet basil."

With one eye open, I laugh and say, "Okay, I agree."

It's not my turn. Awkward pause here.

Tabitha says, "I agree with Mr. Puck."

"Correct!" replies fake Tom Bergeron.

"Okay, guys, lets stop right there and have another person up," says the associate producer. "Paul go ahead and help yourself to a seat. Kevin from Peow, Wyoming, come on up." He says this with his mind somewhere else, like he's trying to remember the number to 911 in case I drop to the ground.

Just like at the Jerry Bruckheimer interview, I float back to my chair, defeated. I know I will never make it to *Hollywood Squares*. The remaining half hour of training feels as long as second grade.

I will never take the Depakote again. Even though Depakote has helped chase away any OCD symptoms and calmed my head a bit, I can no longer burden my experiences with the symptoms this medicine brings. Every time my blood gets pumping, I am afflicted with another plague. I'm done. More importantly, I have lost two big show-business opportunities because of these side effects. I bring enough anxiety into a room. I don't need uncontrollably blinking eyes signaling the boats in Marina Del Ray too.

Humiliation is a complicated thing. I have found that the extent to which I will let it temporarily break me corresponds exactly to the amount of overconfidence I displayed when the embarrassing act occurred. If you display humility and you trip, that's no big deal. It's a shorter distance to fall, figuratively. But when you act like the stud of life and something humiliating happens, then it's time to lock yourself in the bedroom and scream into your pillow for a week. I've found it more difficult to bounce back from the latter scenario. In the case of the twitching Bruckheimer failure, overconfidence wasn't the source of sorrow; it was the massively lost opportunity. But this *Hollywood Squares* episode falls right into the described ego category. It will take something chemical— other than Depakote—to make this pain go away.

I load up L'il Raj's number in my cell. Just hit SEND for drugs. Wait. My last remaining active gray matter shoots me a little reminder of the small vial of coke forgotten and hidden away in my golf bag from last month's Vegas trip. How did I forget about it? Score another for my assigned supernatural evil tempter. What thuh! I've been driving and road raging in LA traffic with that felony-pressing drug in my car? What was I thinking? It could have minimized my rage and given me some peace while driving.

I have to admit that in my relentless search to fill the hole, I make missteps. Concerning my coke night on the radio, I tell myself over and over again that drug abuses like that simply cannot happen. In fact, it's hard to believe I allowed myself to do that while on the air. So it's better to believe I didn't. But you can't simply pluck these events out of your head. Sometimes, whitewashing entire nights is the only protection you have. You do it by saying "too much, too much" a lot. Then you just refuse to believe the past day happened and jump straight into more numbing.

Falling asleep while driving home from Vegas and doing coke while on the air in LA are just the kind of outrageous missteps that make a day need forgetting, for the sake of sanity. That's why my memory of the leftovers stored in the golf bag in the trunk got deleted too, until now. But that little vial sits and waits patiently. It breathes and waits its turn, knowing that crisis will key recollection. That's what happened here.

Cocaine is a living thing. Ask any drug addict; he will twist and turn with excitement at the prospect of inhaling this life-giving powder. Moments later he will curse it. During that denunciation, his position will reverse and he will veer back to coveting.

Once I was at a bachelor party talking to a friend who had just done a line of cocaine. He said, "Guess what? I'm finally going to marry her (his longtime girlfriend). I really love her."

We congratulated him. It was a tender moment, with a side order of evil. Ten mere minutes later, privately, I told him how great I thought his decision was.

He gave me a puzzled look and said, "Forget about that. I was talking crazy."

Cocaine created enough euphoria to cause a man to think he

should make a lifetime commitment. Dangerous. The decisions we make while on the drug are exactly how we feel about the drug itself: all over the place. That's what makes us seem crazy. But more importantly, it is what makes us hate ourselves. Emotional inconsistency like this can only create self-loathing. Oh, how I wished I could just pick a side and stay with it. I didn't care which side.

"Pauly, you gotta lose the guilt," one of my party friends, Ethan, would always say.

I always wondered, "How could you possibly not be riddled with it?"

By the time Jen came home on *Hollywood Squares* day, my Depakote tremors and tics were replaced by cocaine palsies. Many beers would be needed to get me through the night. At one point, about 10:20 PM, I felt whole. It was beautiful, rising from my gut. Other than that, I can't explain it. The feeling lasted about four minutes. After that, I had the sensation of spiraling down like a flushed toilet. It plagued me until I passed out.

Am I past desperate thinking? Have I always been? The credit cards are heavy with debt. We need money and Zyles has hit a dry patch on P.A. jobs for me. I have to admit that a career in food service has always piqued a tad of interest in me. Hollywood is full of people who spend their nights asking "soup or salad" while at the same time dreaming about getting their big break. In fact, I've heard that some found their break in that exact manner. Show business producers and decision makers have to eat too.

Every Tuesday night, Dennis Quaid performs with his band at a hot new place next to The Troubadour on Santa Monica. People here always ask me if I'm related to him. I think maybe I'll impress him and play on his never having had a little brother to mentor.

That will be my way to get inside, and hopefully, I'll earn some cash schlepping chardonnay. Yes, I will begin many profitable relationships at THE LATIN LOUNGE.

CHAPTER 15
Second Language

Everyone struggles for status in this city. LA isn't one huge all-encompassing entertainment industry. Hollywood operates on two levels: there are those who have the information about projects, and there are those who want that information. The wannabes spend massive amounts of time trying to convince everyone they have a pipeline. Nothing ever comes of it. Ninety-nine percent of the projects people will tell you about never happen. They can describe them with the most persuasive proof, using words and phrases like "green lighted," "tested well," and my favorite, "there is already a budget for it." Somehow it all falters in the end. And that means most people in LA are not making their money entertaining people the way they always dreamed.

That is the one way I always have the upper hand. I am a personality on a popular radio station. STAR gets a ton of buzz these days. And whereas being on the radio in St. Louis was lukewarm neat, doing it in Tinsletown is seen as extremely cool for some reason. So no matter how much I fail to make it into their acting world, I always have something they believe they couldn't get. Radio jobs in market number two are very hard to come by. Any sucker could do it, but getting hired is tricky. You must have major market experience, good past ratings, a great demo, and a style that fits into the station's vibe. Even if you have those things, it still can be a feat. Most program directors never call anyone back. I have wasted months waiting for a return call on a well-rehearsed, strategically left voicemail. So I may be sucking it up pretty good in this city, but at least I have radio and you don't. That's the retort I run through in my head to a future conflict that I may have with some snooty person. It gives me the small confidence I need to get up in the morning and walk amongst these people.

You can't measure how much time I waste manufacturing future arguments. If this isn't some form of crazy, it certainly is the epitome of insecurity. I have always told myself that I don't want to be caught off-guard without something smart to say. But I can feel this mental debate team sapping me daily.

The Latin Lounge requires its waiters and busboys to wear all black. The manager seems very curious about me and I'm not sure why. The bilingual beauty tells me to come back tonight for my first night working the tables. Tuesday night, the night Dennis Quaid performs.

When I arrive, I figure out the Latin Lounge manager's curiosity in me. I'm the only blond white dude who will be working here. And she may be bilingual but no one else is. After filling out all my paperwork, I am assigned to Miguel. At least I think that's his name. I can never catch a view of his lips when he says his name, so I don't know what he's saying. I've repeated his name three different ways and every time he has said "Si."

The Latin Lounge does all it can to compete in the very competitive LA restaurant/lounge world. Huge velvet curtains decorate the walls. Kitschy iron tables surround the stage, and other VIP rooms with personalized attendants are totally decked out with big fluffy couches.

Miguel and I fill the candleholders with fresh candles. He gestures to the tiny rectangular menus on the tables and says, "*Juega pelota.*"

My eighth-grade Spanish veers me towards what he's saying, but I'm not sure.

"*Juega pelota!*" he says again.

I take a guess, "Play ball?"

"Si, plahh ball!" says Miguel.

"Okay, play ball!"

I'm not sure what he's talking about, but we are bonding and that's progress.

It's five PM and the lounge is now open. Signature Latin Lounge martinis begin to relieve the stress of a Southern California workday. Four groups of three are already getting in on the early action, talking about projects "in the works." Miguel and I are pulled off our candle project and told to grab empty glasses off the tables. The small talk I attempt with the patrons is received in the same way a transient is avoided at Venice Beach. *Don't answer or look up and maybe the crazy busboy will go away.* That also seems to be the approach used on me by our bartenders when I drop off the empty cocktail glasses.

After clearing off the tables I hear "*Juega pelota!*" from above my head. Miguel asks me to go back upstairs to work with the candles and condiments again. Why does this guy keep yelling "play ball" at me? Is it because we are two men with a language barrier and maybe the only thing he thinks we may have in common is a love for baseball? Or maybe he's crazy. Even though I try to fight them, thoughts that this job might not be for me start to grow. But I push on.

Tables line the balcony of the second floor of The Latin Lounge. Those tables give people the opportunity to look down to the first floor stage. Both Miguel and I have run out of little candles for the tables, so he motions for me to follow him. As I follow him into the deep supply closet he points behind me and mumbles something. I'm taking this thing as it comes so I say, "Okay."

Miguel moves a big box of coffee to the side and reaches to the top of the shelf for a smaller box. I'm guessing these are where we keep little candles. Right when he gets on his toes the door behind me shuts. Miguel goes nuts.

"*Adentro nos traban! Adentro nos traban!*"

"Uh, dude, I told you I don't speak Spanish."

More and more "*traban*" follows a lot of door handle jiggling. Slowly I'm picking up that my little buddy and I are trapped in this closet. He continues berating me in his language. I think I even hear a "gringo" in there somewhere. There's not much I can say. I guess I was supposed to make sure the door didn't close. Personally, I'm thinking we've scored. We won't have to work in here.

Miguel kicks and bangs on the door, but by now, the melodic salsa-club music is blasting away. I can't believe this is happening.

I remember Greg Brady once got trapped in the freezer at Sam's butchery. The Bradys also got locked in an old jail on their vacation to the Grand Canyon. Almost every sitcom takes a stab at this premise at least once. It is at this moment that I realize I must write a book about these crazy LA times. Fate is giving me a gift. Miguel's yelling fades to background noise as I think, "I have to put the beaver suits story in the book and maybe that rain storm in the U-Haul." Then in the one quiet moment my partner takes a breath from yelling at me, I laugh and through a chuckle I say, "Can I use your real name in the book? Wait I don't know your real name."

No answer.

Ten minutes later, we're sitting on the floor, just like we've been trapped in an elevator on *Night Court* or maybe *Shallow Hal*, and the door opens. Our bilingual manager chooses neither language to greet us, just a smile like this has happened before.

Miguel says, "*El muchacho lo hizo.*"

He is clearly blaming me.

She says, "Oh, boy did it?"

This bastard's been calling me "boy" all afternoon.

"Hey, while I have you both here, I have to move my car. They said I could only use that lot till seven," I tell her.

She says, "Go ahead. I have another project for you when you get back."

"Okay, I'll come find you."

"Thanks."

As I trot my sorry ass out through the front, I feel everyone looking at me. I pick up the pace out the entrance. I'm sure they probably frown on employees exiting at the front. Jumping into my car, I see no ticket. Since it's 7:45, I know I got a break. Quaid goes on at eight. This thing can only get better.

I make the left out of the lot onto Santa Monica Boulevard. The Latin Lounge slowly passes my right side as I look for a free space. Should I pull behind the restaurant? No. Looking. Looking. Foot on the gas pedal. Like I'm on autopilot, my car drives me straight home. I can't explain it. I had fully planned to park and go back into the restaurant for more ego deflation, but something would not allow it. I bailed on it before causing more problems. Another job well done.

A bottle of pinot grigio comforts me back at the apartment. I sit and contemplate my two-and-a-half-hour career at The Latin Lounge. Jen enjoys the story.

She laughs. "I don't know what you were doing there in the first place. I can't believe you went."

"Why didn't you tell me that?"

My misadventures are becoming quite amusing for Jen. She must feel deep down that they are temporary. They feel etched in granite to me.

∾◦∾

Back on Roger Dom's couch: "I cannot take the Depakote anymore. The twitches are killing me."

"I understand. There are many great medications out there."

"Ya know, my friend gave me a valium yesterday and the anxiety really ceased."

L'il Raj eats them like Skittles.

"Paul, I believe you suffer from a disorder called bipolar type two. Even though it can, type two does not take you on extremely dangerous trips of mania. What it mainly deals with is anxiety, which you are well familiar with."

"I do over-think things."

"In some cases, a medication that calms you can help. The valium you took is in that family. Do you think something in that family can help you?"

I see my opening. "I don't know, but I'd be willing to try."

"I have one for you that is a bit safer and we've had good results with it. Try it and let's talk in two days. This should help you immediately."

And so my journey with Klonopin begins. A quick Google search reveals that Vietnam vets became very adept at trading their Klonopin for painkillers. I celebrate the potency my new friend will bring with a spirited cold beer. Doc says this new medicine should help immediately. That means I have been prescribed a tranquilizer. I do feel a sense of ease and a let-up on the tension my mind manufactures right away.

However, three Klonopins a day don't seem to cut through my anxiety quite enough. So two days later, it takes little or no convincing to get approval to bump up the dosage in my conversation with the doctor.

"Why don't you take one before eating and afterwards each day?"

In the time I have spent with Doctor Dom, he has gotten to know me and, I believe, like me. Doubling the dosage of a powerful tranquilizer for a known pill-popper might seem irresponsible, but I believe he just wants me to have relief from my "disorder." Also, he doesn't have all the information. I have neglected to tell him about my many dances with painkillers. He says the bipolar type two condition could produce disastrous symptoms of mania. I believe he is trying to save me from a spree that could potentially end my life, marriage or career. I am grateful to him for that, even though part of me knows I'm just searching for drugs.

I'm sure he told me not to drink with this medication, but I don't remember that right now. I do know that he said Klonopin will help me not feel that I need to ingest alcohol as much. However, I have found that it makes me drink more.

Jen was right about me working at a restaurant. I'm not good with food, and working nights would be even more intolerable for me. The production assistant position pays the best since I took this LA plunge, but the work comes too infrequently. I heard about a P.A.-type union that you pay to get into but can offer more frequent work opportunities. I go over to Hollywood to check it out. I drive with two parts disgust and one part hope. What the hell has happened to me? I've resorted to paying for career table scraps. I'm betting Jen will not like the upfront money requirement either. My cell rings.

"Hey, yo!"

"The next big thing, please," a deep voice requests.

My old radio station boss from St. Louis has this deep professional sounding voice and he knows it. During any given conversation, he will play with it like a dog nosing a dead squirrel around in the back yard. He goes from hard movie trailer guy to the devil's whisper right in the middle of sentences. And his name is the topper: Steele Knight. Steele taught me a great deal of what I know about radio today. That's why I care way too much about his opinions of me.

"Hey Steele! How's St. Louis ?"

"Not good, bro. I had to let John go."

I pull the car over.

"What? I'm sorry to hear that."

"Yeah, The River is killing us."

The River is a radio station that plays music similar to what they play at the one Steele runs (my old radio station). He has fired a twenty-year veteran personality of the station.

"How would you like to come back and make it right?"

"Really? Afternoons?"

"I'm going to make us a lot more 'now' and I think you'd be great."

"What a compliment, I would make it great. There will be no other option?"

"Well, let me get some of my ducks in line. But you'd be willing to come back for PM Drive?"

"Yes, if the deal is right."

"Okay, I'll be in touch."

An opportunity to own a daytime shift on the radio back in my hometown is extremely exciting. I left St. Louis for many reasons. One of them was that working nights on the air was killing Jen and me. Afternoon drive would be much better. But can I deliver what I promise? I calm myself because I've heard job talk before and I've heard it from Steele. Sometimes it doesn't happen. But at least something great could be in the works.

CHAPTER 16
Saddled

Hard on the heels of the St. Louis life raft comes the opportunity to prove I can deliver in an intense situation. My track record hasn't been great lately, but maybe I can do this one. Incredibly great ratings have come through today for the full-time air talent at my LA radio station, STAR. A huge celebration is in the works. Our program director, April, is giving Seacrest the afternoon off, so they have called me to pinch-hit and host his hugely popular show. Exciting. Like a reflex, I use a couple Klonopin to kill the nerves. It could be a fun day. After the PM drive show, they want me to join them at the Saddle Ranch on Sunset for the ratings celebration.

I've always been bored in bars with the drinking, standing, sitting, eating and, most loathsome of all, making small talk. It drives me to early fatigue. I guess that's why I have sought out substances to make the boredom immaterial. So I applaud a bar that is willing to give its patrons something unique to do or at least look at. The Saddle Ranch excites and scares its customers with a mechanical bull that jives and jostles. It looks like a brown leather-padded refrigerator. I can't help thinking it resembles a giant beaver-suit torso. The bar also offers outdoor seating with a tiny campfire near each table. The Saddle Ranch is down home yet still very LA. Of all the bars in this city, it has become my favorite.

Filling in for Seacrest is a blast. The phones pop with cool-sounding listeners. On the air, I talk about relationships and workday weirdness. The great reaction is overwhelming. The blood pumps and for the first time in a while, my face is twitchless in a pressure-filled situation. It is awesome to think I am doing a PM drive show in market number two, if only for one day. But maybe my performance today will bring more opportunities.

The show ends and it's time to pick up my pretty wife and head to the Saddle Ranch for STAR's ratings celebration. I have told myself that I need to come across better than at my last station party at the bowling alley. Everything is a performance. Anxiety is barely noticeable this time. Small doses of Klonopin and Jack Daniel's appear to be up for the job tonight. As I walk through the curtain to the STAR VIP wing, Seacrest, the toast of the event, yells, "Hey, it's The Ride with Paul Cook!"

His show is called "The Ride with Ryan Seacrest." The whole station turns to see. For the first time, I allow myself to feel like I belong.

"Ha! No, no. You are the man. But it was fun."

"Oh, I know. You wouldn't believe the bonus I'm gonna get from these ratings!" Seacrest says.

Jen and I sit down at Ryan's table. I don't know it, but we are sitting at a table with STAR's general manager and the vice president of programming on the West Coast for Clear Channel Communications. It is here that Jen and I have our first taste of Dom Perignon. They are ordering the stuff like it's iced tea. Tastes like Asti Spumanti to me, but the cost feels good going down.

The celebration goes on for hours. I even get a few compliments for "the show" I did in a pinch today. Then the Saddle Ranch staff brings out five enormous trays of chocolate, graham crackers, and marshmallows. We are going to roast s'mores over our little campfires not twenty feet from busy Sunset Boulevard. However, all of this excitement put together still doesn't chase away my new fatigue and ache for drugs. Drinking always greases the wheels for drugs. One doesn't happen without the other. It has become an automatic reaction when I'm out.

"I need a pick me up," I announce.

That's all it took. The manager on duty approaches.

"What do you need?"

"I don't know, what do you got? Anything stronger than this?"

He cracks a California earthquake smile.

"Stronger? Of course."

"What's your name?" I ask.

"Shawn."

Discreetly I order. "Cool, Shawn. You can hook me up with some white stuff."

"Yep, after I get off in an hour."

And we're off. The fun button is locked in fast-forward mode; many loud conversations and long stories. With cocaine in my system, I even engage in random small talk with my co-workers. Finally I feel completely normal. The night doesn't end till the sun comes up.

I have a short measure of remorse when I go to bed and much more the next afternoon when I wake up. What did I do at a work function? Did anyone see it? I did it again; I created a drug relationship right out of nothing. L'il Raj is certainly a drug relationship, since I only call him when I need a feel-good. But he's always knocking on our door and he lives two doors down. The Saddle Ranch was about me manufacturing a connection out of a harmless radio station staff party. I lie in bed and wonder how it happened. The quest to feel good drives the search for drugs. But I was coming off a great experience on the radio, a possible huge beginning for me. Why didn't I already feel good?

I partially assuage my guilt by promising myself this will be a one-time thing. It works today. But I find myself going to the Saddle Ranch many times in the weeks to come to "hook up" with Shawn. He is more than willing to help the radio guy from the expensive party as long as I pay well. And so it goes. I have allowed my drug exploits to ruin another city for me. I cannot trust myself to stay away from using my new, easily accessible drug contact.

∽⌖∾

Thoughts of running from my current city once again drive my late-night thoughts. The possibility of moving back to St. Louis is incredibly exciting, but it would also mean I admitted I didn't have the entertainer mettle for Los Angeles. That is a pride hit. I can't sneak out of LA without making a better effort. So while the St. Louis thing is in the works, I decide to give Hollywood my best. I will get an agent and take a swing at the audition bag. And with the gruesome facial ticks behind me, why not?

My best shot at a real agent is tonight when our commercial acting class auditions in front of one. Jen and I have worked our "Do I look 20 percent smaller to you?" Burger King spot to complete perfection. No one in that class will nail this better than I.

Our class begins with a brief question-and-answer session with the agent and our instructor. I sit on the Dudley Moore couch, rehearsing the Burger King script in my head. The agent is a blond man, about forty, with a sunburned face and red eyes. Our instructor brags that this agent has placed his clients in many major ad campaigns.

"If you get hired to do a commercial and you get paid on the frequency of those commercials, who tracks that and calculates how much to pay you?" Teacher's Pet asks.

"Uh, beats me." Ken the Agent waits for the laugh that never comes.

He continues. "Well ya know, uh, one big agency tracks it and they send you your checks and that is suh-weet."

This guy is drunk. My big opportunity to get a foot in the door and the guy is hammered. If I impress him, will he even remember?

Another question, this one from a guy who looks like snuff films are in his future. "Ken, thanks for coming here tonight. How do you stand out among all the other people auditioning?"

Ken the Agent uses his outside voice, "Wow! THAT is one huge sectional sofa! I was originally an actor. So I've been on both sides of it. There is so much less stress on this side, but acting was more fun. What was your question again?"

Mister Tipsy is feeling no pain. How can I begrudge him? Actually, this might work in my favor. I'm picking up some gestures of the ambiguous sexual orientation variety. But this guy is definitely not fully out. Nothing like an after-work cocktail session to loosen a fella's true sexual positioning. And a couple direct eye-contact hits tell me that I may be his type. Either that or he still can't get his interest off Dudley Moore's tweed sectional. Or maybe it's a combination of me and Dudley Moore's couch he's liking and the only thing missing is the three of us together.

I tell myself not to get cocky. However, I do notice one bad thing that is not present again. Absolutely no sign that any eye twitching has taken my face hostage. That is a victory all by itself, because my blood is pumping just like at the *Hollywood Squares* audition.

"Was your question something about working with copy?" asks Ken the Agent.

Our instructor interrupts.

"That's enough questions for now. Let's show Ken what we've got. Everyone go outside and I'll call you in one at a time like a real casting session."

As each classmate comes out looking dejected, I oddly hold my courage. I guess a little batting of Ken's bloodshot eyes in my direction goes a long way. I carry the thought that this agent already likes me as I walk in.

"Hi, I'm Paul Cook."

"Ew, hold on. How old are you?"

"Twenty-six." I'm twenty-nine.

"All right, go ahead with your read."

"Okay."

I get into the body position that Jen and I agreed to, leaning to my right side, head cocked casually, eyes looking up. With a touch of irritation I say, "Do I look 20 percent lighter to you?"

Beat. Hand out, I look at my body. Bit of a sneer.

"Well, McDonald's is now making their burgers with 20 percent less beef, so all I get is a lot more bread."

Tiny laugh under breath into next line.

"I'm taking my bread to Burger King, where there's plenty of delicious certified angus beef on their burgers. And they're flame-broiled, so I don't get bigger."

I strut off-camera, stage left.

My instructor beams.

Ken the Agent says, "I like you. Your look really works in a Midwestern way. Call me."

Finally a win! I am the only person from the fifteen others in our class to sign with Ken the Drunk Agent.

After three calls and a mixed-up scheduling appointment, where I wait for an hour for him to not show up, I finally have a sober meeting with my new agent, and he almost sends me out for an In and Out Burger audition that day. I guess I couldn't adequately hide my distaste for mustard and pickles when he asked.

"We'll get you out to the next one," he promises. "I'll call you the day after tomorrow."

I keep my cool as I officially sign his agent contract. It feels good. My next task is to spend the next two days at Kinko's trying to affix one hundred of my headshots to résumés with Ken the Agent's contact info on them. It is thrilling to know I am no longer going it alone. Hopefully, he can get me auditions as well as he throws back the beers. I bet we'll be "brothers in barley" from this day forward. I see myself eventually telling people "I'm having drinks with my agent. I'll meet you guys there later. He and I need to talk about a part. He really wants me to go for it, but I'm a bit 'iinhh.'"

Having an agent is comforting, but after a few weeks, the feeling fades and things still don't feel right in my gut. A great speaker I once heard named Ravi Zacharias says, "Man feels his most empty and desperate in that moment when he finally earns the thing that he had envisioned to bring the ultimate payoff, and the feeling he had expected doesn't measure up. Because where do you go then?" I always had it in my head that once I got a Hollywood agent, my celebrity spirit would sail and I would feel right. But here I sit with no calls.

Zacharias asks, "Where do you go then?" Personally, I have always gone to the *next* thing that I believe will bring the ultimate payoff. I refuse to learn from the past about empty payoffs. If I don't continue jumping to another blue sky, what is left? Enjoying today? I don't know how. And there is less willingness to learn to do that than to learn the short side of pinning my hopes on failed ventures.

So success is not happening on my schedule here, but what about St. Louis? Being a radio personality on the second most important time slot at a great St. Louis station now dominates my thoughts. I always thought the possibility of that opportunity coming my way was slim. When I talk to Steele a few weeks later, he reinforces that he still wants to move ahead with bringing me back to town. He says I will change the scope and effectiveness of the radio station. His confidence in me is sustaining.

I use the thoughts of this opportunity to get me through another life-sucking production assistant job with Zyles. Thoughts of a perfect future can carry you across time like drugs. These expectations must be what let you down so heavily. I avoided reality by dreaming about stardom on the drive in to LA. And now I'm doing it to carry me out of LA.

CHAPTER 17
Four Easy Payments

The job we're working on is an infomercial for Time-Life "Sounds of The 80s." Original MTV VJ Martha Quinn is the host. The first day of the job, I'm in charge of getting Martha water during production. The second day, I am wrangling the "testimonial talent." These are people who comment on the CD collection on camera. They have been strictly cast, and they suck big-time.

"This stuff, oh this stuff!" Mitchell a forty-year-old actor testifies on camera.

The Time-Life interviewer is off camera.

He says, "Uh, Mitchell, tell me some specifics about this '80s collection."

"Well the CD jacket is totally cool. I love that picture of Devo! Are we still on?"

"The music, Mitchell."

Good God, where did they get this guy? I'm in charge of ensuring they are ready and in order. After that, they are on their own. Also, I walk them to the main stage. The Time-Life people roll their eyes. They have the normal production fear: paying for an entire crew but lacking the talent to make the production good.

Watching them squirm is intriguing. The whispering only increases as I bring in another out-of-touch lamb for the Time-Life slaughter. This time it is a pretty girl in her twenties resembling a cross between Courtney Cox and Drew Barrymore.

"I love this music! "She Blinded Me With Science"? So good.

That title makes me laugh! HAHA."

"The collection is not supposed to be funny," says the Time-Life interviewer. "Can you do that again without the laughing part?"

She says, "Sure!" through hysterical laughter.

The producer of the infomercial pulls me aside. "I know you are on the radio and you play this music. We need you badly."

"To go on camera?"

"Yes. We can't pay you, but we will hook you up with the entire collection of music."

"Huh," I reply optimistically.

Zyles jumps in. "I wouldn't do it without pay."

"Well, we can't pay him," the producer says.

The producer flashes an annoyed look at his production director, Zyles.

"You got it," I say. "I'll do it."

What have I agreed to? My face is puffy and you can still smell the nightcap on me from last night. And due to Zyles's slave driving, I didn't have time to shower when I woke up this morning. He had us up half the previous night sweeping up and then we had to report back to the set at 5:30 this morning. But the expectations are low and I perform best in that environment. What is it about stepping up in a pinch that gives you confidence? It must play on hero elements of your ego. And if I fail at least they can't say, "You had all that time to prepare!"

After getting my hair and make-up done, I'm escorted to the main stage, which feels strange since I was the escort just an hour ago. Lights on. Picture up. An interviewer asks questions off-camera.

"How do you like our '80s music?"

"This is the absolute best collection of music to own. It can totally be the soundtrack to any party!" I boast.

"Tell me about the selection of music."

No twitching yet again. I should sue the makers of Depakote.

"I hadn't heard many of these songs in years. Time-Life's "Sounds of the '80s" really takes you back. If you want to feel great, you'll get this set of music!"

Cut!

I hear an eruption of applause from out of the darkness in the back of this huge soundstage.

"Great job, Paul!" the Time-Life lady cheers.

Infomercial success! I've always seen myself as a game show host; infomercials seem to fall along those lines. Now if only I can get a spot on a home shopping network, I would have all the schmaltzy broadcasting outlets covered. At this time, I do not know that this Time-Life infomercial will play in every market in the country many times, usually in the middle of the night. In fact, the hour-long commercial would play on TV even after they stopped selling the '80s collection it advertised. I guess some TV stations just didn't have anything else to run overnight. Over the next few years I will receive calls from all of my insomnia-inflicted family members, who claim that discovering me on TV deprived them of even more sleep.

⌒⋎⌒

Excitement and glee continue as a deal gets finalized with my old St. Louis radio station. It's going to happen; we will move back to St. Louis for Afternoon Drive. Jennifer's employer is graciously allowing her to do her work from St. Louis as well. Again we are put in a position to win, and I don't want it to go the way of FX and Bruckheimer, so I work every day to develop a great radio show.

Feelings of failure have always been tasty bait for more substance abuse, but for some reason, success can be an even more irresistible lure to an over-indulgent spree. For the next two weeks, I jump back into cocaine with L'il Raj and the bar manager at the Saddle Ranch. And for the first time since moving to LA, ecstasy pills make their way back into the picture. My excuse is that a move back to family and adulthood is about to happen in St. Louis, so I might as well "rock star" it up here before I go back. Somehow I do this with less than the normal guilt.

And now, rather than waiting for my new agent, Ken, to call with an opportunity, I have a reason to call him. He will be thrilled to hear about my out-of-nowhere infomercial booking. Yes sir, I'm hirable! I leave him four messages over the next two weeks saying just that. Discouragingly, that sober meeting in his office a few weeks ago was the last time I would ever talk to my new agent.

I now have the strong opinion that Ken signed me out of guilt. It appears to have been another case of my drive and determination being so great that Ken felt he had no choice but to relent. Figuratively, many situations in my life are similar to my being back in the club bulldogging for ecstasy. My exercise of will is so great it makes events happen that just aren't meant to be and may not be good for me. It happens all the time. In the agent's case and many others, the original vibe they get from me is encouraging enough to open the door, but for them it fades.

Maybe this entire Los Angeles fiasco is a misappropriation of will. I recall doing this with certain radio jobs in the past as well. One exciting summer, I was a top-three finalist for a drive-time show at a great station in Chicago. I sent the program director funny, produced voice mails, e-mailed her my programming ideas almost every day, and sent her shows I had done weekly. I felt like the strongest candidate, but I knew something was missing in her zest for me. Because my effort was far greater than everyone else's, she felt compelled to make me a finalist, even though I wasn't ever going to be hired.

After she hired another guy, other programmers called and told me I was the far more talented and decorated candidate. My follow-through was there too. So why wasn't I the winner of the job? It just wasn't meant to be. She wasn't sold on me for a reason I'll never know and she might not have known herself.

This concept of "meant to be" is totally foreign to me, but it needs to be recognized, because you can will yourself into situations that you have no right to be in. These are places where it is not your destiny to dwell. I forced it, and because of this, I wasted a full summer trying to make it happen, though the signs were not there. I'm not saying achievement doesn't take great effort and determination, because I believe it does, but when it's meant to be, it feels right.

I have a difficult time recognizing this because I haven't felt right in a long time. I do feel a certain "in-tune" vibe about my new radio job back in St. Louis. It's intoxicating to know that I didn't force this one as usual, blindly dragging everyone kicking and screaming onto the hijacked jetliner of my self-will.

It doesn't matter that Ken would never call me back. I was able to get an agent, get on the radio in Los Angeles and even feel infomercial-fulfilled. These would be minor achievements for many West Coasters, but they are things I always wondered if I could achieve. So my time is over in Hollywood. With a steady, fun job back in St. Louis, my hope is that Jen and I can start a family and begin to grow some roots. I have moved her five times in the last six years, covering St. Louis, Northern Illinois, and Los Angeles. It is my hope that this seemingly level-headed move will bring some maturity out in me and possibly save my life.

CHAPTER 18
Pepper Spray

For me, there is no worse agony than that moment before regurgitating the damage done to myself just hours earlier, and lately I've been doing some damage. I'm in the personal business of avoiding pain, but vomit pain is simply unavoidable. You never know when your heart will attack you during an excruciating moment like that. Being a part-time hypochondriac, I believe certain stresses like vomiting can initiate a coronary. Remember the great comedic actor Marty Feldman? He was that genius with huge crazy eyes. I loved him in *Young Frankenstein*. Unfortunately, Marty's bug-eyed spirit left this world in 1982 after shellfish poisoning tripped a heart attack in Mexico City. Marty vomited his way into that *Silent Movie* in the sky, and he had reported no previous heart troubles before that day. See, slapping the wall and retching over the toilet is enough body stress to cause certain death. That's probably how I'll go.

I have vomited in more raunchy places than most people would even dare enter. My regurgitated lunch has bid me how-dee-do behind strip clubs, outside drug houses, on bar dumpsters and in dangerous crime-ridden, wasted neighborhoods. These are places where, if a normal person was forced to go, he would never let his guard down, let alone put himself in the most vulnerable position a person can be in. Imagine fending off a mugging while throwing up. The heaving makes for a difficult defense. On the other hand, maybe barf is nature's God-given pepper spray.

Tonight, my comedian/red carpet friend Seth and I decide to smoke a huge joint with a homeless man outside of a seedy club called Lush. How appropriate.

"Hey, man, you gotta light?" I say to a fellow sitting on the curb.

"I do if I can have a smoke with you."

Oh, the unions that have been created by that vital need for fire.

"You certainly can, my friend. What's your name?"

"Reggie."

"Take a look at this, Reg." Seth strokes the doobie.

What a fine moment of bonding. After the three of us get what we need, we part ways.

"Yeah, yeah, you fellas have fun," says Reggie. "Thanks for the smoke."

I appreciate Reggie. He's no different than us, just doing what it takes to try to feel right.

We head inside. Already loaded up with a ton of liquor, we throw a couple of L'il Raj's valium tablets down the hatch too. Just before they hit me inside the bar, I notice that Seth has lost his mind and shirt in the front of the club. He dances like he's at a Dead show directly in front of the band, alone. The chemicals were a good combo for him, not so much for me. The profuse vomiting began on a damp smoky couch near the dance floor and then moved outside for the people in line to view. Remember, I suffer no black-outs. Luckily Sportscaster Steve had shown up too. He followed me out.

"What are you doing?"

He keeps yelling this at me while the vomit splashes. I cannot answer. I hate him for this. But it is his only defense against the embarrassment of following a puking person. Picture Bob Costas conservatively following a stumbling Jim Morrison to the car. As he drives me home, we make one last stop in front of the most popular coffee shop in the country, The Coffee Bean at San Vicente and Montana in Brentwood. Perfectly primped people enjoy their annoyingly specific cappuccinos on the patio while they talk about their latest fruitless entertainment opportunities.

"Stop!" I yell.

I open the door, spraying tonight's abuse once again right in front of everyone. As I shut the door, I see many surgically enhanced facial expressions quickly spoil. Oh, how many lattes were wasted here tonight?

"Nothing to see here. Just waste more time changing the fonts again on that plagiarized screenplay displayed on your laptop, and the foul odor will be gone soon enough," says Bile Boy.

Obviously, I can never go back to stargaze and slurp on my favorite mocha there again. If I had it to do over, I would have planned something else, but that splish-splashing nightmare turns out to be my farewell to Los Angeles. Of course, this type of embarrassment is familiar to me. I purged in front of my prom date after two warm Budweisers. I threw up in the theater after Madonna's "Truth or Dare." Got sick on salsa after margaritas with Mom. Upchucked everywhere in the club after taking a UFO (PCP-laced Ecstasy). And barfed by my bride before and behind the bars of the K-hole.

∽∾

My first show as Y98's Afternoon Drive personality in St. Louis is set for Monday, September 10, 2001. I arrive in town two days before starting day and head straight to dinner with my family. Jen's job requires her to stay in LA for another month. It feels great being back. My mother is bursting with joy at the sight of her traveling son, home for good. My excitement is genuine too. LA has left its mark on me, but it has also given me some confidence. This swagger is magnified more now that I'm home.

After our delicious fettuccini and cavatelli dinner, I meet up with old friends. We reminisce and begin looking for party enhancements earlier than normal. In just one day, the search is back on. This is made easier by Jen's absence. I have promised her things will be different for us back in St. Louis. I tell myself this drug celebration is just being created from the excitement of being back. It will surely burn out and so will the partying.

Steele has brought me back to bring a freshness and attitude to the afternoon show. The man who was relieved of this job last week had been on the air here for twenty years. I'm here to bring some of that Seacrest hipness and attitude to this newly struggling station. Right off the bat I'm surprised that I don't have the spunky partner I had assumed would be there with me. I hope that this situation is what I expect it to be.

The last time Steele brought me in for evenings, I went out and drank an hour before the show and it went well, but on this day I stay sober. Shiftless confidence carries me. Paul Cook Afternoon Drive dominance begins today, September 10, 2001. My LA attitude-vibing show is riding high, infused with plenty of celebrity news, catty relationship talk and sarcasm, just as I've planned. I am ready for this! It feels great. An extreme amount of preparation has gone into this day, and I've created enough material to deliver a fun, attitude-filled show like this for the next six months.

The first day ends very well. Although it's edgy, the listeners are up for it. I can feel the optimistic anticipation from the station staff too. I'm encouraged when they share with me that they believe the stagnation is over and that my fun show will help Y98 get going in the right direction. I hope they are right. I promise that today was just a preview and I will be even more dominating and cutting-edge tomorrow.

I crack my first beer of the night with thoughts of the radio possibilities ping-ponging around in my head. Hell, I'll probably be doing the much coveted morning show by the beginning of next year if I keep this up. Slurp. Maybe they'll let me hire my own producer. Gulp. Gulp. As the cans pile up, my thoughts slow. And finally, I feel that I'll be able to actually sleep tonight.

CHAPTER 19
9/11

I am shaken awake the next morning by my mother. She flips on the TV in my childhood room where I'm bunking for now. Her shaking feels like a beating because of my hangover.

"Paul! You have to see this. Terrorists are attacking!"

"Terrorists? No way," I grumble while still mostly asleep.

"They are flying planes into the World Trade Center in New York City."

Self inflicted punishment from last night's brew fest causes me to slip back into sleep. My mother comes back a half-hour later.

"Paul, why aren't you affected by this? This is a huge deal."

"Sorry, I'm just a bit groggy. I'll be down in a second."

Gradually, I begin to realize the magnitude of what I'm seeing. Middle-Eastern terrorists are trying to kill Americans. This seems unrealistic, like it could only happen in a movie. As I watch the coverage, I'm disgusted to catch myself rehearsing in my head the witty show I have planned for this afternoon. Reality snaps me out of autopilot when, out of the corner of my eye, a tower falls to the ground. Thousands dead. I keep hearing "horrible," and I believe it, but I'm numb. The New York sky shows only smoke and flames from the other tower.

Watching in the kitchen now, we are speechless. We can only feel a fraction of the hopelessness, but even that fraction is overwhelming. Steele calls.

"We need you early today. We're gonna go in shifts on this

thing. This terrorist attack is the worst thing to happen since Pearl Harbor."

"Okay, lemme print off my show prep for today and I'll be right in."

"Show prep?! Paul, these attacks are all there is."

"Oh, I'm sorry. Okay."

Click.

"All there is." What does that mean? At this time, I still don't recognize that the world has changed. Over the next few hours, drop by drop, I see only how this horrific incident will affect me. Could it be that, on the second day of my big break in St. Louis, the world has been altered for good? The harder I try to feel the empathy that should be automatic for an event like this, the more detached I become. What has happened to me? Is it the Klonopin sedative I'm taking? Suddenly I realize that I totally lack the experience and wherewithal to deliver sincere hand-holding radio, which is the type of execution the listeners and my employer will require. My head throbs and through every jolt of pain I know that this terrorist attack is too big for me.

I struggle through the day's CNN updates and eyewitness reports from Ground Zero. The only on-air verbiage I know lends itself to a lighthearted radio remote broadcast at a car dealership rather than a sensitive event of this nature. After talking to someone at Ground Zero who has lost loved ones, I say, "Thanks for checking in."

"Checking in?" my boss says. "It should be 'Thanks for sharing. We are so sorry for your loss. Please stay safe.' Okay?"

I am not prepared and being criticized for this causes even more balking. The confidence is gone. I have the feeling I am about to drown in unfamiliar broadcasting waters.

There are no jokes on Leno or Letterman for weeks. For those of us who have made our living at satire, here comes a huge period of uncertainty. Taking in more coverage the night of 9/11, the focus falls away from my difficulties. Sadness for what victims have been handed starts to hit me like I'm actually a real live person. What about Jen? How is my wife? The person left behind in LA to organize our move should have been my first thought.

"This is truly the saddest thing I have ever seen," she says over the phone.

"I still can't believe it."

"I am so angry too!" Jen yells.

"There is gonna be hell to pay for this. I just know it," I promise.

"I'm telling you, it is unbelievable. Here on TV in LA they showed people jumping from the burning towers, flapping their arms. How could anybody do this?"

"Horrible. I keep asking myself, what 'cause' could this possibly have helped?"

"It's very scary. I'm not traveling to Memphis this week, obviously. So I'll be able to make sure the moving pods are ordered."

"Thank you so much, Jen. I feel so bad that I can't be there to help. I wish we were together."

"Don't worry. You had to start your job. How was your show today?"

"Not good. I suck at this."

"Well, most people are watching TV anyway."

"I hope you're right, cuz I sound very awkward."

My nightly drinking increases even more after this day. I still find I can even change the way I feel during the day by merely thinking about what I will drink that night. But I assure myself I am not an alcoholic. Everyone drinks to feel better, even non-alcoholics.

Nobody drinks alcohol for the taste. Daily, I'm due at the station by noon. So I manage to do my job adequately.

During this time my sleep pattern changes dramatically. For some reason, I now wake up at three every morning and lie there wide awake. I'm forced to go watch TV for about an hour and a half till the new doses of Klonopin and Tylenol PM kick in. If I don't drink, I don't wake up in the middle of the night. However, if I don't drink, my mind attacks me. Nightly, I beat myself up for many things, one of them being my original reaction to 9/11. "Why didn't I feel the gravity of it more? There is something seriously wrong with me."

So now I try to find balance between too much and too little alcohol, which leaves the over-thinking untreated. The Klonopin provides a distant backdrop of little help, giving me only weakened inhibitions. This causes me to constantly ask myself, "How do I feel?" Am I feeling right? Buzzed? Tired? Have I gone too far? Alcohol quiets those questions. When Jen gets here, I'll be much better. I can talk to her about my thoughts. She will help me get through it. My wife has truly taken a leadership role in my sanity, something I bet neither of us had ever planned.

Eventually, by mimicking the news anchors, I get a touch better at delivering the sad updates to our listeners, but I'm still in uncontrollable "me-autopilot." The 9/11 attacks happened on Tuesday and by Friday I catch myself asking people how much longer we'll be doing radio this way. Two weeks after 9/11, I call Ryan Seacrest in Los Angeles to talk with him about it.

"We have just been doing a lot of handholding with them on the air," Seacrest offers. "Quite a few people out here are from the East Coast. They need to know things are going to be okay."

"Totally. That's what I'm trying to do here."

"Paul, it is what we are here for now. Let them share if they need to. And you can show your heart too."

"Good call. It's hard, but you're right. You still going to the Four Seasons for cocktails with Lisa (his radio partner) during the week?"

"Yeah, that's this town." He throws it away. "But like I said, think of your show as much more of a therapy session than an experience these days. We really try to stay away from cheesy and keep it genuine."

"Thanks, Ryan. I really appreciate your advice, man."

"Good luck, dude," Ryan says.

I wish I were better at the handholding, but this is a muscle I've never exercised. I tell myself I'm a good liar. All I need to do is lie my way to sincerity. I tell myself the only way to be successful is to hold some hands. Obsession with success is all I think about, so that could possibly work.

The next three weekends, I cut loose the only way I know how. I use an old high school friend to find a cocaine dealer. Those nights are spent sniffing, snotting, gagging and talking without listening. The movie *Office Space* loops endlessly on the TV in the background the entire night at my friend Ray's party house. Occasionally, we break conversation to laugh at a funny line from the movie then we get back to our heated conference on anthrax envelopes and terrorism. We don't realize that the white stuff we are snorting resembles cutaneous anthrax identically and that in some circles it had even been rumored that cocaine was replaced with the deadly poison. The enormous danger in this does not deter me.

One sunny Saturday morning, the coke is still in my pocket when I meet my father to return my rental car. My remorse for how I'm living is blinding in the light of day. That afternoon, I'm scheduled to do a remote from outside the YMCA to gather donations for 9/11 families. Like a drugged zombie I stayed up all night. On the way to the Y, I hide the remaining drugs in a plant in front of Jay's house. Giving away drugs is something I have never done. I tell myself, this is it. No more cocaine. I can't afford to be numb any longer. On these days after all-nighters, I'm increasingly feeling that pleasurable, consequence-free drug use is just as dangerous as an overdose, because it reinforces the thought that bringing this dangerous toxicity into the body and spirit is okay. Maybe my use doesn't kill me, but I am sure not living. The slow destruction lies there.

∽◦∾

Waiting for Jen, I continue living with my parents. There's some joy in this. It feels like the days when I came home between semesters in college, sleeping in, going to dinner and engaging in our usual good-spirited family debates. I really enjoy my parents' company. For the most part, I always have. I skipped all my college spring breaks to come home and spend time with them. They are loving, encouraging, conservative, fun people. With the exception of a handful of big arguments, my parents have only been good for me. My insecure neurosis is only mine, not their fault. I wish I could blame this sleepwalking on someone, but it's a me-problem.

Finally Jen arrives in St. Louis and we move into another apartment, the fifth in six years. It doesn't take long for us to jump right back into pretty much the same partying lifestyle as before LA. The only exception is that there is no ecstasy consumed every weekend. Cocaine is still in the mix every time we meet up with old friends.

Now it is generally with small groups in the bathroom, not out in the open at house parties as before. My new dealer connection and improved income increase the amount of coke we abuse. There are no illicit drugs during the week, just drinking. This distinction allows me to tell myself that I don't need help. The fact that I'm still getting refills of Klonopin helps me feel that I am getting some sort of treatment.

But my "treatment" rationale does not satisfy Jen. I wake up after an all-nighter one weepy morning to hear her downstairs having a conversation with a drug hotline. I hear her side of the call.

"No. We can't seem to stop on the weekends ... Uh, cocaine ... We've tried before ... How long is that for? ... Uh-huh ... Immediately? I don't think that will work ... We both work ... Is that the only way? ... I understand. Thank you so much for your time. I will talk to my husband. Thank you. Did you say your name was Lucy? ... Thank you, Lucy. We will."

I can't blame Jen for making this call. It's not the first time we have sought help. This time, the well-informed drug counselor on the other end of the line has told Jen that the only way to overcome our cocaine problem is to enter a treatment facility. Lucy said that we must leave immediately and stay for thirty days. We both agree that will not work for us. I would surely be fired, and I've already paid for the flight to some guy's bachelor party in Vegas this weekend. After sharing our feeling and fighting through another hangover, Jen and I make new promises to entirely quit doing drugs in St. Louis.

It defies logic that I haven't been seriously injured or killed operating the way I do, but even more unbelievable is that I haven't had any legal difficulties. How have I not earned any DWIs or drug possession arrests? I have certainly talked my way out of a few late-night drunken-driving discoveries. Other times, I have just been plain lucky. Whatever luck I have in the can will be riding on empty after another nameless bachelor party this weekend. I'm getting pretty good at this type of fiesta. It is my third bach party in Las Vegas, counting mine.

Many sweet fiancées worry about their guy spending this all-important night or weekend in Sin City with his friends, and they should, because a veering off from Monogamy Ranch happens quite frequently here in the desert. But ladies, there are certain things that you can ask yourself before allowing your man to make this trip. Three red flags almost guarantee infidelity. I have seen these red flags move a man closer than he should be to stag.

Fortunately, my celebration was on the safe side of these warnings, but my bachelor party happened well before my current lifestyle became deep rooted. In fact, I was the responsible guy looking after all the other drunk punks who were having the time of their lives.

If your fiancé is headed to that risky desert for his bachelor party, ask these three questions:

1. Is a brother or father going on the trip? Obviously, if a family member of the groom is there, your man's chances of doing something stupid with another woman are fewer. The mere sight of this family member will remind him of his bachelor party behavior for years to come. Believe me, he considers this and will not want to go there. This rule of the game does not appear to affect my already Hades-bound cousin. That's why it would also be a bonus for you if you could get a member of your family to attend this traveling soiree. Your younger brother might be just the guy for the job.

2. How many partners has your man been with? This one is tricky. If you are his only roll in the turnips, you are safe. This man is committed and possibly too inexperienced to feel confident in a Vegas love-fest. If he's had many partners, that can work in your favor too, tapping off the "been there done that" philosophy. The guy you have to watch is the man who has only partially sown his oats with just a few lovers. Even though he loves you dearly, he may feel shortchanged on his womanly experiences. And now that he has broken the one hundred-dollar bill, those twenties are much easier to spend, so to speak.

3. Most importantly, do your men plan to get a limo for anything in Vegas? Plainly, you don't want your man's group getting a limo. Cabbing it will be much safer. Try to place that thought firmly in the best man's cranium. It's a fact that Vegas limo drivers are the gatekeepers. Generally, if they don't run prostitutes themselves, they get spiffs for directing your group to them. Limo drivers are also the drug dealers in town. As you have read in this book, drugs make men do stupid things. Steer your boys clear of the long shiny bed on wheels.

And this brings us to my act of arrogance here in Las Vegas. It is definitely cuff-worthy. Cocaine is fueling the sleepless weekend, but as always, we have run out. With no sighting of *Scarface*'s Tony Montana in the casino, I decide to whip out our hotel Yellow Pages and start calling limo services. I'm not asking for car service. I want cocaine service. This must be closer than ever to what life would be like with legalized drugs. Maybe someday we'll see advertising in the paper or phone book when that happens.

"Yeah, I got a two-inch ad in the Yellow Pages for my cocaine service, with a coupon and everything! When flipping through that thing, that's when people are ready to buy!"

Right now, I'm an arrest waiting to happen. Even worse, my plan works. The third service I call is bringing coke straight over to our hotel at the Monte Carlo. At least they say they will. I fidget at a blackjack table while a couple of the other guys go out to get it. We were told to pay for one hour of limo service on top of the price of an eight ball, then simply look in the back seat for the product. When the guys roll back to the blackjack table with bugged out eyes and wearing an adrenalin rush like they just jumped out of a plane with Patrick Swayze, I know my idea worked. Although I made someone else go get it, I was still seen as the hero of the night. Ten years peeled off my life on that trip, along with most of my luck.

CHAPTER 20
"A" List

Things start to return to normal after two months of on-air handholding at the radio station. The CNN 9/11 updates fade from our station. Out of nowhere, Steele busts into the studio with a smile and asks me if I'm ready for a road trip. I think, "Time for a road trip? All I am is a human road trip."

"We need to incorporate a bit of fun on the radio again," he says.

"All right. What are you thinking?"

"I'm sending Mr. LA and Greg out to Hollywood for the VH-1 Awards!"

If he wants to be accurate, I'm actually Mr. Couldn't Make It in LA Due to Fear and Addiction and Maybe Lack of Talent, but I don't correct him. "Mr. LA" is fine. Greg is our midday DJ.

I couldn't be more excited to show Greg around the hot spots of LA. His father is nearing the end of his life and helping his dad through this difficult time has taken its toll. Obviously Greg needs and deserves this trip to the West Coast more than I. He helped me get my start in radio, so I want to show him that I made some good things happen while out in LA. Maybe I can take him along the beaver suit transport route. A tour of the places where my big opportunities died due to eye twitching is out of the question.

We are staying at the Wyndham Bel Age on Sunset. The purpose of being here is to promote The VH-1 Big in '02 Awards. We will be set up with about twenty other stations at the Shrine Auditorium to interview celebrities and performers today, which is the day before the awards. Our interviews and our show will be broadcast live back in St. Louis.

The return has me twisting a bit, a mixture of remorse and, mostly, relief. I put Jen and me in a financial bind when we were living in Los Angeles. It's good to know that particular experience is hopefully in the past. That is the relief; the remorse centers around my unrealistic expectation to have "made it" bigger during my year and three months in Hollywood. I've never been good with mixed feelings, so I direct my thoughts and energy toward being a good tour guide for Greg.

The day starts with some excitement when we get on our hotel elevator and see Sean Penn waiting to go down. I say, "Hey, man."

He says, "Hey."

Greg and I look at each other through an awkward silence as we wait for the elevator to ding our arrival in the lobby. Sean Fricken Penn! It doesn't get bigger than that.

Add in LA traffic with our huge star sighting and the blood is already pumping when we get to the remote broadcast for VH-1 at the Shrine Auditorium. A few Klonopin down the hatch and the broadcast goes well. We talk with Jewel, Bon Jovi's Richie Sambora, Creed, and the guy from *Office Space*, Ron Livingston. I don't tell him about the deplorable coke night I recently spent with his movie after 9/11. Not cool. Jewel is stunning in person. Livingston could not have been more down to earth. Sambora seemed buzzed. It is apparent to Greg and me both that Creed are well into their fifteen minutes of fame after this interview: huge egos, very little charisma. They break up two years later.

Evidently the Wyndham Bel Age is a preferred hotel for huge celebrities. We learn a very useful thing about seeing celebrities

I checked a childhood dream off the list when I met Flav from the legendary rap group Public Enemy back stage at VH1 awards. Like most of those childhood dreams, the payoff fell short. Flav made a comeback on the VH-1 hit show Flavor of Love.

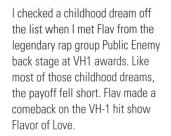

I do a smackdown TV interview with the WWE's Mr. Kennedy at KMOV in St. Louis.

John Mayer with Greg Hewitt and me a night before he won his first Grammy.

Ed McMahon in Hollywood in 2006 with me and Y98 traffic reporter Lance Hildebrand.

on this trip.

"They like to drink, but not at big bars. Usually, the huge celebrities hang out in their hotel bar," the concierge tells us.

The Wyndham Bel Age bar is small, dark and intimate. It is lined with low couches and cozy chairs. The sitting area has two partitions that split the cocktail area into three small spaces. People can be seen through small glassless windows in each partition. The entire bar is decorated in mauve/purple. When Greg and I arrive, the area is empty. We sit down in the middle and order two Bud Lights. Reflecting on the day at VH-1 causes some loud laughter. This experience has been fun. We are eager to hit the strip and see the LA people.

While we pay our tab, we notice that another group has gathered in the sitting area to our left. The Wyndham waiters are standing behind this threesome that is now seated. I look.

"It's Sean Penn," I whisper loudly. "Sean Penn again."

Greg slowly peers through the partition.

"He's with the guy from *The Legend of Billie Jean*, uh, Pete Coyote," Greg whispers back.

"No way."

Peter Coyote has been in many films. He is also the deep-voiced, good scientist in *ET*.

One of the Wyndham waiters comes to get my credit card.

"Is that Sean Penn over there?" I ask.

The polite Middle Eastern man says, "Yes, sir. Also the author Hunter S. Thompson and Peter Coyote are having cocktails with Mr. Penn."

"Hunter S. Thompson! I'm reading *The Rum Diary* right now," I whisper loudly. "I have it in my toiletries bag."

"Well, that is nice sir," the waiter replies.

Toiletries? I have lost all remnants of cool. By now, we've been drinking for five hours since our broadcast ended. We are buzzed heavily.

"Ya know you should go up to them and say hi," Greg suggests.

"Nah, I don't do that anymore. It's cool to be here with them, but believe me, that is always awkward."

"Okay, I'm just saying you will probably regret it if you don't."

"You do it, Gee."

"No, I don't have that in me. This is a job for Paul."

Greg orders two Jack and Cokes.

"I see what you're doing," I tell him.

"We just need a little Jack. You *are* going to do this."

"Easy there, fella."

As I sit there, the disturbing Smash Mouth incident runs through my head. This celebrity approach has the potential to end even worse. I reluctantly recall a story about Hunter S. Thompson that proves he doesn't appreciate strangers. Evidently, he had some legal issues when he lived in Colorado that his fans thought he didn't deserve. One day, getting back to his farm after a court date, he noticed that a group had gathered on the edge of his property to support him with "Free Hunter" signs. After a while, the spirited chanting of his name was interrupted by the popping sound of close-by gun shots. As the Hunter S. Thompson faithful scrambled for cover, they noticed that their hero was the one shooting at them. That's the kind of distaste for approval I can respect. So tonight, how will he respond to a spiky headed punk disturbing him in a closed meeting with his "A List" friends? And what if he's packin'?

Some food is what we need to soak up all this liquor. We order two cheeseburgers at the bar. They help level us a bit, but Greg is still working it like *Wall Street*'s Bud Fox.

"You gotta do this. That's Sean Penn."

I don't answer. I am in a bar where the reclusive legend Hunter S. Thompson is drinking. I have to try to at least flash him a smile. Greg is right. In as little as an hour, I will feel major regret for not making a story of this wonderful opportunity.

"All right, I'm goin' in."

After all that pushing, Greg now looks shocked, like he's awakened a sleeping pit bull, and he has. His surprised expression reveals that he didn't actually think his pressing would be successful. By now, there are five people sitting having drinks. Hunter S. Thompson and Sean Penn appear to be telling an animated story together. Peter Coyote is gone. Sean wears all black with a black sports-coat. Standing in a guard position is our waiter. He steps closer to me as I approach. Then Sean sees me out of the corner of his eye. It's too late to bail now. I clear my throat. Dead air.

"Hey, guys, the last thing I want to do is bother you."

Silence, with all eyes on me now.

"But I would hate myself if I didn't tell you that you are my favorite author, and that I believe you are the best actor of this generation."

"What are you a cop?" Hunter says without missing a beat.

"Uh, no, I'm an abuser."

"Ha! Well, have a seat!" says Thompson.

"No, no," Penn interjects. "But thank you very much."

Penn shakes my hand. I immediately turn and head back to Greg, who is now cross-eyed on a bar couch. His mouth hangs open to the point of an unhinged jaw.

"I can't believe you just did that."

"I can't believe it either. That was crazy."

"You talked to Sean Penn. What did Hunter say to you?"

"He thought I was a cop. So I ... Oh my God, Nicole Kidman is behind you at the bar."

The statuesque beauty is wearing an off-white dress with her hair up. She is three feet in front of the bar, standing with two handlers. Greg and I give each other a "This is *not* happening look." But it is. I'm still reeling from my Sean Penn drive-by. With no prodding, I get back up and walk to the bar immediately to Nicole's left.

"Two Jack and Cokes please," I order.

Then, like it was just chance, I pretend to discover her on my right.

"Oh," I say softly, off-handedly.

Kidman looks straight ahead, then right at me.

"Hi there. How are you?" I say softly.

She lowers her chin and says, "I am quite fine, thank you very much."

Her beauty stuns me. Before this day, I would always say I didn't see her attractiveness. But this encounter changes all that. Looking into Nicole Kidman's eyes, I realize that she is one of the most beautiful women in the world. She possesses the kind of beauty that makes everyone else you see appear ugly.

It is unsettling. I am frozen. She appears to be a foot taller than me. I snap out of it and begin to shuffle. The man standing behind Kidman makes a gesture and just like that our drinks are free. After getting them, I head back to Greg. What an incomprehensible five minutes I've just experienced.

Both Nicole Kidman and Sean Penn would be nominated for Best Actor Oscars this year. Neither wins, but they don't get more A-List than that.

After a couple of minutes, Penn approaches Kidman and they leave together to go to the dining room. She was there to meet him to talk about a project. That project turns out to be a movie called *The Interpreter*. It saw mild success in 2005.

Greg and I are absolutely flying about our star conquest, so we hit the strip to tell everyone. Our first stop is my favorite LA destination, Red Rock. It's totally packed and we have to wait to get in with a group from some other radio stations who are also in for the VH-1 awards. We share our story with them. No one can believe it. By the time we get into the packed bar, grab a drink, and move to the back of the place, the rumors buzz that Nicole Kidman and Sean Penn are partying on the strip. Our experience has traveled the entire bar faster than us, and now people are telling us about it.

On a Friday night on the strip, people stand almost elbow to elbow in the bar. A blonde on my elbow says, "I hear Nicole Kidman and Sean Penn are at one of the bars nearby."

Greg and I blurt out together, "We saw them!"

"Paul chatted with them."

"No way!" she says.

Talking to her for a couple of minutes reveals that she is also here from St. Louis and she was on the *Wheel of Fortune* today. She was on the NFL Special with Rams quarterback Kurt Warner. Evidently, she totally sucked on the show. Red Rock is her oasis destination tonight to drink away all woes with her husband.

"I need to meet Sean Penn!" she yells.

"Seanny!!" we yell.

We agree to go back to the Wyndham.

The blonde and husband bring her mother too. Another group of people staying at the hotel follow us as well. When we enter the Wyndham bar, it is much more crowded, with no sign of the celebrities. We grab our middle-seating area position again. The group we have assembled now takes up all the couches and chairs in that section. Energy is high. Having that experience is literally like taking a drug for Greg and me. We talk, laugh and display good-natured arrogance about the fact that it happened only to us.

A guy from another radio station says, "Well, where are they now? You gotta prove they were here."

Proving it doesn't matter to Greg or me; we know it happened just as we described it.

"Oh, I wanted to see Sean Penn!" Blonde Girl is disappointed.

It hits me that I need to call Jen and tell her about what happened, so I sit in the back of our little section in the center of a low couch dialing my phone. People standing fill the area now. Jen answers. The bar is loud, and I shout.

"Jen, you won't believe who I talked to!"

"Who?" she answers in a muffled tone.

"Nicole Kidman and …"

Suddenly, I see our group of fifteen people separate like someone has been shot. The bullet is none other than Sean Penn. He splits the crowd and heads right for me. Everyone in the group goes quiet. He's right over me now.

"I wanted to thank you," Sean says to me in a Brooklyn accent. "Your enthusiasm is much appreciated."

He extends his hand.

"Oh, no problem. Thank you, Sean."

"My friend Hunter was complaining that people of your age don't get him right when you walked up and said you loved his work."

"Wow, that's great. I'm glad I could help."

"Thank you."

He turns and walks back through our stunned group. Greg stands to my right.

"What in the hell? Sean Penn just approached you." Blonde Girl scurries up.

"He was talking to you. What did he say?" Blonde Girl begs.

"He thanked me for my, uh, enthusiasm."

I realize I never hung up the phone.

"You still there?"

"Oh my God. I heard that!"

Whatever excitement tipped the scales before is now at a dangerous level, and it has caused everyone to throw back the cocktails. It makes me wonder if it turns into this at every bar a major celebrity attends. What must it be like to have this swarm of energy around you? No wonder they have a hard time with long-term relationships. Celebrities are used to constant puppy love. When the fresh love dust fades, all they know to do is search for another supply of fuzzy.

This hotel bar is so small that you have to leave and enter the lobby to go to the bathroom. I need a minute to gather myself. The light of the lobby strongly contrasts the low lounge light of the bar. The beams are sobering. While walking, I run into Mr. Gonzo Journalist himself, Hunter S. Thompson. Actors are made for the camera and daylight, and they "make" the cameras quite often, but obviously writers are more reclusive and mysterious. To me, the presence of Thompson is a bigger thrill than even Sean Penn. Penn is in movies, but movies have been made *about* Hunter S. Thompson. This living legend is leaving the bathroom as I'm entering it.

"Hi there," I throw at him.

Hunter says, "Howdy, sir!" then makes a half-Nazi salute. "Hold on."

I stop, and so does a girl leaving the women's room.

"May I see your lipstick?" he says to her.

She roots through her bag and hands it to him. I stand next to her and watch him apply the red lipstick, purposely going outside of his lips. He then puts the cap back on and hands it back.

As he walks away, he says, "Thanks."

I never see him again.

This transcendent writer would die of a self-inflicted gunshot wound to the head in 2005. He was sixty-seven. In his books, he talked frequently about "getting the fear." I can't help but think we suffered from similar demons and afflictions in varying degrees.

By now I'm dealing with a great measure of awestruck excitement overload.

"This is too much," I keep saying to myself, but we're just getting started. In the small two-urinal bathroom, I'm semi-stunned to notice I'm peeing next to Sean Fricken Penn. More accurately, he is peeing. I am stricken with a mammoth episode of gun-shyness. *This is crazy.*

While washing up he turns to me and says, "What crew are you with?" in a thick Brooklyn accent. Sean is from Santa Monica.

"Uh, I'm with a radio station. We're here from St. Louis."

I now feel myself slipping into Sean's east coast accent.

"Well, I'm gonna come and talk to you in a minute," he promises.

"Okay, I'll be in there."

I trot back to Greg.

"Seanny just told me he's gonna come and talk to us."

"Truly an unbelievable night," says Greg.

By this time, the bar has cleared out a bit. It's past midnight and most of the sightseers have gotten this week's story to tell and now they are on to the bigger clubs. It's just Greg and me sitting now. *Wheel of Fortune* girl's husband sits in the background. Greg and I are talking when Sean Penn walks up and grabs a chair next to me.

"So, yeah, that was just great timing when you walked up earlier tonight," Sean says. "It was something Hunter really needed to hear."

"Well it was honest. I really love his work."

Greg says, "Oh yeah, he's done some great things. *Fear and Loathing on the Campaign Trail*, too. Does he still do some stuff for *Rolling Stone*?"

"Some."

I catch Greg's eyes. We can't believe we are having this conversation with one of Hollywood's coolest bad boys.

"So you guys are from the Midwest?" Sean lights a cigarette.

"Yeah, St. Louis," Greg replies.

"I just moved back there from here a couple months ago."

"LA?" asks Sean.

"Yeah, I had a screenplay."

He says nothing. Yet another person the word "screenplay" fails to impress. I do a Chris Farley-esque "Damn, why did I say that!" in my head. Then I pick it back up.

"Traveling has certainly changed with 9/11," I offer.

"I was trapped in London for 9/11," says Greg.

"Oh really? Yeah it's all a mess. Afghanistan," Sean replies.

Standing three feet away is the bar manager who has been following Sean all night, attending to all his needs. His name is Demitri. Demitri has been freshening up Sean's drinks repeatedly. He is also the guy who almost blocked me out on my first approach of the night.

"I fuckin' hate that Bill O'Reilly guy," Sean says.

Greg and I agree. I fail to tell Sean about my experience with O'Reilly in the FX lunchroom. I have no clarity of recollection right now.

"He doesn't get it and he is so fuckin' arrogant," Sean continues.

By now, the husband of the *Wheel of Fortune* girl has sidled up. His wife and mother-in-law are on the other side of the bar where Sean has spent most of the evening. Some of Sean's people are still there.

Husband nervously interjects, "What was it like working with Susan Sarandon in *Dead Man Walking*?"

"It was good. She is very talented."

"Where is your wife?" I ask the husband.

"She's over there."

"She's talkin' to my friend," Sean warns. "Let me tell you, he's the middle-weight champion of Prussia and I would get over there, dude."

We all laugh. The husband gathers his drink and wanders away.

"Not to sound like a simple fan like that, but I can tell you are really enjoying the directing," I tell Sean.

"I'm glad you see that. I can express and convey my message best that way. I find my head working more and more in the directing mindset."

Sean puts his hand up.

"Demitri, please get three Fernet-Branca's for me and my friends."

"My pleasure, Mr. Penn."

"You are going to love this," he tells us.

"What is it?" asks Greg.

"You won't find it many places," he says. "Fernet-Branca will give you pep."

"Sweet!" I yell.

"Speaking of great directing, I watched *Apocalypse Now* again this week. Great stuff," says Greg.

"Marlon is an amazing individual," Sean tells us.

We are actually having a conversation with Sean Penn about Marlon Brando. *Nuts.*

"You know him?" I ask.

"We studied with the same teacher in New York."

"Is that Stella?" I offer.

"Yes, it is," he says, surprised.

Demitri is waiting for his break.

"Here are your spirits, sir."

He puts three snifter glasses down on the cocktail table that only Greg, Sean and me surround now.

"You just take it all down," says Sean.

He drinks it like water. We try to do the same. It burns severely. My eyes feel like they are melting in my head. Sean slams down the glass.

"You, my friend, will have a great shit tomorrow!" laughs Sean.

I yell with victory. Sean laughs with that jack-o-lantern grin. Unfortunately, the drink isn't done with us. Greg and I can't stop coughing. We feel rude because Sean is trying to get back into more talk about his politics.

"Demitri, two waters!" Sean orders.

"Yes, sir."

Water helps slow down the coughing, but it can't stop the world from speeding up. The next hour is a bit blurry. I recall having a ton of fun yucking it up with him. I even remember grabbing his thigh during one of my animated stories and he didn't seem to mind.

When the bar closes at about two AM, Sean gathers his cigarettes and glass to leave. Greg is in the bathroom; it's just us two now.

"Hey, Sean, do you have a bump (cocaine)?" I ask.

In that one instant, his face changes completely. That huge expressive smile quickly turns to disappointment. Watching his expression turn is one of the saddest things I've ever seen.

"No, man, I have to get up early tomorrow," he says looking past me.

He walks over to the area where the middleweight champ of Prussia is and then he disappears. At first, I thought that maybe he thought I was a cop trying to trap him with drugs, but after a while, I realized he wasn't into drugs anymore, if he ever was, and it was sad for him to see that a guy he had bonded with was. Somehow, the movies *Hurlyburly* and *Fast Times* took over and I could see Sean Penn no other way. Or maybe it had nothing to do with those excuses and I just needed drugs.

On the lonely elevator ride up to my room, I use all my powers of mental distraction to get his heart-stopping reaction out of my head, but it's no use; acting or genuine, with one response Sean Penn has stomped my lungs. How does anyone share a deep scene with him without fleeing for higher ground? Neither of us knows on this night that Sean Penn has two Best Actor Oscars yet to win this decade, in 2004 and 2009. And bringing Paul Cook coincidence to a full figure eight of unbelievability, the 2009 Oscar came under the producing direction of Dan Jinks, none other than the dark, redheaded guy Tom and I ate next to on Rodeo Drive on our first reconnaissance mission to LA.

The next morning in the lobby, *Wheel of Fortune* Blonde Girl tells us that she and her mom were up in Sean's suite talking with him and his friends all night. This is an invite I figure I blew with my drug request.

CHAPTER 21
AA Meeting

This roller coaster of drug and alcohol abuse is not abnormal for me and the people I associate with. One of the craziest drinkers I've ever known was also a guy with promise. Jim and I were inseparable in early high school. In our junior year, his parents got divorced, and his drinking really escalated. Soon the risks he was willing to take became too great for me and we had to go our separate ways. A couple years later, he became a hard-core drinker with a drug problem. On top of that, Jim would usually become violent when he used.

Four years ago I went to an engagement party he attended and he looked completely different. His big smile and bright eyes were startling. I learned then that Jim had been sober for five years. Jen and I were headed out for more partying that night when we saw him, so Jim's sobriety seemed lame to me. But his confidence stirred me and I always remained curious. Since that party, we talk about four times a year about life and his sobriety.

After I got back from the LA trip, I was miserable—depressed, tired and lost. Jim must have picked up on this when I ran into him at a restaurant. He convinced Jen and me to come to a Thanksgiving Alcoholics Anonymous meeting with him. The first beer I ever drank was with Jim, and after all the trouble the drink caused him, I figure I at least owe him a visit to the thing he claims saved his life.

This is one of those things that you agree to do, but right up until the time you go you dread it.

"I hope they don't make us talk," I say to Jen on the way over.

We meet Jim at the church and follow him to one of the kindergarten classrooms on the lower level. Children's drawings of Moses' stone commandments decorate the walls. We grab a seat in a middle row where thirty chairs all face one direction. I feel like I am back in preschool. I even experience that familiar absence-of-mommy anxiety that I felt so much back then. The only thing different now is the overwhelming aroma of fresh coffee. Stimulants! We get up to grab a cup while Jim talks loudly with another alcoholic. Jim has a dark crew cut and blue eyes.

"How long does something like this last?" Jen whispers from sugar and cream coffee-pouring duty.

"I think an hour, but we can still bail," I say this more for me than her.

"I'm good."

We take our seats again. Directly to my left is a giant construction paper cut-out of Jesus with a big crown of thorns.

"Well, I'm glad Kerry made it back," Jim announces. "He's got quite a story."

We sit quietly. Jim notices us.

"How are you guys doing? I'm glad you could make it," he exclaims.

"We're good."

I say that a lot, but the fact is I have no idea what "good" is.

Suddenly I feel a heavyset gentlemen in overalls approaching from the other side, hand outstretched. Is he going to stop or bowl us over? Bogie three o'clock!

"Hi, I'm Mick!" He seems to shout.

Watch the personal space, fella.

"I'm Paul and this is my wife, Jennifer."

"Great, great! Jim, so you're moving to Kansas City on us huh, bro?" says Mick.

"Yeah, I've got a new job," Jim confesses.

Wait, this is news to me. Jim is moving to Kansas City?

"Well KC has just gotten some great sobriety," Mick tells him.

"Thanks, Mick."

Here comes another. Flanker! Eight o'clock!

"Becky!" She says with a smile.

Becky is bright eyed and very masculine. We're under attack from happy people!

I say "Hi" with raised eyebrows, which is code to my wife that this is getting weird.

What the hell is everybody so cheery about? It's Thanksgiving and this "meeting" is taking place during the Macy's Thanksgiving Day Parade. Is this a meeting of the Communist Party? Nobody forsakes relaxing TV couch-time and beautiful floats, do they? Why is everyone hugging and laughing all around us? They are genuinely happy to be here. I'm not there. But I'm glad we got a seat, because thirty chairs are not enough for this crew. It's standing room only. Jim told me there would be a speaker at this gathering. The guy must be pretty entertaining to draw this kind of crowd.

After a couple of minutes, the girl at the front of the room silences everyone with: "I'm Maggie and I'm an alcoholic!"

"HI, MAGGIE!" everyone yells.

Startled, I defensively jerk my Styrofoam coffee cup up high, like when you're sitting on the couch and someone's huge annoying dog is running around at a party. The 1,000-degree rocket fuel spills on the top of my hand. It burns, but I say nothing. Maggie then leads us in a prayer about being controlling or something. I can relate. Then Frank, our speaker for today, stands.

"Frank, alcoholic," he throws out there.

"HI, FRANK!" the room shrieks.

Good Christ!

Frank talks about how he was in the military. He says it was okay to be drunk there, and it was free. He talks about soiling himself. This is pretty depressing stuff. I wonder if Jim thinks I live like this. I want to tell him, this is not me. Frank continues to talk about his life before AA. He describes his divorce, DWIs and losing his job. I feel for the guy, but none of this has happened to me. And frankly, it's starting to get a bit boring. I can't get over the thought that everyone is staring at me. Am I responding to his story with the correct non-verbal? Having nothing in common with this guy, it's hard to know how to act.

Then Frank starts talking about seeing true beauty, feeling whole and enjoying the moment. My interest perks up. I have been a self-help nut from birth. Sure, I've had some scrapes, but I've always appreciated practical motivation. I notice similar feel-good endorphins that speeches from Zig Ziglar have activated in me are starting to flow as Frank shares his enlightenment.

He tells how it happened for him with these "steps." Frank even says that he was previously unable to be a good son to his dad before he died. He describes the pride he felt in cleaning up some of his father's messier moments of incontinence. I appreciate his message, but somewhere in there he loses me again. When he finishes we all clap. Then, one by one, people talk about how great Frank is, how much he has helped them, how Frank helped them get "off the pity pot" and quit blaming everyone for their problems. They speak a lot about changing and that seems pretty cool to me. Then some old codger in the back jumps in and hits me right between the eyes with his comment.

"I'm Bob, an alcoholic."

"Hey, Bob!"

"Thanks. Ya know we love to blame, but we get some help too. I have been around for fifteen years, and every young alkie who goes to a psychiatrist for help always comes home with the same diagnosis: bipolar. I have never-not-once seen it come back any other way. They go and describe the fear, agitation, remorse, anxiety and depression and they stamp you bipolar so you get to avoid taking ownership a little while longer. What you are describing to the psychiatrist is a thing called alcoholism! Get the program and you get well, without all those bipolar meds. Worked for me and I've seen it work every time," Bob promises.

A bit freaked out, I grab Jen and we hit the door before the "Thanks, Bob!" chorus fades.

"What do you think?" I ask her.

"It was powerful. Do you think that is something we need?"

"Totally not. I'm happy for Jim, but we just like to drink. Life isn't perfect, but it's never gotten that bad," I remind her.

"What do you think of that bipolar stuff?" Asks Jen.

"Well, the doctors say I'm bipolar two, not just plain bipolar. That guy looked crazy to me. Did you see his overalls?" I try to reassure Jen and myself.

I learned later that Thanksgiving is a big holiday in AA because gratitude is a theme of the program. This is another thing I cannot relate to. We don't go back.

∽◦∽

I was at the exquisitely gaudy Fox Theater introducing The

Sing-A-Long *Sound of Music* when I got the call.

"Paul, the test is positive! I'm pregnant!"

"No way! Incredible. How great! Are you sure?"

"This is the second test that has the solid line!"

I have had four glasses of wine at this point. I had even made the call to the drug man already.

"I love you! We have to celebrate!" I tell her.

"I love you too!"

"I'll come and get you."

Rushing home from The Fox I think about how I'd always had the fear that maybe I was not fertile. This is wonderful. *I helped make a baby!* What a feeling.

This night would be one of the last times Jen would have more than one drink in a week during this pregnancy. Every once in a while, she would partake in a glass of wine, but for the most part she was able to stop drinking altogether. And luckily, the drug man never called me back. Doing coke the night I found out about this incredible news would have created more unbearable remorse.

The hypochondriac in me is happy that Jen is not drinking, but now I feel alone more than ever. What do you do when you lose your best drinking buddy? If you are me, you drink alone, and you suddenly begin attending every office-related cocktail party, as if you are really interested in building great work relationships or possibly shooting for CEO. On top of that, you offer to get carryout food every night for dinner so you can drink at the bar while you wait. Many husbands' lives are changed positively upon hearing they will be a father. For some reason that does not happen for me. I beat myself up about this too. I use more wine and Klonopin together to help quiet that anxiety. Those are my weekdays.

On Fridays and Saturdays, adjusting reality is one of my

priorities. Drinking, drugging and "feeling the heat" are my top exhilarations, but on Sundays, my head is full of remorse. The pattern is to spend Monday through Thursday swearing off the bad stuff, while building up a tad more confidence of entitlement each day. When Friday arrives, last week might as well be last lifetime. The only constant is the despair you can hear in my every footstep, seven days a week. If you don't hear it, I'll make sure you do. My self-pity excuses my abuses.

CHAPTER 22
Employee Of The Month

Cocaine is the drug of choice now. Painkillers that are "found" are just a rare bonus. By now, I have minimized the possibility of getting busted because my "friends" are the ones with the coke, so I don't have to search among strangers at clubs. But that only lasts for a few months. I mentioned in the beginning that, to me, these people are not friends, they are people I do drugs with. Oddly, Jen cares about many of the girls in these groups of couples who happen to do coke recreationally on the weekends, and these people care about Jen. That is a bad thing for me, because soon my pregnant and uncontrollably morning sick wife sends out the word:

"Don't give Paul ANY drugs."

Parties, gatherings and late-night soirees that I attend alone due to Jen's being sick change dramatically now. In my arguing with them to "Just come on, a little, it's no big deal," I come off as desperate, and desperate is a destination my ego won't let me publicly visit too often. Now I'm more than lost, sleepwalking through life armed with only a must-feel-better awareness.

Is this how it's going to be? I keep rolling it over and over in my head. What did I do to get like this? Does it run in my family? Did a simple painkiller after my wisdom-teeth extraction trip all of this? I have no answers and only two solutions: continue to put things in me that make me feel good and keep trying to surround myself with things that make me feel even better. One of those things is work success. In spite of my extracurricular activities, the ratings on my afternoon show soar to number one in the desired demographic of women eighteen to forty-nine. That feels good. Drinks make it better. Already I have been ending most every day with the thought that "I worked very hard to put a good show on the air today. I deserve to wind down with drinks."

For me, the two go hand in hand. And when ratings are with you, everything seems to glide, even getting a little too drunk at a station event.

⌒⌒

Steele has decided to send me out to a four-hour remote broadcast in the center of St. Louis's enormous Mardi Gras celebration. This is the same event I attended last year on a visit from LA, with an embarrassing trip to LALA Land. The horrible remorse I felt after exposing my drug problem to my old college friends is something I'm looking to avoid this year.

Another year lived, another year wiser, right? No. Being on the clock does not deter me. I take one of my last Klonopin and begin drinking at my tiny pop-up tent after the Mardi Gras parade. The first hour goes well in spite of receiving a new free drink every five minutes.

"I'm gonna find a bathroom," I tell my traffic reporter, Lance.

"Cool," he replies. "Come right back. You gotta do weather in five minutes."

"Oh, that's plenty. Hold down the fort and I'll be back in a sec."

That was two and a half hours into the four-hour show. By the time I stumble back to my post, they are breaking down the booth. I have been gone an hour and half. Lance had to finish the radio show by himself. What a flagrant howler of a misstep. I will surely

Grammys in 2003. Vince Vaughn was exhausted but funny.

Y98 Artist Matt Kearney performs for my afternoon radio show. His songs were featured on the popular shows *Grey's Anatomy* and *The Unit*.

be reprimanded.

"You sounded very drunk on the air," an engineer scolds me that next Monday.

"It must have been the reception. That equipment is old, you know." I reach for an excuse and blame the problems on our technical equipment. After the engineer leaves the studio, I realize I have been holding my breath for over a minute. I let it out.

The silence grabs me. *I have to stop this!* I'm tired of giving a new excuse every week for messing up. My boss, Steele, is a micromanager. He doesn't miss a minute of the broadcast day. When he asks me what was wrong, I'll just come clean for once. I drank too much. I've been drinking too much. Can you help me? Let him do the damage control rather than me. Maybe he will fire me. No, he won't. That might even be illegal. That's it, though. I'm making a deal with myself. When he asks why I sounded so weird on the air, I will tell him. I make a note reminding myself:

*Do not fearfully cave to deception just to save face. This is what I need.

I wait and I wait for him to ask.

Steele never mentions it. With each hour and day my arrogance builds back up. I got away with it. Approaching him about this would be crazy. I have others to think about, a baby on the way. Maybe ratings are good enough that he's decided to take the good with the bad. Good numbers make everyone happy, but just like a drinking buzz, they never last.

As if ratings aren't enough to make me arrogant, the St. Louis Radio Awards are being presented this week. This year, I am nominated for Best Afternoon Show and St. Louis's Best Music Host. This is my second Best Host nomination. I accepted that award two years ago while completely hammered. The horrible speech I gave that night in front of my boss and many other potential employers totally ruined the glee my underdog win should have produced. This nomination gives me another opportunity to make things right from the last time I won an award in Steele's presence.

Of course, doing this one right will be more difficult. First, I have to actually win one of these awards and then I need to be much less drunk.

Incredibly, I go two for two, winning both awards. Even though I drink Bud Lights during the ceremony, I give two brief and lucid acceptance speeches. I sit with Steele, just like two years ago. He appears proud of my conduct and my awards. There was no way I was going to create that kind of depression for myself again. Maybe I'm getting better, growing up a little bit.

During the awards ceremony I convince Steele to run Ryan Seacrest's new syndicated show on our radio station. *Live From The Lounge with Ryan Seacrest* is a cool little unplugged show where many of our core artists perform then have a chat with Ryan. A few days later Ryan calls my show to talk about this new venture.

"Paul Cook Show!" he yells into the cell.

"Ryan Seacrest, the host of Y98's new show *Live From The Lounge*. I think I hear an airport, man. Where are you headed?"

"I'm just now leaving Chicago to head back to LA. We shot part of another new show I'm doing here. Paul, it's called *American Idol: The Search for America's next Superstar*," Ryan says on our speaker phone.

My intern Rico and I roll our eyes. Sounds like a clunker.

"Exciting, what is that about?"

"*American Idol* is the next great talent competition for the new millennium. I think it's gonna be huge for FOX."

To us, this great radio talent is basically describing *Star Search*, and I can't get Rosie O'Donnell's mullet out of my head.

"Well, we're just happy to have you getting intimate with all of our great Y98 artists for *Live From the Lounge*, but let me know when this new talent show airs and we'll let our listeners know when to watch," I pander.

"You got it."

After the Seacrest interview ends, I attempt to enlighten Rico with a ten-minute tutorial about how you need to make smart career choices. In this case, it appears Seacrest has definitely not. *American Idol* sounds like someone Ace and Gary would try to save on *TV Funhouse*.

CHAPTER 23
Beware, You Just Might Get It

The ratings and awards create a big opportunity, which scares the crap out of me. Afternoon drive for a radio station is the second most desired position on the air. The big money and power come from being the morning host. It's a pressure-filled position, because you are the storefront for the entire station. Steele has decided that I should fill in for our veteran morning show host when the host goes on his extended vacation next week.

Guy Phillips is a legend in St. Louis and a member of the Missouri Broadcasting Hall of Fame. Until now, not many people have been allowed to take the chair when Guy is on vacation. The rest of the show members usually just run the program in his absence. This test run is a huge vote of confidence from my employer, and it has everyone curious about why it's being proposed.

"I want to see what you can do. I think you'll be great," Steele says.

The compliment brings a wonderful feeling, but when the feeling fades, why am I ruled by the desire to do everything in my power to make it not happen? I am terrified. Not just nervous, my body reacts as if I'm headed into physical combat with no hope of survival. My mind races. I have the jitters. I am being asked to deliver on all the promises I have made of "being your next great morning host." All I can think of is how I can make this tryout not happen. Instead of preparing to make it a great show, I focus all my energy into achieving one result and one statement from Steele:

"Sorry Paul, it's not in the cards this time. Maybe you can do it the next time Guy is out."

"Oh, too bad, Steele!"

How do I make this happen? Call in sick? No, too disappointing and that would be my fault. I need someone else to take the blame. I decide to meet with some salespeople and have them make my afternoon endorsers threaten to cancel their advertising if I move off my normal time slot for that short time. Possible money losses—that will do it. I alert them that the advertisers will be unhappy that the guy they are paying to talk about their products is replaced for two weeks by a part-timer filling in. They take that argument as their own. These questions of continuity are brought to the GM and Steele. Those men do not want angry advertisers. After a rocky period, it looks like it's going to work. I will not be required to put my money where my mouth is. My scheming has prevailed yet again.

Then, out of nowhere, Steele goes to bat for me and tries to get my commercials moved. He personally talks with the endorsers to get their approval. *No!* He does all of this not knowing that I am trying to sabotage it behind his back. If he finds this out, I'm in a ton of trouble. What the hell is wrong with me? I stand to gain the most, but I still don't care. This fear has taken over. I get the call.

"Pauly, it was a lot more difficult than I had planned, but I'm proud to let you know you are in to host the morning show for Guy."

"Awesome. I can't wait," I say like there's a gun to my head.

My lame attempt at circumvention has failed.

I sit home alone that night, appalled by my actions. Why do I have such a fear of doing what I have always believed is my dream? This anxiety in me is extreme. For the first time in my life, it dawns on me that I have used alcohol to cover up my natural feelings for too many years. I have faced nothing as a man. Instead, I've used alcohol and drugs to do the job. It hits me like a lightning bolt: the solution I have chosen has caused me not to experience real maturity. I've even regressed in age. This revelation is profound: the only way I have been able to deal with the negative emotions I create is with artificial substances. It's Wednesday, June 12, 2002. I promise myself not to drink again. I can't afford to.

The Sunday before doing the Monday morning show I walk around in a non-alcoholic daze. The fear has not lessened. Even my balance is off, and I feel a little crazy. The pressure to be great is huge, but getting up at four in the morning is also something I'm not sure I can deliver on. I sit in perpetual stun at our family dinner at my mom and dad's house. My brother-in-law endured extraction of all of his wisdom teeth this week. He struggles with the aftermath. Like many, he has tried to bounce back quicker than advised. His prescription of Vicodin provides some relief for him.

The bottle of Vicodin sits on the wooden island in the middle of my parents' kitchen. I can't take my eyes off it. I remind myself that a painkiller hangover is a bad thing, usually taking most of the morning to get over. I do not have the option of dealing with that on my first day of morning radio. Still, I cannot take my attention off that damn bottle.

In the past five years, I have become a full-fledged, self-taught pharmacist. I know the effects, dangers and potency of medications. The sight of a sticker that reads DON'T TAKE THIS MEDICATION AND OPERATE HEAVY MACHINERY AT THE SAME TIME makes me tingle with excitement. Any caution not to drive while taking certain pills is a red flag that you have good stuff. This little bottle of Vicodin has stickers all over it.

My crazy daze has me staring across the room at that pill bottle like Leonard from *Full Metal Jacket*. I am in a trance. I slap myself with the reality that my brother-in-law is in real pain. He needs these pills! That plea will deter me from pilfering. Swiping these pills is out of the question. I have made up my mind.

My dad yells from the other room, "Pujols just went deep again! No way!"

One of the baseball Cardinals has hit an important homerun to win the game. Everyone goes into the family room to see the replay. Now it's just me and the bottle, alone in the kitchen. Opportunity has caused me to lose my resolve. It's too tempting. I quickly open the bottle and put two of the powerful Vicodin into my mouth. Down they go. Lid back on, the bottle goes into its old position, appearing undisturbed.

Nobody sees my theft. The thought of the ease and comfort these pills will bring me sends a charge of energy through my body.

"Prince Albert is gonna be a hall-of-famer," I offer. "This is our year!"

After I calm down a bit, I see how excited my dad is about today's baseball conquest. It's natural, genuine glee.

As I wait for my stomach enzymes to break down the opiates in these pills, remorse swirls around my head and heart. I have sucked the love out of another day. My only hope now is that the narcotic warmness will wipe away my regret. Twenty minutes creep by: no flush of euphoria. I feel a bit off kilter, but these pills are not working. All they do is put me back inside myself, creating more grief. How could I have taken pills from a loved one who really needs their benefit? And more importantly, how can they not work?

When we get home that night, I can barely lift my head. All

five senses are drenched in remorse and self-pity. I have sapped around for the last two years, but this time it seems more fatal and hopeless. I need to do something. I can't live like this. I tell Jen about swiping my brother-in-law's pills. The expression on her face is of sad irritation. I can tell she feels for me, but she is also getting tired of these confessions from her husband.

"Paul, you should go to a meeting."

"An AA meeting? Tonight? I have to get up early."

"This is not good. Don't you think you'll feel better if you go?"

She's right. I have attended a few AA meetings over the last year. They do make me feel at the very least like I'm not alone and hiding, even though I know this type of treatment will never work for me. Maybe Jen will feel better about me if I do the meeting.

"I will go."

At the AA meeting, I meet an extremely content looking guy named Mark. He seems strangely grounded, yet cool. We have a conversation before the meeting begins.

"I have done so many bad things," I whimper.

"What? You haven't killed anybody have you?"

"No."

"I felt like you do right now a couple years ago. You know, we do stupid things when we're sick. But I have found that with the help of the program, you can make almost everything good again."

"That's nice to hear. I appreciate it."

"Call me if you want to."

"You got it."

Very nice dude. I give him credit for what he has been able to do, but he doesn't know me and what goes on in this head. I do not take him up on his offer.

I get home late from the meeting. The Vicodin has caused

extreme brain fuzziness and restless legs. I can't sleep. By the time I doze, the alarm clock wakes me up for the morning show. I fight the remorse about my pill theft during the show. I don't wow them, but I don't completely suck either. I keep my vow not to drink at all that week so that I will stay sharp. My shows get better, but my head gets crazier as the week progresses. My mind continues to attack me over the smallest things, which sometimes makes for good radio discussion.

CHAPTER 24
Drinking Requirement

During the short time Jen has been pregnant, I have done my best to show concern for her morning sickness. She is truly plagued at least fifteen hours a day by nausea, but I find that any attention I give her always drifts back to me within seconds. I can't take it if the people around me aren't happy. I feel their despair so intensely.

Jen's prolonged sickness is hard for me to stomach. How can I think like this? I can't handle the pain I feel for her discomfort. It is like a reflex, no matter how hard I try. When I attend to her, it usually comes with a time limit. "Okay, when will this be over." Fortunately, I don't voice it, but I regret that my face and body language must convey that message.

Reinforcing the boycott of drugs by my "friends," Dr. Dom has now cut me off from the nerve pills. He says it's wrong to prescribe Klonopin to Missouri from California. *Pansy.* Where do I go? Life has gotten sticky and closed in and I'm unwilling to tell anyone about it. I'm too paranoid to take the old risks to get drugs, and now the more comfortable methods are restricted. The notion of not drinking gets quickly jettisoned like a blown out tire, and my alcohol consumption surges way out of control. Gallons and gallons of liquor, beer and wine fill the day, before going on the air, during long songs and after work.

The alcohol helps me feel more together. Others begin to sense my loss of control, though I do not.

"You were really having a good time last night at my birthday dinner," my mom tells me. "You were so loud."

I stopped at the liquor store after work and killed some beers the whole way to the restaurant. I hardly remember any conversations at that dinner. It's one big "swoosh" sound. I struggle to figure out why I felt the need to drink on the drive over to the birthday party, when I knew I could readily have alcohol when I got there. Most free moments now, I drink on autopilot. The harder I try to turn off the reflex, the more I think I need it. Maybe I'm crazy, severely messed up. I have heard no experience like this at the AA meetings I have attended. Of course it is hard to hear anything with all those eyes on me. Am I worse than alcoholic?

My over-thinking is killing me. Just *be*, don't think, I coach myself. But that advice doesn't last long. There is simply too much to work through these days. The fatherhood scenario becomes more real and distressing every day. Adult life does not yield one bit to my effort to slow things down.

I use all my might to resist drinking on baby ultrasound day. Scans from a couple of weeks ago showed that we are on track to have a healthy baby. The gratitude we feel for this is massive. We agree that we could not handle a special-needs child. I joke to Jen that she already has one in me. As we sit in the sterile room waiting for the news about the sex of our baby, I think about the nurse. She looks rushed. Is she happy? How many of these ultrasounds does she do in a day? Does the sparkle she sees on our faces at this moment seem plain and ordinary to her?

. I overhear heated conversations in the hallways. How do hospitals handle all this life-and-death activity? Even though my thoughts are always on me, my ears take everything in and my mind must figure it out and feel whatever emotions people around me are dealing with. Hospitals always do this to me.

It happens with the same intensity on airplanes. How do they know the wings are okay? Who organized this vast system of air traffic control? I can't help but include all of these things in my world, even though literally none of it is my business. Perhaps this truly is an anxiety disorder I have. Do I believe that I'm bipolar type two? I'm not sure, but this need to figure out and absorb outsider feelings has always been there.

Finally the ultrasound reveals that we are having a baby girl. I don't see the vagina they see on those little pieces of paper, but I do see a time limit on my substance abuse. Obviously, I can't live this way with a baby in my life. I feel both encouraged and frightened. That is my baby. This reality is unreal to me.

At work, I watch myself create conflicts early in the day, just so I have an excuse to escape with some liquor. Steele takes the brunt of this. Basically, he has hired a know-it-all who judges everyone else's radio performances but is stricken with sweating and extreme defensiveness when it comes time to look in the mirror. During these months, I feel myself getting deeper and deeper into what must be alcoholism. This is a place I never thought I would go.

Every morning, I make new promises that I won't drive to the liquor store I find myself standing in right now. I am going at it alone. In 1999, when Jen and I decided we were going out and doing ecstasy too much, we sought help together. We talked about overcoming this huge pothole in our lives together.

Now that she is pregnant, I rarely communicate what is going on with my consumption. I don't want her knowing how far I've fallen into drinking. She has helped with the occasional drug slip, but she can't know this. She absolutely can't know that I wake up, drool around, check in at the station then leave to buy liquor, which I start drinking before the show. Trips out to the car kill the remaining booze while I'm on the air. Then I either grab some beer on the way home or pick up food while drinking at the bar. While I'm at home, I doze. Then I start the whole process the next day.

That is the physical representation of my life. It's the kind of description a private investigator paid to log my comings and goings might report in an unmarked manila envelope. Just the facts. But my mental journey is far more disgusting. The investigator might demand an increase in his stalking per diem if he is required to capture the treachery in my thoughts. He will find it a tricky maneuver to angle a telephoto lens out of his Mercury Monarch driver's window to snap a few pics of my twisted self-hatred, euphoric promises never kept, and that anxious search for a new distraction. They just don't make cameras like that yet.

It is a long winter. My abuse finds the ketamine K-hole again right before Christmas, only this time at a club, not a house party. Mandarin is a kitschy kind of club, all in white, with huge beds surrounded by curtains. Guests generally sit on the beds while they drink and talk. They must be intended to make everyone feel close and chummy. Physically I'm there, but mentally I'm nowhere close to chummy. My deflated torso rests on my lap in drug-induced motionlessness as people move around me unaware of my dire presence on the corner of the bed. Jack from Phoenix sits with me in the metal-spiked, freezing cold Siberia I've created. Our fight is long behind us now. My head is in my lap. Without moving, I throw up on our shoes. After another hour of the most disgusting mental torture you could imagine, I snap out of it. I had promised Jen it would be a quick night out, and I didn't lie. It only took me till nine PM to get this way. While I wait for Jen to pick me up, Jack tells me over and over again how he hates seeing me like this. Instead of thanking him for babysitting me, I tell him he should worry about himself, not me.

Two nights later, I snort heroin for the first time. With all the coke I've already done, I barely notice any heroin effect. When I am dropped off at our apartment, Jen is asleep upstairs with our unborn future in her belly. This is the first time I wonder if I'll be around for the baby, either the birth or the life.

Earlier in the day, doctors had told us that Jen's pregnancy had given her high blood pressure. My thoughts and actions should be focused on the effects of this pregnancy on Jen's life. I walk up and look in on her. She breathes peacefully. I stare, drenched in bar smoke, ears loudly ringing in the silence. Where have I been? I know I try to act like the good husband, but I am incapable of true consistency. I will probably always be this way. A trite thought hits me: maybe she actually would be better off without me.

Early the next morning, Jen has to drive me to get my car because I was too messed up and scared to drive. I know that a night like last night causes worry and concern for her. On the awkward drive to get my car, I lightly salt in some inquiries to see where she is on the subject of me.

"So, how are you feeling?"

"Fine," she says.

Minutes pass.

"What's going on today?"

"You know, we're going to see your parents."

"Oh yeah, yeah."

I'm tired of sapping around. I hate this! I can swear it off, but I know I'll be right here again in a week. "Jen, this is it. I'm done doing this to myself, to us."

"I'm just glad you didn't drive home."

"But, you know what I mean. It's over."

"Paul, I feel very bad for you."

"For me! Don't."

"I do. I hope that you will find a way out of this someday."

"Jen, I will. That is what I'm telling you."

Promising is all I know to do. And she knows that's all I do.

"There's your car," she says.

I stand outside her car, leaning down.

"I'm going to do this."

"I know you will," she says without looking up, only to make me stop talking.

Driving home that early Sunday morning in the bright sunshine, I realize this problem has taken me to new lows. All I am is alone with huge regret and self pity. At a stoplight, I bang on the steering wheel and cry.

"Heroin!"

I am losing myself. I take a second and try to gather my composure. Grabbing a big deep breath, I look up to where I think God is. "Help me," I whisper. "Help me. Please, God, help me."

The traffic signal changes to green. I make my left. A car directly in front of me makes a right turn on to the same street at the same time. We are side by side now. The guy in the car waves his hands. He motions to me. Oh, no. This guy must have seen my tantrum. I speed a car length ahead of him. I hope he will stay back there, but that's not going to happen.

After a couple of blocks, he pulls even with me and gestures again. I cautiously look over. It is Jim, my childhood drinking buddy who got us to go to the AA meeting. There is no way it's him. He moved to Kansas City four months ago. Why is he here? He's motioning for me to pull over. With tears in my eyes, I pull over to a parking lot. Just our two cars occupy the lot. His window comes down.

"Hey, buddy, you don't look too good."

"What the hell are you doing out this early, and in St. Louis?"

Jim gets out of his car and into mine.

"I'm not sure, but it looks like you need some help," he says.

"I can't believe you're here."

Jim puts his arm around me. He knows where I am. "I can't do this anymore," I cry.

He says, "I know."

"I'm just so damned beat up."

As I cry, I still can't believe Jim is here. Until now, I had always tried to paint my drug and alcohol uses to him as very light. Now he knows the truth.

"I just can't stop."

"It can be done. Look at me. I stopped."

"You are a miracle. Being here now is a miracle," I say.

"Yep, it is."

"God, I can't believe it. You wouldn't have believed what I was doing before seeing you."

"I saw you. How about we get you to a meeting tonight?"

"Okay."

That night, Jim has a guy he sponsors in the program take me to another AA meeting. The speaker is amazing. His charisma cuts through. I sit and quietly cry in my seat.

This event would cause me to stay dry for almost two weeks, my longest period without alcohol in fourteen years. I attended that same meeting the next week and completely freaked out when they called my name to talk.

"Uh, me, Paul. Uh, no, no. How'd you get my name? Me ... just visiting."

I speak for a living. How could I have been so reluctant? After that, I could think of nothing other than how stupid I must have looked to them.

Six days later, I decide I need to drink some beers after smelling the scents of summer and an outdoor barbeque. Just like that, my days of hard-earned sobriety are gone. Occasionally, I think about praying in my car and the impossibility of seeing Jim at that very moment, but then I tell myself it was just a big coincidence.

For the next four months, I drink every day and night. Many times I catch a look at myself in the rearview mirror, sitting in my car, drinking. That guy looks like a different person to me. I say, "I don't know who it is, but it certainly isn't me."

Jim and me at fifteen. I promise you that is not a coonskin hat I'm wearing. It's my real hair! He introduced me to recovery fifteen years after this picture. Also joined by my beloved Grandma Dorty. We called her Dorty because we couldn't pronounce Dorothy. Quinn's middle name comes from Dorty.

CHAPTER 25
Same Old Rock Bottom, Thank God

What am I so troubled about? I have been given a great job and the greatest gift a man can have, offspring.

"Do you even want this baby?"

Jen hits me with this when we're backing out of our driveway to go to our required parenting class. She asks after I appear numb at the presentation of a canary-colored baby bib that says, "DADDY'S LITTLE GIRL." I have pushed off the class as long as possible. It's a month before the due date and we have to do it today. Other times would have been more convenient for us, but my procrastination has caused a double booking. We have to rush from this class at the hospital to a wedding for a couple we have become friends with from our partying group.

"No, I thought the bib was cute. Guys just aren't into that stuff like women," I explain.

"You don't seem to really care either way, though."

"Look, it's a great bib."

"Not the fucking bib! The baby, do you even care?" screams Jen.

"Yes, I care. There is just a lot going on. Let's not argue before this class."

My wife is at her wits' end and I can't blame her. She is waiting for her man to engage in this reality we have in front of us. Instead, I toss and turn in the background, helping no one.

The class is pretty informative. We learn how to give a bath and change a diaper. Jen warms to me because of the interest I take in being cautious about unforeseen hazards in the crib that can cause injury and death. It is appalling to me how easily a baby can be killed in an improper crib. The video they show hits me hard. Obviously, my anxiety rises at the thought of this. I would be the guy who this happens to. To avoid this, I take copious notes.

During our lunch break, we sit on a bench outside the hospital in the grass. We look out to the road in the distance. She grabs my hand.

"I know you are having a hard time with all of this. I also know that when the baby comes, fathering instincts will kick in and you won't feel so lost."

"Thank you for saying that. I just don't know how to feel, but I think you are right about when she is born."

"Can you believe she's almost here?" Jen asks with her hand on her belly.

"No."

"Do you think we'll be okay?"

"I love the way you have done everything you could to make this a healthy pregnancy. You will be a wonderful mommy."

"Thank you."

We both know I have not found my courage or parenting gene.

"I hear it is harder for the dad because he doesn't have the baby growing in him," Jen offers.

"Yeah, I could see that."

In spite of all my wrong actions, she still tries to give me a way to feel normal. I haven't felt normal in years.

"I love you," I tell her.

After the class ends, we rush home and get into our wedding clothes. It's summer now and the ceremony is hot and simple.

Every wedding I have seen since my own serves as a reminder of how my pledge of unconditional love falls short each day.

Today I've gone later than any day without a drink. I'm feeling shaky. On the way to the banquet hall, Jen cautions me not to drink too much at the reception.

"We have a big day tomorrow, and if you drink a lot you might want to do other things (drugs) tonight."

"That is ridiculous! This is a wedding," I lambaste her.

"You know how it is," she replies.

"Yes, and I think I can control myself. It is hurtful to hear that you don't think I can."

"I just know how tough it can be."

"Bullshit! Can I even have a drink?"

"Yes, but I can't," she reminds me.

"You can have some wine."

"Oh yeah, that will look great from the pregnant chick."
Silence.

"Just promise me you won't overdo it."

"Okay."

Walking into the reception we are both off kilter from the argument. I order an iced tea for Jen and a Coke for myself to prove my resolve. I do it only to make her feel bad for asking me not to overdo it. It's funny how I can take such offense at her worries, even though I know she is 100 percent right.

People approach in delight at Jen's pregnancy. They touch her belly. Interaction is awkward. In between approaching groups, I hug her and lightly push my face against hers, giving her a kiss. This is usually the way we make up from our standard "on the way to the party argument." My nerves and anxiety have caused many of these. Now we hold hands, feeling more connected.

Jen whispers, "You can have a couple of drinks."

"Thank you. But I do understand what you were saying. And you were right," I tell her.

When we sit, I am stunned to see that our table is right next to the table of a cocaine dealer our group has sometimes used. I'm not sure why this surprises me. They go to wedding receptions too. I look away for a minute, telling myself his presence matters little. I have to block out all thoughts about drugs. This wedding reception is a sacred moment. On top of that, I told Jen I would take a low-key path tonight.

I stare at the salad that has just been placed in front of me. My heart begins to beat quickly. Finally, I look up to glance in his direction, hoping that I have identified him incorrectly and all this anxiety is over nothing, but no, he looks right at me and it's him. I reflex a huge smile and look away quickly. It's on me now. I can think of nothing else. Small talk at our table hits me and slides to the floor.

"What's wrong? Still mad at me?" Jen asks.

"No, not at all. That was all my bad. I'm just tired and hungry."

After my untouched salad gets picked up, I excuse myself to hit the bathroom. To be cordial, I stop by the dealer's table on my way.

"What's up!"

He can see it in my eyes. I bet he's become very adept at spotting this look. "Great to see you, Radio Boy," he says with a dirty grin. "How you been?"

"Good." I lean in. "You hittin' it tonight?"

"Oh yeah, let's talk after dinner."

Walking back to my table I feel no remorse, only excitement. I will feel good tonight. I cannot sit still, and now I can't take my eyes off him. My discovery has also killed my appetite. Dinner lasts as long as major heart surgery. Finally people begin to mill around the dance floor. I grab him and we go out to the car. He sells me two grams of cocaine. I do some quickly in the bathroom stall. Now my head is calm. Now I smile. Now I feel whole. Now I compliment my wife. I even begin to hear and respond to the small talk at our table, even appearing to enjoy it. And now I talk about my upcoming fatherhood. Jen notices the difference, but attributes it to a full stomach. She has heard the "low blood sugar" excuse many times and now believes it.

Cocaine is an extreme stimulant. You would think it would bring me anxiety, but within the first few hours, it does just the opposite. I'm as calm and collected as one of those huge one-hundred-year-old turtles. In this state, I take life as it comes.

On the way home I tell Jen I promised to make an appearance at a small party a guy from work is having.

"Okay, just drop me off first," she says.

I have extended my night.

"But promise me you will put together that diaper-changing table tomorrow morning."

"Oh totally, we will have that baby room looking great. I won't be late."

"I really want to have that done," she says.

"Totally, I'll do it." I say all of this through the excitement and release I am stealing from the drug.

I've been using for three hours now and the chase is on to get back to the early serenity. Drug-induced paranoia is an odd thing. There is no fear in the willingness to ingest a dangerous, life-threatening substance, but driving in a car after doing that can be full of so much anti-courage that collision is inevitable. You may think that fear to drive would cause more care and caution on the roads, but it doesn't. The state of alert isn't for safety. The caution to drive well is so that you don't get pulled over and charged with drug possession. Add that paranoia to an energized head and racing thoughts and you have a driver jerking his head toward every moving vehicle that could possibly be a cop. Imagine pulling up at a light next to a life-sized bobble head driving a compact. My huge pupils alone, staring you down, could cause you to quickly dial 911 on your cell.

It's eleven PM when my toxic self-party arrives at this innocent party of beer drinkers. I clean up my gagging, snotting face before knocking.

Nothing stands out about this gathering: music, talk, locking the bathroom door to snort cocaine off a CD case while other people with pressured bladders beat on the door. Other than forcing career advice on another DJ, it is a typical all-talk, no-listening event for me.

The party continues at home. I've never been able to stop until the drugs are gone. Even though the euphoria I felt is long gone, the narcotic-soaked brain always lacks the sense to cease.

Viewing a sunrise is typically lauded as one of the more beautiful natural things a human can experience on earth. If you asked, "What's the most beautiful natural thing to view?" on *The Family Feud*, it would "DING" as at least a top three answer. But there is no more depressing thing in the world for a guilt-ridden person doing drugs than the wrong side of the morning witnessed without a second of sleep. I am seeing this again now. Hatred of Self is the feeling. But whispering in Self-Hate's ear is Survival.

Self-Hate says, "Oh my God, I did it again. How?"

I say this to myself as if I wasn't there last night. In the basement, alone, I have another mini tantrum, beating my fists on my lap as I sit on the couch I haven't left for six hours.

"How will I get through this day?" Self-Hate says.

A family dinner is planned and before that I must keep my promise to prepare the baby room. My jaw is locked, pupils look like grape Spree candy. I hear the toilet flush. *Oh, no.* I'm dead tired and geeked up at the same time. You would have to be blind not to notice. And Jen is up.

Survival talks now. "Don't tell anyone."

She's not blind, but maybe, in her uncomfortably pregnant and tired state, if I stay busy, she won't notice my broken promise.

Survival says, "Last night's consumption will fall off you as you work."

So, I fire up the Dirt Devil and start vacuuming big old cobwebs that cover the ceiling of our laundry room (last week's promised chore). I don't notice the comic parallel of using this inhaling machine to suck up huge strands of a white substance, even though the irony feels familiar after the night I have taken on.

"What are you doing!?" Jen startles me.

The high-pitched engine has brought her downstairs with two piping-hot cups of coffee. *She still serves me.* I flip off the Dirt Devil.

"I need to take care of this. I have been putting it off for weeks," I say without looking at her.

She laughs. "Okay, you're still gonna do the baby changing table, right?"

"Totally, I'll get it. Do you know where the Phillips is?"

"It's up next to the box, freak. You okay?" Jen asks.

"Yeah, I'm just sorry I haven't done those things for you."

She puts the coffee on a table. With a curious look, she carries her huge stomach back up the steps.

"No problem," she says.

I flip the engine on because that is what she would expect, but I don't vacuum. I focus my attention on a nail coming out of the ceiling from the upstairs floor. I think, what if I jam my miserable head into that three inches of sharp steel? This massive pain I feel would change, and the fatigue might go away. A nail through the brain is what I deserve.

"You're fuckin' crazy," Self-Hate says.

"She doesn't notice your hangover. Keep going!" says Survival.

I push through, entirely cleaning the webs from our laundry room. The second I flip the machine off, all my energy is cut off like the electricity going to the Dirt Devil. I'm screwed.

I overturn the trash where my cocaine-filled plastic cigarette wrapper rests. Over the table I straighten it, relieving every crevice of the tiny white powder. Enough for one line gathers on the table. Excitement. My phlegm-filled human dirt-devil sucker sniffs it up. Most of the last of the two grams doesn't make it past my nasal cavity. It's just clogged in the tip of my nose, but I get a bolt of energy. That and more paranoia are enough to send me running up the steps to check if everything is all right.

It is nine AM. Jen is watching an episode of *Baby Stories* on TLC. This show takes you through the whole pregnancy up to birth. She sits with her feet up and hand on her belly. A young mother does the same thing on the show. I sit on the loveseat and watch quietly. What is she thinking? Does she know?

"Do you think this is really gonna hurt bad?" she says without looking from the TV.

"Honey, your epidural will take care of you." My mind goes to drugs before anything.

"But what about afterwards?"

"I bet you'll be so happy you won't feel it."

The two minutes of chemical release are gone. My head is once again crazy. Any type of communicating has always greased the wheels of honesty in me. I am aching to confess to her how bad I've been. She is the only one I can tell, but if I tell her she will freak. She will insist on rehab. If I go to rehab for thirty days, I'll be fired. I am hopeless. I head back downstairs.

She yells, "We have to get that changing table put together before your mom's at one."

"I will."

MTV is running a rerun of its movie awards. I sit and watch from the exact location of my exploits last night. Two crunched beer cans and an empty bottle of wine adorn the coffee table in front of the couch I sit on. Strong beams of sunlight blast through the two windows at the top of the basement wall. I hear my neighbor's hose splashing water on his driveway while he washes the car. Now my spinning wheel of emotions has stopped on unrelenting remorse and fatigue. I'm forced into another mini tantrum. During the bashing of my lap, my attention catches Marilyn Manson's girlfriend, Rose McGowan, walking down the red carpet in a completely transparent mesh dress. Nothing conceals her butt. The whole thing is visible. They close up on it. I sit and wonder how they can allow this on basic cable. She has a great butt. I'm out.

I wake to a loud noise from above my head. It sounds like someone is kicking around a vacuum cleaner upstairs. I'm sweating, my head pounds and I'm short of breath. How long have I been out? I run upstairs. The noise is from the unfinished baby room. Jen has unboxed the giant wooden changing table. My forgotten promise surrounds her unassembled. Her eight months pregnant body awkwardly sits in the middle of all the pieces. My puny cold heart breaks.

"What are you doing?" I yell, like I don't know.

"I told you this has to be put together today." She can't look at me.

"Oh, hon, let me do it."

My contact lenses feel like cornflakes in my eyes. It's obvious I have been out cold. She probably yelled for me a couple times, then rather than bringing her body down the steps, decided to go at it alone. This isn't the first time. Besides the energy-sapping excursion down to the basement, just seeing me there would be enough of a letdown to turn her away all by itself. Wisely, she saved herself this viewing.

"No, I got this. I will be just fine," she says. Survival has kicked in for my wife too.

"Come on. I'll hold up one side."

"No! You are going to mess up my system. Go back downstairs."

"Jen."

"Please, Paul!"

I lumber back down to the second replay of the MTV Awards. Sitting on the couch, uber-anxiety hits me like I've never felt before. Until now I believed I had experienced every color of nerves on the spectrum. Flashing thoughts and a racing heart torture me.

I cannot stop. I cannot stop hurting my wife. I cannot stop hurting myself.

My head feels like a tumor, and now my heart spikes with pain. It has hurt emotionally all morning; now there is physical pain. It reported a few hours ago as a small tinge, and now, two inches to the left of my sternum, the ache increases. I lie back on the couch.

Maybe if I control my breathing it will go away. *Calm down.* I keep my thoughts away from the notion of a coronary, but after a night of cocaine, I cannot control my thoughts. Am I having a heart attack? Am I dying? I won't be able to keep this a secret. Will my life end here? This has happened to people like me before just like this. The sadness and anger swirl. Deep breaths. Just like Chris Farley, I will have wasted my life in my early thirties. For me it's probably long overdue. The baby! My child! As always, I play out the future scene in my head.

"Your Daddy was a good man. He died a month before you arrived," Jen will say to our child some day.

"But why?" our daughter asks.

"He was very sick."

"Did you take care of him like when I'm sick?"

"Yes, I did. As best I could."

It hits me for the first time that Jen will be plagued with remorse, thinking she didn't do enough for me. She will ask herself, "Why didn't I force rehab? Why didn't I threaten to leave?"

The truth is, she shares no blame. She could have done nothing to change this. Now my chest has a hard time containing my heart. The pains feel like lasers of acid shooting out from the muscle.

Survival and Self-Hate banter again.

"Lie here," says Self-Hate. "Talk about this and it's all over— marriage and career. Don't tell, it will go away. You'll never do drugs again."

"This is very serious," Survival says. "Call to her now, or die."

I sit up and my blankets fall to the floor. My heart pain leads me upstairs to the living room couch. I pass the baby's room on the way. The baby changing table stands in the middle of the room completely assembled, but with a quick glance, I see that she's assembled it backwards.

Jen sits in the living room on the loveseat watching TV. I go to the couch.

"We have to leave for your parents' in a half hour," Jen says with a disgusted tone in her voice.

Tears run down my face.

"I have to tell you something." My voice shakes.

"What!"

"I did it again last night."

"What? Coke? Where?"

"I am so—"

She jumps up.

"No, no, no! You lied to me. You said you wouldn't."

"I know."

Her disappointment hits me far more than I expected it would.

"Oh, my God. You need serious help!"

"I can't go to rehab. They will fire me."

"Maybe they won't."

"They will. You talked to the drug hotline yourself. I can't disappear from the radio station for a month."

I hold my chest.

"What about your mom and dad? They're expecting us."

"I'm telling you this because I'm having very serious chest pains."

"Where? Okay, okay. We have to call someone."

All we have built together is leaving us right before our eyes.

For more than three years, my life has been an interminable roller coaster. Days like this (without the chest pains) happen all the time. Eventually, I make it back to good health and jump back on the ride again. The truth about my drug use has always been a secret to my loved ones, a secret that fuels the roller coaster. Pride keeps the secret. If the roller coaster is to end, I need to break the cycle and cut its power.

"I will call Mom and Dad and tell them. They will tell us what to do."

"Tell them all of it?" Jen asks.

Tears cover both of our faces.

"I will."

My heart still pounds. The pain is still present, but it's not worsening. I dial the phone. My breath shortens with each number. The phone rings. My dad answers with the usual zest for a phone call received from his only son.

"Hey, Boy! Where are you guys?"

"Dad." Words muffle. I never wanted him to hear this. I swore I would die first, and I might. There's unbearably sharp pain in my chest now.

"What's up? Everything okay?"

"No," I reply, sobbing

"What's wrong? Is it Jennifer?"

"No, Dad. I have a problem … to tell you … I am an alcoholic and a drug addict."

Two seconds of nothing.

"Okay. Are you all right?"

The chest pain begins to fade. I'm numb. It might still be there, but I don't feel it.

"Yes, it has been this way for a while. I have kept it a secret for too long."

His voice breaks.

"You stay there. Mom and I are coming to you now, okay?"

"Okay. I'm sorry, Dad."

"It will be okay. We will be there soon."

"Bye."

I can't believe I told them. The anguish is smothering. Jen comes in from the baby room.

"You did good ... did good," she struggles to say.

I grab her.

"I am so sorry," I cry.

"How is your chest?"

"For some reason the pain is gone," I say into her neck.

"Paul, all the pain is gone?"

"For the most part, yes."

"What did your dad say?"

"They're coming here. They were very shocked."

As we wait for their arrival, I wonder if there will ever be a way to make right all the lies I've told. During a pause, ego dashes in, telling me I have shared too much, that I shouldn't have done this. It nauseates me. I run and cough over the toilet. Nothing comes up. My head feels like bombs are going off. My shocked parents are coming over to rescue me and the chest-pain catalyst that caused this confession is now completely gone. Forty-five minutes ago, I was convinced I was having a heart attack; now there is no sign of pain. But I cannot undo what I've shared.

Their arrival starts with tight hugs and worried eyes. I cannot stop the truth from running out of me with the tears. Details of my addiction do not rattle my parents like I always envisioned they would. Now they are calm, listening in fix-it mode.

"We will make you good again," Mom promises.

That comforting declaration shows me that the love I had shut out for so long is fired up and beaming. I had always thought that this was my problem, my cross to bear, and to tell my parents would mean I had lost, that I was weak. In my crazy head, I played out a scenario in which I told my mother about my problem and she said, "Who knows about this? Keep it quiet!"

All this time I had twisted in hell, unfairly pushing my pride and need for secrecy unfairly on my parents. They just want to love me and help me. Finally I am letting them.

Not many grown children receive such amazing love and respect from their parents. That is what makes my fall into addiction so difficult. I had wanted them to be proud of where I was, not scared. Together we decide to jump right into the program. My dad tells me he will attend a meeting with me tonight.

The shooting heart pain is gone, but my erupting stomach makes me feel like I might pass out at any moment. Like any mother does, my mom insists that I need to eat something. Although that concept is the furthest from my mind, I say okay. I have given up. From now on, I will do it someone else's way. I'll never forget sitting with my parents and pregnant wife at an empty Steak and Shake on a Sunday night trying not to throw up. I have wrecked my stomach for the last five years. The restaurant is cold and bright. About every five minutes the realization that I'm getting honest hits me, and I want to bawl.

CHAPTER 26
Tunnel Light

My parents deliver on their pledge to get me right. My first day of sobriety starts with another "recovery" meeting at seven AM at a hospital. While still extremely embarrassed, I feel mostly grateful and relieved to finally be going down this path. Chest pains hit me again that day. A trip to the emergency room, along with other doctor appointments, reveals no heart damage. Doctors tell me I have costochondritis or possibly strained ligaments near the ribs and heart. The cause is never discovered. The pain fades after two weeks. Maybe it was that my heart could not continue to let me live that way.

After just a few days of staying dry, I declare some basic realities. I do not want to die, not before this baby girl is born. If I go back to the old behavior, I am confident I will die. If I don't die of some overdose, at least incarceration is in the cards. These are ideas I have never fully realized about my use: if I drink, I will die.

It's appalling to think about all the times I have been pulled over while using, only to work my way out of it. I'm sure that craftiness kept me living in this black hole longer than necessary. Driving or not, I have arrogantly purchased drugs in unstable environments many times. I now believe that if I do these things again, the outcome will be very bad. These broad conclusions keep me following the recovery plan.

In the first anxious week, I find myself trying to walk away from people to find an empty room, but when I get there, the pressure is still built up in my head. I realize I am trying to go to that place where drugs and alcohol used to take me, so I wouldn't have to deal with the nerves. Now there is nowhere to go. I have to take life on without insulation. In my weak moments, thoughts of letting my parents down keep me from taking that first drink.

Mom or Dad pull into the driveway every morning at 6:30 for the next thirty days to take their thirty-year-old son to recovery meetings. Without that, I would not be alive today, because even though I'm ready to try recovery, my lack of courage makes it tough to actually walk into meetings. An awkward stumble into the meeting at Missouri Baptist Hospital becomes part of my daily diet. It is my only choice as Mom and Dad sit outside in the car reading the paper and watch me go in. Once in the room, I slide to the back and listen to the chipper people talk about recovery.

"My name is Page. I'm an alcoholic."

"Hi, Page!"

That blow horn of a welcome still surprises me. Page is a heavy but attractive American Indian-looking lady of about forty-five. She talks about the struggles that she's facing with her ex-husband and her young daughter.

"My ex is being as nasty as he can possibly be about custody, and he's really hurting our daughter with this selfishness. He told her on the phone that I was probably cheating on him and her the whole time, and he says he won't even visit her because of me," she says.

As I listen to Page, the morning sluggishness falls away from my head. What a jerk her husband must be. I don't even know this guy and I'd like to hurt him.

Page continues, "And you know before the program I would really let him ruin my day. His attempt to hurt me would even make me drink. But today I'm okay. I mean it's rotten what he's doing, but that's his choice, not mine."

What? Come on, Page! I want her to talk about taking this dude to court or throwing his crap in the street. What a dick.

Her comments are foreign to me. "All I can do is what I'm doing. My sponsor tells me that the most important thing is to not talk negatively about my husband to my daughter. She doesn't need that. And it would only hurt her."

I know that Page's reactions are probably the good way to be, but I know I couldn't do that with someone behaving that way.

"Most importantly, if I acted on the emotions that my ex-husband is working to cause, I would only hurt myself. Nope. He doesn't have that much power. Not anymore."

At the end of the meeting we gather in a circle and hold hands while saying the Lord's Prayer. It definitely feels weird. I fight off a flashback of holding hands at the Agape church in Los Angeles. After the prayer everyone sticks around to chat. I fly out the door.

I didn't expect to learn such insightful things at each meeting. These thoughts about sick thinking are very interesting. I hear it over and over again. I'm starting to learn that I have allowed people's reactions to rule my life and run it into the ground. Like a small child, I have acted out only on emotion, nothing else. This type of fruitless living caused me to seek constant escape. In those meetings I learn that I have a disease. My cravings for alcohol, once tripped, were unbeatable when I tried to cease drinking using only my human will.

I find that sharing many of these things with my parents on the ride home is rewarding. I know they are privately dealing with grief over how I had been living, but they always manage to put on a pleasant face to greet me. Telling my parents the things I am learning helps them to see that their son is learning to live all over again. It feels that way for me, too.

In that first week, I repeat little sayings I hear in the meetings. Sayings like "Live and let live" really hit me hard, as well as the often stated claim that while I'm in a meeting, my alcoholism is out in the parking lot doing push-ups, getting stronger, so I have to work hard on my recovery to beat it. I keep hearing "There are no coincidences. Everything happens for a reason."

Every time I hear that I stare into my coffee and think about my sober friend Jim. If that phrase is true, how incredible was that morning when I was driving home hung-over and yelling for help and he appeared out of nowhere. Was he sent to help me? That is too much for me to comprehend these days, but I should talk to him.

"Coincidences are God's way of staying anonymous. I told your dad that I was sure you were going to die if you continued on the path you were on," Jim tells me.

"I believe it. I think I came close too many times."

"Well it's awesome to have you in the program. And just don't drink today, Paul."

"I'm never drinking again!"

"No, Paul. Don't drink today."

"I see what you're saying, getting too lofty," I admit. "Man I feel so bad for how I made everyone feel. They have been great, but I sort of wish I didn't have to tell my parents. It just feels weird now."

"You're embarrassed?" Jim asks.

"Yeah. I know there's no going back now—"

"Who would want to?" Jim interrupts.

"Not me, but I'm scared I hurt them and they will look at me differently."

"Paul, you had to do it that way."

I didn't fully recognize it, but many forms of fear directed my life. Despite every advantage in life, I rarely felt right. They tell me this emptiness is a common symptom of alcoholism. The hope I find at these meetings is beginning to make me feel less empty, but it is a process. I broke so many promises to myself that I know it is going to take a while to live with me again. So for now I keep my attention on the program and my family, trying not to ask myself that dangerous question: "How do I feel?" During these months, I struggle quite often with wanting the ease and calm that a drink would bring. My thoughts drift to that happy place of moderation before too much consumption made me a mess. But the only substances I put in my body are the two prescribed to me for bipolar disorder: a mood stabilizer and an antidepressant.

Getting back to good with Jen is much more difficult. The lies have left marks, and I had stolen time from her during this difficult pregnancy. It's been a week since the big event at our house and Jen still isn't really talking to me. At this point, I'm tired all the time and I have completely lost the sense of taste; all food is simply matter that I chew and swallow. These nagging symptoms of early sobriety have made me impatient.

"Jen, I hope that you will be able to forgive me someday soon."

She picks up around our bedroom while I try to make the bed I was oversleeping in.

"You know, I'm glad that you are gonna live. But your anger and that final lie you told me about the wedding reception is really sticking with me. I can't seem to shake it."

"Okay," I admit.

I try to give her a hug. Bad idea. Her arms stiffly stay by her side.

I let go. She heads for the exit.

Then she turns back. "I will be okay. I will. Don't worry."

Hurt and angry, she still looks out for my delicate sensitivity.

My actions were surely a factor in Jen's pregnancy blood pressure problems. When I was supposed to be pampering her, it was all about me. My sponsor, Mark, tells me that consistency in my actions is the only medicine that will fix the harms I have done. Yep, the Mark I met at the meeting after stealing a few of my brother-in-law's pills has graciously become my sponsor. A sponsor takes you through the twelve steps and tells you when you're being stupid.

Unexpectedly, I do not miss even a single day of work during this time of early recovery. I hope that others who are suffering like me are getting better information than we got about seeking help. When Jen called about my problem she was told that I had to immediately leave for rehab for thirty days. I used the incorrect information that I would have to leave work for thirty days as a great excuse never to try recovery. Thirty days is nothing when your life is in question, but it seemed like an eternity to me. I bet I'm not alone in that thought. I'm far away from recovered, but I hope that I can prove that no matter how lost to addiction a person is, they can get well without leaving the world for a month. To my surprise, many people I meet over the next few weeks have already done that. Maybe I can follow in their recovered footsteps.

At two weeks dry, I feel like I haven't had a drink in ten years. My sponsor, Mark, helps to keep my self-pride about this "achievement" in check. He knows that many times the trigger to a relapse starts with over-confidence and a feeling of invincibility. Mix that outer arrogance with low self-esteem and that's what got me drinking myself into a twisted hell.

"Did you read the book today?" Mark asks.

"Yep. I gotta tell you, I feel great, man."

"I don't care how you feel, Paul. This thing is about how you act."

He tells me that if I'm ready, I will do recovery his way. If not, I'll probably drift back into using. From this point on, we start taking the "steps" as he took them. Many times I have no idea what I'm doing other than taking his direction.

"Show up here. Go stand there. Shake these guys' hands as they walk into the meeting. If you want what I have, you'll do it."

I do it because I remember the desperation I felt that last night after drinking and drugging and I don't want to feel it again.

Mark reminds me that I will do everything better once I find a God of my understanding, and he says the steps will help me find a God of my own. This concept of doing things better with God is foreign to me because I truly believed that I did most things better while drinking. I was deceived. I actually thought I performed on the radio better after drinking. I used to brag to people that after a few drinks "the wall of doubt" is removed and a creative, fun personality thrives. I was partly right. You could have listened to me on two different shows, one after drinking, the other without, and the drinking show would have been more energized, entertaining, and original sounding.

Mark promises that "this wall of doubt" will be removed when I learn that radio and approval are not the most important things in the world. He even tells me I will make love to my wife better as a sober man. The coming months would prove that all of his promises were legitimate. The quality of the first two hours of radio after drinking were good, but then fatigue always caused me to fade. In sobriety, there is no fading and each hour's performance is leaps and bounds more creative than all of the buzzed hours. It's pretty simple: now I feel good about where I am, so I do a good show. What an exhilarating discovery this would be to a guy who is as concerned as I am about making the show great. I thought I was making my show better all these years when all I was doing was holding the true Paul back.

At three weeks sober I sit in a very unspectacular meeting. The people look a bit depressed, the coffee has no taste, the folding chairs all creak loudly when people fidget, and every five minutes the air conditioner blasts on, drowning out all the talk and even the noisy chairs. For some unknown reason, all I hear is my head blasting away with disgust. Mark told me this would happen one day.

"When it happens, look for something to be grateful for. You have a lot, Paul."

In this state of anxiety, all I can muster to be grateful for is that at least we have an air conditioner in here with the thermometer pushing ninety-five degrees outside. I know that more gratitude should be dawning on me, but I can't think of anything. Actually I really pushed myself to muster the A/C acknowledgement. This Frigidaire 28500 must be running on NASCAR fuel:

"BBUUUUBBBBBSSSSSSSSHHHHHHhhhhhhhh..." Then the engine shuts off.

"Ahem, I'm Dennis. Wow, that thing is loud. But it's great to be here," a gray-haired guy wearing a red baseball hat says from the back. "I didn't know how to love before this program. The feeling always missed me. I knew I should be feeling it, but it never came and I hated myself for that. After coming to these rooms for a while, I realized that love is unselfish. And how are you going to feel it when you never do anything for anyone? Everything had always been about me," he says.

Stay off, A/C! I push myself to try and comprehend what this guy is talking about.

He continues, "Now I feel love and I feel alive. It takes work, but I'm never letting that feeling go. Love is a gift of the program."

Walking into the parking lot after leaving that meeting I didn't want to go to in the first place, it hits me, first in my eyes and then in my heart. The cars in the lot shine brighter and the detail of the trees is greater than I remember seeing before I walked in. My ungratefulness has disappeared. Dennis's words have hit me right between the eyes. At that moment, I realize that the "meaning" I have been searching for could be in my near future if I follow the course I'm on. Only this meaning is not consumed or performed, it is lived. Act right, feel right. Not the other way around. My constant quest for comfort has never paid off fully. Dennis says I will feel that warm comfort if I try to live unselfishly. I get into my car and call Jen.

"Yeah."

"How are you feeling?" I ask her.

"Hot and fat. How 'bout you?"

"Good. I'm bringing home dinner. Stay off your feet. You know, Jen, I can't argue with how you are feeling, and I'm calling to tell you that there is no pressure to feel better about me. I was so wrong. And on top of being hurt, I don't want you feeling like there is a time limit on your pain. Feel how you need to feel. I'll be here if you want me to be."

Silence.

"Thank you, Paul."

"I love you, Jen."

"I love you too."

When I get home, I re-assemble the baby changing table and don't say a word about it. Soon Jen is willing to smile around me, and that's a start.

But I'm not perfect at the new life. There was so much bad thinking on top of bad behavior packed in over the years that it takes a while to straighten out. And I do experience moments of self-pity and selfishness, but as never before, I see that I am being given the tools to fight those destructive emotions. I had conditioned myself to look at life in totally the wrong way. Fancying myself a self-sufficient hero of life, if I felt weak, I would put into my body what I thought would keep the hero going. This caused massive overshooting, lying and stealing. Being such a taker, I was more like the villain than the hero. All I did was over-think and paint the world black and blue everywhere I went, while always maintaining a semi-realistic smile. The program helps to take all of the power from me and put it on something higher.

I'm learning that before now I had taken God's victories as my own, confirming self-reliance and taking me further from him. I was allowed to cheat death many times over the last few years. And every time it happened, I told myself that I alone had done something great. I said, "My will is bulletproof." This unintelligent notion kept me unhappy far too long. When I reflect back on my crazy days, I am humbled by the memory of falling asleep on the road home from Las Vegas, but being awakened just before hitting the median. How did I make it through that? I will never have all the answers, but I have to believe God was with me that day, keeping me alive so that I may be useful to him one day.

Men in the program tell me, "You were spared so that you could help others find this great truth of faith. But you must not leave before the miracle happens."

I hope I don't leave before the miracle. And I certainly don't want to leave after it.

"Just do the next right thing, Paul," my sponsor preaches. "Keep it simple."

The main source of knowledge about the disease of alcoholism is a book written in 1939, simply called *Alcoholics Anonymous*, and it describes me perfectly. The book's author, Bill Wilson, speaks to me like no therapist could because he shares from his own desperate alcoholic experience in this divinely inspired book. Another alcoholic I listen to named Chuck C shares a nugget about our condition that seems to connect a missing link in me. He says that in his thirty-plus years of studying alcoholics he has come to believe that most alcoholics are up to two hundred times more sensitive than most people. Chuck says that this handicap has served us well from time to time at reading situations and people, but mostly we have allowed it to hurt us incredibly. Hearing his claim causes an "Ah ha!" moment for me, as Oprah says. Until this moment I had always hated myself for being the only person alive to allow such "emotional overload." Thinking of it as a condition rather than a choice gives me some great peace. I also learn from these men that this condition can be overcome, and that gives me more than great hope for a happy life.

But, the inconsideration I displayed wasted many opportunities where I could have been useful. Horribly, when I allow myself to drift toward my recent past, remorse overtakes me and I actually want to drink again. Drinking was the only tool I had used to deal, but not now. I caution myself that I have to be here for Jen no matter how anxious I get. And for the first time, I am not too selfish to be a real husband and actually help with our pregnancy.

I have read stories about men on the path to recovery, doing the right thing, and then a big business opportunity develops that will get our recovering alcoholic back on his feet financially. Obviously, the notion of drinking before the big meeting is flat-out ludicrous to this man, but on the day of the meeting he fools himself by thinking a drink or two will make the anxiety go away. Soon he's drunk once again and his lucrative business deal dies, once again. I am reminded of this man's experience time and time again. I know that I have to be present for this birth. My sponsor tells me to keep my thoughts on Jen, and that helps. But this selfish disease is relentless. I think about me and making outcomes go my way even when I think I'm being unselfish. It's tough to realize that I have always been the great manipulator. Hopefully with work it will fade someday.

CHAPTER 27
Natural High

With Jen experiencing high blood pressure, we have been asked to attend weekly doctor appointments. It is Monday, September 16, 2002. We go to the doctor before my two PM air shift.

"Yes, it is high. We will do it today," our Indian doctor says after taking Jen's blood pressure.

"Sounds good," I say. We think he is talking about an examination, maybe another ultra-sound.

"Are you free?" the doctor inquires.

"For what? When?" asks Jen.

"To deliver baby," the doctor replies. "Today."

"Today!" we say in unison.

"Yes, is that good? To induce labor?"

We look at each other with excited energy. We've entered a lot of new ground together in the last month. This will be the most colossal. It's not like we didn't expect the thrill of childbirth—we just didn't expect it today.

We have time to return home to notify our families and work. Also, we need to complete a mission Jen has been sweetly neurotic about.

"I need to get a really cute sweat suit to wear during the next few days after the baby is born. There will be a ton of family and friends visiting us."

So, off to the mall we go. We scurry into the mall at noon like uninvited giddy squirrels. Zig-zagging through the mall, Jen leads me to The Gap. We have a purpose.

"How about a baby blue one?" She holds it up.

"Looks perfect. Can you believe we are doing this?" I am beaming.

"I know. No, I can't." My round wife chuckles.

"I love you." I grab her.

"I love you too. Blue or tan?"

"They are both perfect! This is perfect."

The elation we feel is hard to contain. We carry over the same emotion when we are filling out the paperwork at the hospital. Confidence is the baseline. It's like we're running a tank up a mountain. I can tell that underneath the giddiness, we both feel a quiet joy that we have made it here together. Immediately after getting our cozy birthing room, Jen is put on two medications: pitocin and magnesium. The pitocin will cause her uterus to contract, making her go into labor. The magnesium is for her blood pressure. It will cause her to break down in tears for no reason and then occasionally laugh about that same crying. It becomes a bit unsettling for both of us.

I stay very close by to comfort her during these swinging emotions, just as she has stayed with me during my wildly seesawing emotions over the past few years. The nurses tell me that this medication keeps her out of a very risky blood pressure zone. The high blood pressure is not as dangerous for the baby as it is for the mother. Of course while holding Jen's hand, my overly dramatic thoughts drift to the fear of having a beautiful baby girl but possibly no beautiful wife. I correct myself and concentrate on being strong by measuring my emotions.

But it's difficult not to ask the question: is it possible that the woman who has gone through hell for me is now in jeopardy of losing her life because of our baby and the stress I have caused in our lives? Doctors and nurses watch her very closely for the next few hours. We learn a great deal about ourselves during this time. If we stick together, we can handle serious circumstances like adults. Soon the magnesium serves its purpose. Jen's dangerous blood pressure slowly decreases as her contractions start.

After hours and hours of contractions that separate each other by many minutes, finally they gain in frequency. The epidural goes in. Our loving families wait outside.

"It's time to start pushing a bit, Jennifer," the nurse tells her.

"But where's the doctor?" I ask.

"He'll be here, but we do a lot of pushing without a doctor."

I can't believe this is happening. We will have a baby within an hour.

Jen then launches into some magnificent pushing. She really goes after it. I am so proud of her. Her red and tan sweaty face looks so incredibly beautiful to me.

Another extended push. Damn, she's hanging on to it like the *Battle of the Network Stars* Tug of War. I've got a star here.

"Look at that, Dad," the nurse says.

She points to a little tuft of short soft hair. It's the top of the baby's head. I've never seen anything so slimy and red that represents something so beautiful and innocent. Our baby girl is right there. And still no sign of the doctor. The nurse and I look at each other.

"I have called him," the nurse promises.

More anxiety.

"He will be here; we need to push just a bit more."

She is so wiped out, but Jen really gets after it.

"Okay, stop."

The nurse leaves. *What the hell?*

After two long minutes of my telling Jen, "Everything is normal. You are amazing!" the nurse and our small out-of-breath Indian doctor come running in.

Meekly, he says, "Hi."

He straps on these huge blue boots and jumps in there.

Two more big pushes and tiny Quinn Cook pops out. She mutters something, but doesn't cry. She is absolutely gorgeous. We hug and kiss her wet chalky head. My wife has done it!

Quinn lies on the examination table moving in slow motion, taking in her first air. What a sight. At half open, Quinn's eyes appear larger than a full grown adult's eyes. Irony hits me. Holy crap, did we just have a Marty Feldman. Her eyes are big and beautiful, but not buggy. All the infant tests come out "normal." I'd rather they said gifted, but I'll take what I can get. Then a younger nurse comes in. She has red hair.

"What a beautiful baby. My name is Rainbow. I am going to wash this little girl."

After the scrub bath, Rainbow hands me my daughter. I look down at this new life. At this moment, I am given the meaning I have been searching for. Early sobriety has helped to change me dramatically, but this baby is the final piece. This gift is like painting a thick lacquer over all the fragmented cracks of my selfish existence. My blanks have been filled in, making me whole.

I carry our baby to Jennifer and place the bundle on Mom's chest. She looks down at the baby and giggles. The baby swings her head to Mommy's familiar voice. Quinn's huge eyes open a bit more to see her hero for the first time. What a beautiful moment. We are a family.

As I look at mother and baby together, I am eerily given the assurance that she will sustain me. In times of remorse and self-centeredness, Quinn will draw me out of me. It's hard to say why I know this, but I do. How can I look into those little eyes and feel sorry for myself for not being able to drink alcohol normally? How petty that complaint sounds to me now. My only option is to serve her. It is my duty to keep this tiny gift alive. This show of love through action is why I was created. Baby Quinn Cook has saved my life and given me a purpose. And she has proven that there is a God who loves me.

CHAPTER 28
Team Cook

In the months to come, I feel a combination of joy and pride watching Jen care for our tiny baby. She operates as a world-class mom with such ease. Gratitude can't help but be my number one sentiment. I have once again been put in an incredibly fortunate position, and finally my eyes are open to it, appreciating it and not taking it for granted or spending my useful time trying to grab more. All the while, I'm constantly being told that developing a spiritual life is key in this process of healing for me.

Is it possible that a guy always searching for wholeness, living on the edge, close to dishonorable peril and addiction, can straighten out before ruin with the help of a baby and a God of his understanding? Yes. It is possible. I am looking at my existence with a whole new set of peepers. These eyes aren't as big as my beautiful daughter's, but they are as new.

I have been sober for such a short time, but the change in me is sudden. I wanted to feel right for so long, I guess I was ready for it and just needed guidance and willingness. I learn that this spiritual life can be lived to its fullest if I stay in this moment, remain teachable, and continue to do what I'm told without question. These things keep me in a position of service to man. I've noticed that trying to achieve those simple goals helps calm my anxiety like no medicinal fix I've ever tried. I think that Bob was right in that first AA meeting. I don't have a bipolar brain disorder; my past craziness was merely acting out with untreated alcoholism, but

September 17, 2002. Quinn is born a healthy 8 pounds 8 ounces. I am twenty-three days sober.

Jen, Quinn and me. That was the most surreal moment of my life. Jen answered the bell like a champion.

that can be just as dangerous as being bipolar. Soon I learn from many people in recovery that many psychiatrists diagnose the fear, hopelessness and anxiety of alcoholism as bipolar disorder. I'm sure some people are truly bipolar, but I'm just truly alcoholic.

I'm nowhere close to cured, but this new plan of action shows me beauty I never thought I would see. I have also learned to look back with gratitude at the bad things I have done. Sharing those unfavorable experiences helps me be useful to the man who still lives in the darkness I know too well. These discoveries are new to me, but people in recovery have been passing them on for many years. My sponsor, Mark, has only asked me to do the things that his sponsor, Murph, had him do. I do them because they worked for these guys and their past experience feels eerily similar to mine. One time in a meeting Murph talked about being "mugged by his mind" while he was on a paradise vacation: even though his surroundings should have made him happy, his alcoholic mind wouldn't allow it. That description of alcoholism hit me right between the eyes, because it's exactly what happened to me when we first arrived in LA. I thought I was crazy, but really my alcoholism had just taken over. It's a thinking disease. Hearing these similar things at meetings keeps me coming back.

And now for the first time, my life feels in sync. I have had great luck and exhilaration before, but something always felt wrong. I forced things, causing life not to flow. As I look back I see that I wasn't fulfilling my purpose. I was running up the down escalator of life. I willed some good outcomes, but they were always followed by some sort of loss.

I wasn't supposed to be sweating it out in Jerry Bruckheimer's conference room waiting to be his assistant. I even have to be willing to believe that those debilitating facial twitches were not

Top: Jen and Baby Quinn at ten months.
Bottom: My Dad and Quinn grab a Sunday nap.

caused by some powerful bipolar medicine but were simply the manifestation of extreme fear. Doesn't that seem more likely? Or maybe massive eye twitching in front of Bruckheimer was a sign that I was going against my true current. They were like my own little built-in Spidey Sense. I thought that Bruckheimer job would save me, but deep down I knew it wasn't the right place to be. More suitable and rewarding things have been planned for me. As devastating as it was, Jerry Bruckheimer did me a favor by not hiring my flinching, ticking, jittering self. And obviously he did his business a favor too. I see that now. I'm far from perfect at the new life, but now as I float along the current, I know when something is right.

I heard someone in a meeting say that it's important to remember we will never achieve better than human status. Even with these wonderful discoveries, the occasional moment of ungratefulness can slip in. When it happens, all I have to do is look at that baby and get to a meeting, and as fast as it crept up on me, it leaves. If I do those things, the pressure is not on me to be great, funny or perfect anymore. I just have to be—just be. That's it.

Another idea has given me great peace too. It is the acceptance that all we have is this moment. This is paramount in my recovery. As cheesy as "living in the moment" sounds, it really does work. Both the past and the future are untouchable. I spent my life worrying about and dabbling with the untouchable. What happened before is gone and somehow it got me here. And that is enough. On top of that, fear about the future is by far a sillier notion than living in this moment. I learned that the fear I was riddled with was basically just faith in the bad. I thought having faith in a bad result (fear) covered my bases and kept me guarded against a life-deflating failure. But all I was doing was slowly letting the air out of my life

Backstage at the Grammys with Ed Kowalczyk from the band LIVE. In their song "Heaven" he sings that he "knows Heaven exists every time he looks in his daughter's eyes." Me too, Ed.

Lenny Kravitz in 2006 with Jen Myers and me. She is the DJ I was giving career advice to my last night of drinking. Thanks for the patience Jen.

I've never worked for a more compassionate radio station than Y98. From top to bottom they have always done their best to do the best for me. Radio is struggling these days, yet Y98 continues to prosper. It's no wonder.

with that thinking.

I constantly needed to escape that negative feeling, so I did it with drugs and alcohol. Now trying to stay optimistic helps keep me full of life. Even faking positivity when I don't feel it can do the trick. Generally I am rewarded for this state of mind. I don't walk around with a fake smile while saying "It will work out" all the time, but I don't lean on the negative like before either. Too many parents have brought their kids up to live in their negative state of mind. I wish not to do this to my daughter.

These concepts are just the beginning for a guy in recovery. I am grateful they have been taught to me, but I must build upon them if I am to survive. I have been urged to develop a deeper relationship with my God. This pursuit is a true gift. To my surprise, I have found that I have an insatiable drive to learn all I can about my new friend.

CHAPTER 29
A Test At Seven Months

A few weeks ago, I hurt my rib while playing with my niece and nephew after jumping across a chair. At the time it just popped, but as days have passed, it has become increasingly painful, and now I'm having a hard time sleeping. Jen is getting tired of my morning complaints.

"Good God, you have to get that x-rayed!"

I have put it off because I know my old instincts might take over with a doctor, working him for painkillers. But possibly it is broken and maybe I need some kind of treatment. So I go to the ER for x-rays.

As I sit in my gown waiting for the x-rays to come back, my heart pumps. I know a possible painkiller prescription is within my grasp if I seek it. Can I rely on all of the new discoveries I have bragged about to steer me around this? Maybe I've become too cocky.

The disinterested doctor enters.

"Well, there is no major fracture to your rib, but there could be a very small contusion. That can be quite painful till it heals."

There definitely is pain. But how much is too much, knowing my history?

"Yeah, it's definitely uncomfortable to sleep," I complain. What? I feel my drug instincts seizing me and taking over. Doctors hate to hear you can't sleep. They always want to help with that.

What am I doing?

"Well, I can give you some pain medicine that should help."

NO! NO! NO! My head screams. I even hear Mark, my sponsor, saying it with me in chorus.

Pause. The doctor squints at me. I need to do the right thing. Now is the time to speak up.

"Okay, that prescription would be fine," I say.

It was automatic.

"Okay, this is Darvacet. Make sure you take it with food. You should be able to sleep better till it heals more."

Last chance to come clean.

"Oh, okay. Thanks."

I must not be as well as I think I am. As I put on my shoes, my gut doesn't feel right. I know that I am lying to myself about needing these pills for a medical reason, when Advil will probably be enough.

I float out of the ER with the newly earned script in my hand, feeling scummy. Before, this used to be exhilarating. Hold it, there—I *am* physically hurt. This wasn't manufactured like before. I *need* these pills. We are going to visit Jen's parents this weekend. These pills could help me sleep and be more patient during their traditional kitchen table confabs. And remember, I'm hurt.

For the first time in six months my thoughts race rapidly. This is a familiar episode. My head twists as I drive to the Walgreen's Pharmacy. In the past, going to the pharmacy with that legal prescription paper was a proud and validating moment. This trip used to be the equivalent of taking your newly hunted ten-point buck to the weighing station. Today it feels sneaky with just a dangerous tiny dash of excitement. Will all the work I've done on the steps go down the drain? Alarms ring in my head. I'm in jeopardy. This is insane. I felt completely sober a day ago. What got me here?

The thought hits me: I am still sober, I have done nothing yet. Then what am I doing at the pharmacy? I wait for them to call my name with my painkillers. The pressure in my head is blinding. What should I do? Abusing these pills will almost certainly cue another drug and alcohol spree. I need to use my recovery tools. I don't want to call my sponsor. He will be mad I let it get this far. I'm getting the damn prescription filled for God's sake!

I'm startled as the armband tightens around my right bicep from the do-it-yourself blood pressure machine near the waiting area at Walgreens. My head is so crazy that I forgot I am sitting in this contraption. The reading comes. My blood pressure is normal. What? My pulse is through the roof.

"Mr. Cook." The pharmacist calls my name over the speakers.

"Here is your prescription. Any questions about taking this medicine?"

"No, thank you."

I know this painkiller better than she does. I've seen it from every angle and abuse. I tuck it away and slither out of the store. Usually pride carried me out to the car; this time it's total unrest. I'm back to resembling Whoopi Goldberg in *Ghost*, stomping across the parking lot tensely in red high heels.

"Call your sponsor!" I tell myself as I get in my car.

But all I do is drive in silence. From the pharmacy, I travel home to grab my show prep for the afternoon show. I leave the pills in the car. My head is packed with twisted thoughts. It is totally the devil-on-one-shoulder-and-an-angel-on-the-other scenario. The devil tells me I'm in pain and this is justified. The angel reminds me that the cost is too great and I'm in no real pain. I should have told the doctor about my pain pill problem. I feel like crap and I haven't taken a single dose. Suddenly I remember I have leaned on one thing over the past months. That thing is the floor and the God I have found down there. So I drop to my knees.

"Help me with this," I whisper. "Tell me what to do. Give me the strength."

After a few more moments down there, I rise and jump back in the car and head for work. My thoughts are still crowded, but now I feel less agitated. I'm on the highway now. Again I think about going to my weekend and the mental "check-out" comfort these opiates can bring. But then, I would probably take some of my mother-in-law's pills that she really needs. I remember that I took pills from Mom and Dad in the past, too. Do I want that life-crunching guilt again?

I open the bag, grab the full bottle in my hand and read it. "No operating of heavy machinery" and "Don't drink alcohol with this" stickers are all over it. Before I can savor the potency of the medicine, my window is down and I hurl the bottle at the highway's center median. The bottle smashes to pieces. Cars behind me poke holes through the big cloud of white pill powder hanging in the air.

I can't believe I just did that!

What just happened? I actually did the right thing when it came to drugs. I have never done this. The desire has always been there, but the action to back it up never was.

The feeling after doing this is indescribable. Ironically, it is comparable to the good feelings taking the pills would have given me, but it is natural. I feel a healthy pride—pride in my God, whom I asked for help. I could not have done that by myself. After telling my sober savior, Jim, about this, I realize that the strength to do this was not given to me for free.

Jim yells at me, "Show your thanks by helping other addicts, bone head. And you can do that by sharing this experience with them. That's it!"

What a gift. I have received the opportunity to help other men overcome their gripping fear. This great responsibility always secures the strength to make the right decision, as long as I am carrying the message of hope. What a rewarding agreement.

It's a joy I can never fully repay. I never feel more relief than when I share my experience with a guy who believes he has lost all hope. There is nothing like watching a man light up in sobriety. I find myself always saying to them, "There is light on the inside!" I say that because you can actually see it when a man finds hope and recovery. His eyes shine brighter and his face has life. I wish that every person suffering from alcohol and drug addiction could find that relief and light to happiness.

∽⚬∾

As I look back at the last year, I think about that legendary author I met in Los Angeles. I am convinced that Hunter S. Thompson suffered from my disease for far too long. People who knew him say that he was born angry and he died angry. I fear that Hunter's unwillingness to try the recovery solution caused this creative man to take his own life, ending his pain. But that was only the beginning of the pain for his family. Suicide always works that way. Many of Hunter's books talk about "getting the fear again." Alcoholics are riddled with fear, and as you have read, one of fear's most common forms is anxiety. It dominated me for most of my life and many times I didn't even know it. Strangely, writing this book helped me to see how my days were rife with it.

Hunter S. Thompson's forms of fear might have been different, but they were still fear and mostly they caused him not to feel right. They sent him constantly searching for something to fill that hole. It's interesting: drug users unwilling to face the facts will tell you that they just like to have a good time. Or they'll say it "expands their mind." These are rationalizations to explain away not feeling right in the first place. But that's okay. People like this are not yet ready for recovery. Unfortunately they have to do more harm to themselves before they can recover. Hopefully, they have this realization before they take their lives and steal many moments from their families and themselves. Maybe guys like the great Hunter S. Thompson and my late cousin Ren are good examples for other folks to not accept living in anger.

ᖇᢇᖇ

I truly believe that drug addiction is waiting for all of us. All it takes is finding your drug of choice. Some drugs do nothing for you, others make you sick, but if you keep experimenting you'll find the drug that fills you up. Then life changes, as it did for me when I took that first painkiller. Then I was off and running and all bets were off. There lies the danger in living with an "I'll try anything once" mentality.

Exhilaration has a new definition. Clubbing and Numbing no longer matter. We took a Disney Cruise with the girls in 2007 and we had the time of our lives. This is Jen on Disney's own Island Castaway Key.

CHAPTER 30

To Feel Human Again

My empathetic heart has been returned to me, and just as Dennis said, it comes from action. My original reaction to 9/11 was the ultimate act of self-centeredness. It was all about me and how this event would change my job. I have finally been able to grieve for those who lost their lives that day. This blessing was given to me in an interesting way.

In 2007, I was asked to emcee an event for The Delta Gamma Center for children with visual impairments. The speaker for this event was a man name Michael Hingson. He was on the seventy-second floor when the planes hit the World Trade Center. The planes crashed just fourteen floors above him. He had to scramble to get out alive before the building crashed to the ground. As a manager, he walked his staff down all seventy-two floors successfully just minutes before the tower fell. Michael Hingson is blind.

He accomplished this amazing feat with the help of his guide dog, Roselle. As I sat off to the side of the stage listening to his miraculous story, all of the missed emotions of 9/11 hit me. He told the story of briefly meeting a brave young fireman passing him on the stairwell. The firefighter was on his way up to save some injured people on one of the higher burning floors. I could not fight back the tears when he told us that brave fireman would die just a few moments later when the tower fell on Michael's heels. At the end of the night, I thanked God for letting me feel what I should have felt six years earlier. It is truly a blessing to be able to face adult emotions as an adult.

CHAPTER 31
Don't Eat That

Sober almost eight months, smooth sailing. Guess again. Life happens. Evidently my twelve-step "home group" throws a big potluck meeting every year so family members can see what we do every Tuesday night. For this we move the show to the church gymnasium, which has vacation Bible school kickball written all over it. Upon entry I trip over the powerful blast to my nostrils of seventy cumulative years of Lenten season fish fries. For me "potluck" has always been a bad word. Potlucks are where you optimistically approach the card tables piled high with starchy food while clutching your paper plate only to find yourself back at your seat a few moments later with a slice of wet ham and some chopped potatoes with Corn Flakes sprinkled on top. And if the food doesn't get you, the small talk will. The endless lists of boring biographies and obsession with life's progression could suck the life out of even the chicks on *The View.*

"Got married? Great. When are you getting a house? Really? A starter home, nice. Won't be too long before there's a house full of babies."

Yuck! That's why I always drank before the potluck. For me it made everyone, their food and the conversation more bearable. But not tonight. Tonight, I'll take an interest in someone else and really try to listen. That's what Mark has told me to do.

"You won't believe how the time will fly when you try to take an interest and really engage someone about their life," my sponsor promises.

I'm just now getting better at this, and it does work. Grab a big icy Coke and probe away.

Tonight will also be special because my dad is here with me. I'm excited and nervous to introduce him to the people I've been spending all this time with. We enter with our St. Louis Bread Company pastry desserts and grab a seat. The format for this potluck is that we eat and then a sage old member of the group shares his experience, strength and hope about recovery.

Once we penetrate the cod-flavored force field, we see it's crowded and chirping with energy. Kids run and circle after each other through the folding chairs. There must be a hundred and seventy people in here. While picking through a variety of cereal-encrusted casseroles and some lunch meat, I point out people I know. I even manage a few introductions. The vulnerability in this is actually very warm and beautiful. I'm calm. My dad is nice, complimenting someone else's dessert.

The speaker begins. Teddy P. has quite a story: from upper management in a huge company to living on the streets of St. Louis and carrying a gun. Men in the program aren't solely responsible for a man's recovery. That's a God deal. But Teddy has contributed heavily to the resurrected lives of literally hundreds of men in the last twenty years. He's a pillar and I've been too nervous to ever even say "hi" to him. We sit at a table in front, just to the right of Teddy, who's at the podium. The table that was hidden at the back of the room when we were eating is now front and center for the speaker. Great choice on my part.

Our tanned, bald speaker says, "I was a gun-toting freak who no one could trust. And now I get to go into men's homes and show them hope. Never let someone tell you a man has gone too far to recover. I've seen miracles."

My heart flutters at the potential of this program. I glance at my dad for agreement. He is surprisingly washed-out and looking down.

"Dad, you all right?"

I see pain on his face.

He whispers, "Indigestion, I'll be fine."

This damn potluck food, it got me again. Can't we just all throw in a couple bucks and have a professional bring in food? The speaker is background chatter now, I can't take my attention off my dad and that wincing that has gotten more expressive with each minute. I really wanted him to have an enjoyable time. Hopefully that TUMS I just saw him pop will calm his stomach.

"Our experience is our greatest asset. It gets through to the newcomer when nothing else can. He has to know his problems are not unique, even though he thinks blah-blah-blah ..." That's all I hear from Teddy.

"Dad, you sure you're gonna be okay?" I whisper with a purpose.

Head down, no answer. Another white tablet goes into his mouth. It looks smaller than a TUMS.

"Dad," louder whisper. "What is that pill?"

His bloodless face slowly looks up. "Nitroglycerin. I think it's my heart. Just gimme a minute."

"Okay. You sure?"

"I think ..." fades out of his mouth.

"No, let's go." I demand.

He follows me as we get up in front and shuffle around the back with all eyes on us. Dad stiffly makes it to the exit.

"Wait here, the car is really far away. I'll be right back to pick you up."

Sprinting faster and farther than I ever have, I finally make it to the Jetta parked all the way over at the normal meeting site. I zoom up and Dad stumbles in. In the middle of a heart attack, we zoom away from a potluck with at least three doctors sitting in attendance. This is not happening!

Through restricted breathing, all Dad says on the drive to the hospital is, "Slow down."

I keep asking myself, how bad is this? He was popping nitroglycerin like Tic-Tacs, why didn't they work? We arrive at the emergency room at the same time as my mom and sister. From their eyes I can see that they are quietly panicking.

I help him on to the stretcher, "Chest pains. He'll be okay!"

My dad is a tough man, but I've never seen him in this much agony. It's overwhelming him.

"Can we go in the room with him?" Mom asks.

"Yes, please do," The ER nurse says.

My sister Shannon holds his hand as they put all the monitors on his chest. There is no familiar, "I'll be all right" coming from him. He is locked up in pain. I stand over my dad watching life leave him. Just an hour ago we were laughing about bringing too feminine desserts to the potluck; now we're thinking about goodbyes. My mom is silently distraught, occasionally probing for hope. Could it be that we are losing the man who has brought us so far, the man who helped me out of drug addiction and active alcoholism? The doctors and nurses spend none of their time assuring us he will make it. All of their intensity channels into tests, IVs and medicine.

Dad tries to explain where the pain is to my mom.

"Now you all have to step back for a while, please," an older nurse warns.

I sit on a hard black chair in the corner by the empty coat rack. We still wear our coats. My mind flashes with thoughts. I have not been a good son these last four years. I want to make him proud. Please. I begin to quietly pray with my chest resting on my legs.

"Save him. Let me show him I can make it. Please, five more years. I will work for you. Save him."

"Okay guys, talk with me really quick here." The nurse herds us out. "We are finding a significant blockage in your husband's heart. The Cardio Catheter doctor is rushing here now. We are going to prep your husband for surgery and then go in to attempt to remove the blockage."

"Okay, how successful is that usually?" Mom asks while gripping our hands.

"It all depends. We'll know more when the doctor gets a better look. So we're taking him in now, you can come back in for a quick second."

We all stonewall the thought that this could be goodbye.

A tapestry of "You'll be all right and we love you," piles on top of each other from all three of us. Then we all stop with no prompting and Dad says, "I love you," through tears.

And they wheel my father away.

ༀ

"That was five years ago today," I announce at the potluck podium.

My speaker notes are written on the back of a flyer that reads:

"Paul C. is Your 2007 Group #477 Speaker. Bring your favorite dish!"

This year, I'm the sage old speaker, even though neither of those descriptions applies.

"Five years sober," I declare, "and I hardly recognize that guy who was drinking in his car before going on the air. But I'll never forget him. The healing started that week in 2002 when you guys stuck out your hand and said 'Hello' to me. Thank you for that."

The 200 people in the crowd look at me with curious intensity.

"Oh, and Dad, please hold up your hand and let everyone know you made it."

My brothers in recovery stand and applaud for Dad.

"When they got inside, the doctors discovered that Dad had a 90 percent blockage in one artery and a 75 percent blockage in another. He shouldn't have made it, but our prayers were answered."

More applause.

"They say nitroglycerin tablets could not have saved him. But Alcoholics Anonymous did. With my mother out at a party, Dad would have been alone that night. And knowing him, he would not have wanted to bother anyone with his pain. This potluck gave God and those doctors the opportunity to save him. What a gift!" I say, voice shaking.

I grab a moment to breathe.

"Such a great thing to have been able to face my dad's heart attack as a sober man rather than just going to the liquor store to deal with those thoughts of losing him. Without this program, that is where I would have been. This is an incredible thing. To men who are dealing with alcoholism and addiction, I describe the joy of recovery like this: 'The high you get from using is like a tiny slice of one color in a rainbow. Fully taking the steps in recovery is like having the whole rainbow. You get all you were seeking with substances and so much more. Thanks for allowing me to share my story tonight. God Bless."

Our young family makes a presentation at our church in 2008, Webster Presbyterian.

Halloween, 2007. My favorite holiday has become even more fun now that I have two beautiful bees of my own.

Quinn and Ryan Cook in 2008. I am the luckiest man in the world. I look at this picture and none of my struggles seem real. I am so blessed to be able to share my story with you. Hopefully my life has helped to illustrate the point that no pain is permanent and that if God brings you to something, he intends to bring you through it as well.

RESOURCES

Recommended Reading
- *Alcoholics Anonymous*, Anonymous
- *A New Pair of Glasses*, Chuck C.
- *Recapture the Wonder*, Ravi Zacharias
- *See You at the Top*, Zig Ziglar
- *The Rum Diary*, Hunter S. Thompson

Alcoholics Anonymous
There are hundreds of thousands of Alcoholics Anonymous meetings all over the world every single day. All 12 Step programs began with the foundation AA teaches.
http://www.alcoholics-anonymous.org/

STAR Supporting Teens At Risk is an incredibly useful and groundbreaking program in many St. Louis Schools. STAR works closely with students to change the drinking and drugging culture in our schools.
http://starforteens.org/

Recovery Radio
The most reachable place on earth for recovery audio in an "on demand" streaming-media format.
http://www.recoveryradio.net/

Keep anything you value away from baby Ryan's mouth when she goes apple picking.
Apples and pumpkins filled the Cook trunk after a trip to Eckerts Apples in 2006.

A B O U T
Paul Cook

Author Paul Cook is a radio and television broadcaster. He can be seen daily on CBS St. Louis's News 4 *This Morning* and heard on CBS Radio's famous Y98FM. Paul has twice won the award for St. Louis's Best Music Format Personality.

Paul is extremely active in the St. Louis recovery community.

As a member of S.T.A.R (Supporting Teens At Risk) he frequently talks to schools about the lures of substance abuse and other dangers. Paul also sponsors men who struggle with alcoholism and works closely with the National Council on Alcoholism and Drug Abuse to raise money for substance abuse awareness.

Cooked in LA ■ Paul Cook

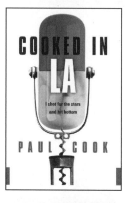

How does a successful young man from a "good" home hit bottom and risk losing it all? *Cooked In La* shows how a popular, middle-class young man with a bright future in radio and television is nearly destroyed by a voracious appetite for drugs and alcohol.

Non Fiction/Self-Help & Recovery I US$ 24.95
Pages 304 I Cloth 5.5" x 8.5"
ISBN 978-1-60164-193-9

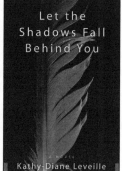

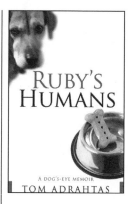

Against Destiny
■ Alexander Dolinin

A story of courage and determination in the face of the impossible. The dilemma of the unjustly condemned: Die in slavery or die fighting for your freedom.

Fiction I US$ 24.95
Pages 448 I Cloth 5.5" x 8.5"
ISBN 978-1-60164-173-1

Let the Shadows Fall Behind You
■ Kathy-Diane Leveille

The disappearance of her lover turns a young woman's world upside down and leads to shocking revelations of her past. This enigmatic novel is about connections and relationships, memory and reality.

Fiction I US$ 22.95
Pages 288 I Cloth 5.5" x 8.5"
ISBN 978-1-60164-167-0

Ruby's Humans
■ Tom Adrahtas

No other book tells a story of abuse, neglect, escape, recovery and love with such humor and poignancy, in the uniquely perceptive words of a dog. Anyone who's ever loved a dog will love Ruby's sassy take on human foibles and manners.

Non Fiction I US$ 19.95
Pages 192 I Cloth 5.5" x 8.5"
ISBN 978-1-60164-188-5

The Unbreakable Child ■ Kim Michele Richardson

Starved, beaten and abused for nearly a decade, orphan Kimmi learned that evil can wear a nun's habit. A story not just of a survivor but of a rare spirit who simply would not be broken.

Non Fiction/True Crime | US$ 24.95
Pages 256 | Cloth 5.5" x 8.5"
ISBN 978-1-60164-163-2

Save the Whales Please
■ Konrad Karl Gatien & Sreescanda

Japanese threats and backroom deals cause the slaughter of more whales than ever. The first lady risks everything—her life, her position, her marriage—to save the whales.

Fiction | US$ 24.95
Pages 432 | Cloth 5.5" x 8.5"
ISBN 978-1-60164-165-6

Screenshot
■ John Darrin

Could you resist the lure of evil that lurks in the anonymous power of the Internet? Every week, a mad entrepreneur presents an execution, the live, real-time murder of someone who probably deserves it. *Screenshot:* a techno-thriller with a provocative premise.

Fiction | US$ 24.95
Pages 416 | Cloth 5.5" x 8.5"
ISBN 978-1-60164-168-7

Touchstone Tarot ■ Kat Black

Internationally renowned tarot designer Kat Black, whose *Golden Tarot* remains one of the most popular and critically acclaimed tarot decks on the market, has created this unique new deck. In *Touchstone Tarot*, Kat Black uses Baroque masterpieces as the basis for her sumptuous and sensual collaged portraits. Intuitive and easy to read, this deck is for readers at every level of experience. This deluxe set, with gold gilt edges and sturdy hinged box includes a straightforward companion book with card explanations and sample readings.

Non Fiction/New Age | US$ 32.95 | Tarot box set with 200-page booklet | Cards and booklet 3.5" x 5" ISBN 978-1-60164-190-8

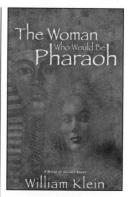

Sleepers Awake ■ Patrick McNulty

Monstrous creatures invade our world in this dark fantasy in which death is but a door to another room of one's life.

Fiction | US$ 22.95 Pages 320 | Cloth 5.5" x 8.5" ISBN 978-1-60164-166-3

The Nation's Highest Honor ■ James Gaitis

Like Kosinski's classic *Being There*, *The Nation's Highest Honor* demonstrates the dangerous truth that incompetence is no obstacle to making a profound difference in the world.

Fiction | US$ 22.95 Pages 256 | Cloth 5.5" x 8.5" ISBN 978-1-60164-172-4

The Woman Who Would Be Pharaoh ■ William Klein

Shadowy figures from Egypt's fabulous past glow with color and authenticity. Tragic love story weaves a rich tapestry of history, mystery, regicide and incest.

Fiction/Historic | US$ 24.95 Pages 304 | Cloth 5.5" x 8.5" ISBN 978-1-60164-189-2

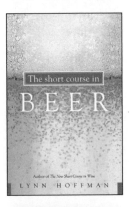
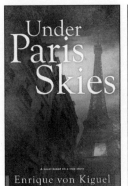
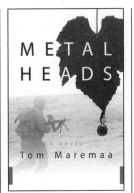